CATALDO

Managing
Software
Acquisition

Managing
Software
Acquisition

Open Systems and
COTS Products

B. Craig Meyers

Patricia Oberndorf

 **Addison-Wesley**

Boston • San Francisco • New York • Toronto • Montreal
London • Munich • Paris • Madrid
Capetown • Sidney • Tokyo • Singapore • Mexico City

Carnegie Mellon
Software Engineering Institute

Many of the designations used by manufacturers and sellers to distinguish their products are claimed as trademarks. Where those designations appear in this book, and we were aware of a trademark claim, the designations have been printed in initial capital letters or in all capitals.

CMM, Capability Maturity Model, Capability Maturity Modeling, Carnegie Mellon, CERT, and CERT Coordination Center are registered in the U.S. Patent and Trademark Office.

ATAM; Architecture Tradeoff Analysis Method; CMMI; CMM Integration; CURE; IDEAL; Interim Profile; OCTAVE; Operationally Critical Threat, Asset, and Vulnerability Evaluation; Personal Software Process; PSP; SCAMPI; SCAMPI Lead Assessor; SCE; Team Software Process; and TSP are service marks of Carnegie Mellon University.

UNIX is a technology trademark of X/Open Company, Ltd.

The tables on pages 106–107 reprinted with permission from IEEE Standard for Information Technology—Standardization Application Environment Profile—POSIX Real-time Application Support P1003.13 Copyright 1983, by IEEE. The IEEE disclaims any responsibility or liability resulting from the placement and use in the described manner.

The authors and publisher have taken care in the preparation of this book, but make no expressed or implied warranty of any kind and assume no responsibility for errors or omissions. No liability is assumed for incidental or consequential damages in connection with or arising out of the use of the information or programs contained herein.

ANY MATERIAL FURNISHED BY CARNEGIE MELLON UNIVERSITY AND THE SOFTWARE ENGINEERING INSTITUTE IS FURNISHED ON AN "AS IS" BASIS. CARNEGIE MELLON UNIVERSITY MAKES NO WARRANTIES OF ANY KIND, EITHER EXPRESSED OR IMPLIED AS TO ANY MATTER INCLUDING, BUT NOT LIMITED TO, WARRANTY OF FITNESS FOR PURPOSE OR MERCHANTABILITY, EXCLUSIVITY OR RESULTS OBTAINED FROM USE OF THE MATERIAL. CARNEGIE MELLON UNIVERSITY DOES NOT MAKE ANY WARRANTY OF ANY KIND WITH RESPECT TO FREEDOM FROM PATENT, TRADEMARK, OR COPYRIGHT INFRINGEMENT.

The publisher offers discounts on this book when ordered in quantity for special sales. For more information, please contact:

Pearson Education Corporate Sales Division
One Lake Street
Upper Saddle River, NJ 07458
(800) 382-3419
corpsales@pearsontechgroup.com

Visit AW on the Web: www.awl.com/cseng/

Library of Congress Cataloging-in-Publication Data

Meyers, B. Craig.
   Managing software acquisition : open systems and COTS products / B. Craig Meyers,
Patricia Oberndorf.
         p. cm.—(SEI series in software engineering)
   Includes bibliographical references and index.
   ISBN 0-201-70454-4
   1. Acquisition of computer software. I. Oberndorf, Patricia. II. Title. III. Series.

   QA76.76.S95 M49 2001
   005.1'068'7—dc21

                                                         2001022976

ISBN 0-201-70454-4
Text printed on recycled paper
1 2 3 4 5 6 7 8 9 10—CRW—0504030201
First printing, June 2001

Craig thanks Donna and the boys—
Zac, Andy, Ben, and Tim

Tricia thanks Alyson and Ryan

Contents

Illustrations

Tables

Preface

In the rapidly changing world of software acquisition, open systems and commercial off-the-shelf (COTS) products continue to grow in importance because of their expected functional and economic advantages. This book will help you understand the many issues surrounding acquisition of open, COTS-based systems. Although our focus is on software acquisition, this book can equally apply to hardware and system acquisition. You also need to understand the relationship between open systems and COTS products. If you understand these issues, you can more easily deal with the dynamics of today's acquisition environment.

Audience

The intended audience of this book is project managers and their staffs who are involved in designing, developing, procuring, maintaining, funding, or evaluating computer systems in both private and public sectors. We use the term *project manager* to denote the individual responsible for completion of the acquisition activities for systems in government and industry. We use the term *project staff* to denote the many professionals who support the project manager. Each of these professionals has different responsibilities, concerns, and technical expertise, but the use of open systems and COTS products will affect each person in some way.

We recognize that readers may very well have experience in basic project management. We include some basic management information as background so that we can get all readers on the same page. The real difference arises, however, when we apply our management skills in the context of open, COTS-based systems. That's the challenge we want to help you address.

Purpose

The purposes of this book are to

- Define basic terms, concepts, and processes related to open systems and the use of COTS products
- Explain the potential benefits and difficulties of using an approach that relies on open systems and COTS products
- Describe how open systems and COTS products affect the project manager and the project staff
- Illustrate how to incorporate open systems and COTS products in the acquisition process
- Highlight special concerns for government managers

Terms associated with open systems and COTS products have many different definitions. Experts may not agree, and you may find a lot of hype. We need to share a common understanding of what these terms mean, and we take care in defining relevant terms.

The use of open systems and COTS products has both potential benefits and potential difficulties. In this book, we discuss both. Emphasis on an acquisition approach that uses open systems and COTS products will change the way you do your job. We hope that this book helps you identify—and be able to successfully deal with—the challenges that lie ahead.

Emphasis on principles
In writing this book, our emphasis is on *principles* related to the acquisition of systems that are based on open systems and COTS products. If you are able to understand the principles, you are more likely to be able to deal with management issues. Thus, our focus is *not* toward

- Detailed technical issues. A detailed discussion of particular standards or sets of standards is outside the scope of this book. For example, we will not present a discussion of all the networking standards you may hear about. Instead, we concentrate on what such terms as *standard* and *profile* mean and discuss such topics as how standards are developed and selected and how they relate to COTS products.

- Checklists. An acquisition approach based on open systems and COTS products can be complex and challenging. Despite the temptation to reduce this complexity to a simple set of checklists, we resist such an approach. Instead, we place emphasis on the specification and application of principles that govern the acquisition process. Maybe you can develop your own checklists, appropriate to your system, based on what you will learn in this book. But don't confuse a checklist with the understanding of basic acquisition, open systems, and COTS principles.

We believe that emphasis on principles will help you more than lots of details will. In many cases, a particular approach for your system will *depend:* on your situation, your goals, and your approach to meet the problems you will face along the way.

Open systems and the use of COTS products present **Government** unique challenges for government programs. Because the **concerns** government's business practices are inherently different from those of industry, we devote special attention to government concerns. We hope that, to some degree, we can build a bridge and develop a shared understanding between government and industry regarding acquisition issues related to open systems and COTS products.

Organization and Content

This book consists of five main parts, which contain **Organization** related chapters, and four appendixes.

- Part One, Getting Started, consists of the first four chapters, which introduce the basic elements of open systems and the use of COTS products. These chapters present an overview of acquisition, describe the promises and pitfalls of the open, COTS-based approach, explore the paradigm shift to open systems and COTS products, and present the elements of an open, COTS-based approach.

- Part Two, Understanding the New World, explores various aspects of open systems and COTS products. Chapters 5–8 look at reference models and architectures, standards, commercial off-the-shelf (COTS) products, and acquisition roadmaps.

- Part Three, Managing the Transition, provides information to help you maneuver successfully in the world of open systems and COTS products. Chapters 9–12 consider how open systems and COTS products can change your business, discuss special concerns for managers, describe engineering practices, and discuss procurement practices.

- Part Four, Considering Acquisition, focuses on the acquisition context for open systems and the use of COTS products. Chapters 13–15 describe an acquisition framework used to describe various acquisition models, particularly acquisition models for open, COTS-based systems.

- Part Five, Closing Thoughts, consists of one chapter, which looks at anticipated future acquisition issues, both general and specific to the government.

- Other information is provided in the appendixes: a glossary of terms, a list of acronyms used in the book and what they mean, sample questions to help you analyze your system, and references.

Notations   This book uses two types of special notations to help you as you read this book. When we define a key term, we present it as follows.

open system ⇢ A collection of interacting software and hardware component implementations, and users

- Designed to satisfy stated needs
- Having the interface specification of components
  - Fully defined

- Available to the public
- Maintained according to group consensus
■ In which the component implementations conform to the interface specifications

The second type of notation is for material that you may find interesting, enlightening, humorous, or thought provoking. Sometimes, we have included anecdotes from colleagues. We present this special information in a gray box like the following.

Leadership

All acquisition managers are expected to provide leadership to their organizations and their people, who must achieve the goals established by management. In a special message to Congress on urgent national needs in May 1961, President Kennedy gave a speech that included the following text: "I believe that this nation should commit itself to achieving the goal, before this decade is out, of landing a man on the moon and returning him safely to the earth. No single space project in this period will be more impressive to mankind, or more important for the long-range exploration of space; and none will be so difficult or expensive to accomplish. In a very real sense, it will not be one man going to the moon—if we make this judgment affirmatively, it will be an entire nation. For all of us must work to put him there."

Each chapter includes a number of open-ended questions in a section titled Food for Thought. These items have been taken from our experience over a number of years teaching this material to audiences that include people who are involved in acquisition on a daily basis. We include these questions to illustrate some of the issues that may confront you as you conduct your job.

Food for thought

Few "right" answers apply universally to all project managers or systems. For this reason, it is difficult to give answers to these questions; in many cases, *it depends:* on the circumstances that are unique to your system. It is possible, however, to trace various approaches back to the principles discussed in this book. When you complete a chapter, look at these questions and spend a bit of time thinking your way through them. You may find some of the questions difficult, but don't be frustrated by them. Deal with them in the same way you would deal with any other difficult issue. You're also encouraged to discuss them with your colleagues.

Acknowledgments

Many talented people contributed to the development and production of this book. We would like to thank all of them.

We as authors accept the ultimate responsibility for the book's content. Part of the credit, however, belongs to the following extraordinary people who donated their time as expert reviewers during the book's development. Although we did not always agree, all the reviewers' comments were carefully considered and had impact on the final manuscript: Sandra Borden (United States Coast Guard), Joe Gwinn (Raytheon Systems Corporation), John Hill (Compaq Computer Corporation), Jim Isaak (Digital Equipment Corporation), Petr Janecek (X/Open), George Prosnik (Defense Systems Management College), Chuck Roark (Texas Instruments Incorporated), David Spencer (Massachusetts Institute of Technology, Lincoln Laboratory), and Stephen Walli (Softway Systems Incorporated). We are also grateful for review and comment from John D. Eikenberry, Elaine M. Hall (Level 6 Software), Steven M. Jacobs (TRW Systems and Technology Group), and David A. Umphress (Auburn University).

At the Software Engineering Institute (SEI), some reviewed the book's contents, others suggested improvements to the book's graphic design and stylistic aspects, and still others helped with administrative aspects of the book's development. We would like to thank the following persons in particular: Ceci Albert, Rick Barbour, Lisa Brownsword, Peter Capell, E. T. Dailey, Jon Gross, Donna Mahoney, Terry McGillen, Bill Pollak, Sheila Rosenthal, Skip Shelly, and Barbara White.

Much of this book was derived from courses we developed at the SEI on open systems and on using COTS products. A number of key people participated in the team associated with that effort. We thank Sandy Shrum for doing an early draft of this text. We also thank Ellen Ayoob for helping research many of the questions that arose during the development. Carol Sledge also contributed to this work as part of additional course development at the SEI, and we appreciate her comments.

It is also a pleasure to thank two other people who were part of our team: Kimberly Brune, who served as editor and helped with the expert reviewers, and Mary Glendinning, who searched far and wide to find things that would help in the development of the book. We also appreciate the good humor they both brought!

Finally, we say thanks to a new friend and editor at Addison-Wesley, Peter Gordon.

PART ONE

Getting Started

In beginning this book, we want to develop some common background to understand the importance of open systems and the use of COTS products. Our context is acquisition, including procurement, development, and maintenance of a system. Various opinions are readily offered about open systems and COTS products, and those opinions often shape the opinion of a busy manager. We will look at some of the opinions—both pro and con—and then describe the essential features of why an open, COTS-based acquisition is fundamentally important to your future acquisition.

Chapters in Part One

1

An Overview of Acquisition

Our concern in this book is the role of open systems and COTS products in the context of acquisition management. Although our focus is on software acquisition, the principles in this book apply to hardware and systems as well. In this chapter, we set the stage for examining these topics. First, we consider primary concerns of typical project managers. We then discuss some aspects of acquisition strategies. Together, these topics provide a common background on which to later address how open systems and COTS products affect acquisition.

1.1 The Project Manager Perspective

By the term *acquisition*, we mean

> **acquisition** ⇒ The set of activities performed to procure, develop, and maintain a system.

Note that we have taken a broad interpretation for what we mean by acquisition. Some might limit it to procurement only, but we feel that such a view is too narrow. We believe that an open, COTS-based acquisition is much more than simply procurement activities. Projects need to understand development and maintenance activities in order to succeed in procurement aspects of acquisition.

Acquisition activities can be technical or managerial in nature. The primary concern of most managers is with management activities, and this is to be expected. However, most managers also provide oversight to project technical activities.

Some examples of technical activities are requirements specification, design, development, modification, integration, and testing. Some examples of management activities are planning, budgeting, risk management, and contracting. The acquisition may be accomplished through in-house staff, contracting out some of the work, or a combination of in-house and contract work. The resulting scheme is shown in Table 1.1.

The acquisition of any system is a human endeavor, carried out by people who work together to achieve a common goal. The most visible of these people is often the project manager, who is lauded or berated, based on the result of an acquisition process. Managers are concerned with a myriad of issues, but several themes are common in discussing the role of the project manager: cost, schedule, performance, people, and synergy.

Cost Every project manager must address cost issues. Most managers face decreasing budgets, owing to ever increasing pressure to develop systems more cheaply, thereby increasing profit. The pressure of meeting the bottom line ripples through an acquisition. Sometimes, those ripples can be pretty big. Successful project managers are able to present realistic cost estimates, provide honest input concerning cost trade-offs, and are prepared to execute an acquisition in the face of sometimes volatile cost/budget projections.

Schedule A system must not only be acquired within cost constraints but also be acquired according to a schedule. Too often, the schedule is dictated by others; "now" seems to be used a lot! But even when a project manager gets to determine a schedule—and feels comfortable with it—

TABLE 1.1 Organization of Acquisition Activities

	Acquisition		
	Procurement	Development	Maintenance
Management			
Technical			

there always seem to be slips. The reality is that we do not have accurate ways of predicting schedule and costs in acquisitions of any reasonable size. This means that the project manager must deal with uncertainty, some of it self-induced. All project managers face the challenge of developing approaches to handle this uncertainty and trying to find opportunities to "buy back" schedule.

Along with the difficulties of dealing with cost and schedule, the project manager recognizes that the system must exhibit some specified performance characteristics. In this area, the project manager must rely on technical staff to provide guidance. Let's face it: Many senior project managers are not technical folks. But good project managers have a knack for finding the right technical folks and trusting their judgment. The more technically astute managers are, the more likely they can evaluate input from their technical staff. When faced with acquiring a system that must also be fault tolerant and real time and reconfigurable—name your favorite list of characteristics here—some project managers feel like finding something else to talk about.

Performance

One characteristic of outstanding project managers is the way they deal with people. Such managers are not autocrats but rather colleagues attempting to develop their people to build a successful team. This approach helps develop shared understanding and mutual respect. When an organization faces change, as with the use of open systems and COTS products, the effort is more likely to be successful if the people share the same goals and are lucky enough to have the support of their project manager.

People

Dealing with an individual aspect, such as cost, of a project is one thing. What makes things especially difficult is when a project manager must deal with the synergy among various aspects. Managers have to deal with questions like the following.

Synergy

- We need more staff but don't have the time to train them, so the schedule will slip, either way. So how do you want to deal with this?
- If you *really* want that feature in the system, we either incur a schedule overrun due to testing, or we need

more budget for testing. Or, do you want to consider hiring an outside agent to help with testing?

- I can meet your schedule but can you give me more money?
- I can't meet your schedule even if you give me more money. So what do you want me to do?

In each of the preceding situations, the project manager is faced with a choice. These situations involve combinations of cost, schedule, performance, or people issues. Some managers seem to apply an intuitive algorithm: Cost is highest priority, then schedule, and so on. Others struggle along, wondering why someone else didn't solve the problem in the first place. ("Bring me solutions, not problems!") Finally, some managers recognize that their job is to help others find a solution and will act more as facilitators. Regardless of style, project managers are responsible for finding the best balance among these aspects and for ensuring system success. Some will succeed; some won't.

The players
A project manager must also deal with a larger synergy. This synergy involves the players who participate in the overall acquisition context. These participants include

- Acquirers: you as project manager, your staff, and contractors
- Vendors: companies that produce and maintain COTS products
- Upper management: the people higher in your food chain
- Customer or sponsor: the person who funds the acquisition you are responsible for
- End users: the people who use the system you deliver
- Peer managers: individuals responsible for other systems with which yours must interoperate
- Other affected parties: those whose business processes are indirectly affected as a result of processes supported by your system

As if this is not enough to worry about, you also have to deal with standards organizations and the commercial marketplace.

1.2 Acquisition Strategies

Understanding acquisition activities is an important consideration for a project manager. Another important element that must be accounted for is the acquisition strategy.

> **acquisition strategy** ➡ A pattern of acquisition actions designed to accomplish the goals of a project.

Note that the strategy is a high-level concept. In contrast, a plan is a particular implementation of the strategy and contains more detail. Some of the questions that a project manager must consider when developing an acquisition strategy are the following.

- What are our overriding goals and constraints; for example, is the schedule rigid but the cost somewhat flexible?
- What acquisition approach is most relevant?
- What are the key assumptions on which we base our strategy? For example, what do we believe about future technologies or the likelihood of changes to the system?
- How much of a given activity will be performed by our staff rather than others, such as contractors?
- What alternative plans do we need, and when do we change our current plan?

Throughout this book, we address acquisition strategies and the impacts of various decisions that the project manager faces when developing and executing the strategy.

1.3 Looking Ahead

It is worth taking a moment to look ahead and see how an acquisition changes when we incorporate aspects of open systems and the use of COTS products. In that case, some of the activities that we will need to include deal with

- Identification, evaluation, and selection of standards

- Identification, evaluation, and selection of COTS products
- Life-cycle considerations for COTS products

One point that you need to keep in mind is this: Traditional acquisition approaches are based on a *build* philosophy, whereby an organization is *developing* a custom system. In contrast, the inclusion of open systems and COTS products forces one to change to a *buy* mentality. The problem shifts to one of identifying, buying, and then integrating implementations that are built by others. This shift from build to buy is fundamental to the role of open systems and COTS products in today's acquisition environment. One characteristic of the change is the increased complexity of acquisition in today's world over that of five or ten years ago.

A second point to understand is that open systems and COTS products go hand-in-hand. The result is that they will *collectively* impact your acquisition in the future.

A final important point: In a build mentality, you can insulate yourself from much of the external environment, as you are in control. Now, however, you must interact with that external environment. Managing that interaction is one of the major challenges you will face. Your fundamental challenge is to handle the myriad external events that will arise.

Dealing with complexity and the ever present external environment are two fundamentally important aspects of an open, COTS-based acquisition approach. But the path between our looking ahead here and the development—and your understanding—of a particular acquisition approach is long and sometimes winding.

One of our goals in this book is to help you deal more effectively with the issues associated with open systems and the use of COTS products. In addition, we develop an acquisition model that addresses open, COTS-based systems. So to begin, we want to describe some of the promises and pitfalls of open systems and COTS products. That's the subject of Chapter 2.

1.4 Summary

This chapter has helped to set the stage for what follows. We addressed several areas of key concerns that typically face project managers:

- Cost
- Schedule
- Performance
- People
- Synergy

We also touched on the notions of acquisition and acquisition strategy.

1.5 Food for Thought

In this and succeeding chapters, we end with questions for you to consider. These questions are drawn from our experience in working with real acquisition projects. There are few simple answers, and we recognize that the "correct" answer will depend on your particular acquisition project. We readily admit that some questions are especially difficult, yet they represent challenges that successful managers must meet and conquer. Don't let these questions stump you; deal with them in the same way you would deal with any other difficult issue. They give you a realistic idea of what may lie ahead. You're also encourged to discuss these questions with your colleagues.

1. How many times have you heard "better, faster, cheaper"? What does it mean? How do you react to this phrase and why?

2. In many situations, when a project starts falling behind, blame starts being cast on the technical staff who have to build a system. A senior technical person

said this when things started going sour: "Look, before you start blaming me and my people, let's be honest here. We have a schedule and we're not meeting it. That schedule was basically concocted because we really don't know how to predict how long things will take, whether it's integration testing, unit test, or risk management. So before we get blamed, let's just admit that the problem is we can't predict a schedule. You shouldn't be surprised we are either on or off the schedule." How do you respond to this statement?

3. How would you describe your organization's current acquisition strategy? If you were in charge and your organization were undergoing a merger with a competitor, how would you change the strategy? If you acquired another organization, what would you do differently?

4. Flexibility in acquisition can be very important for a project. How much of your management resources do you apply to developing and modifying alternative acquisition strategies? How important is this for you? For example, what if your budget decreases by 10 percent? What if your budget increases by 20 percent? How will you make your acquisition strategy flexible enough to respond to these changes?

2

Promises and Pitfalls

What are people saying about open systems and about commercial off-the-shelf (COTS) products? There are a lot of strong opinions, both pro and con. This chapter discusses the variety of opinions you might hear. It is meant to give you a taste of the complexity that surrounds open systems and the use of COTS products.

We present the pros and cons as promises and pitfalls in the context of situations in which someone might tell you about them. The promises are the *claimed* benefits of open systems and COTS products, whereas the pitfalls are the *claimed* shortcomings. The promises and pitfalls can apply to hardware and/or software in a system.

Many of these opinions, both pro and con, may not be supported by empirical evidence, but they represent much of what you might hear. As you read these opinions, keep in mind that we cover the issues raised here in greater detail later in the book. We give you information to help you evaluate and decipher claims and criticisms about open systems and the use of COTS products. Unfortunately, the answers are not always easy, but if you are knowledgeable about open systems and COTS products, you will be more likely to make informed decisions. An informed decision should also help you minimize and mitigate risks.

2.1 Key Definitions

Before we present some of the promises and pitfalls, let us define what we mean by *open systems* and *COTS products*. Many definitions of "open system" exist, and it is important for you to be aware of which one is being used. We use the following definition.

> **open system** ➧ A collection of interacting software and hardware component implementations, and users
>
> - Designed to satisfy stated needs
> - Having the interface specification of components
>   - Fully defined
>   - Available to the public
>   - Maintained according to group consensus
> - In which the component implementations conform to the interface specification

The key aspect of the definition hinges on the interface specification and the context in which it is created and used. The importance of this specification lies in the following elements:

- *Fully defined:* The interface specification must fully define the behavior and other aspects (pin size or application programming interface) for a component. Without a full definition, it is virtually impossible to integrate an implementation of the component in a system. Being fully defined also requires that the interface specification have no hidden, or secret, interfaces.

- *Available to the public:* The interface specification must be not only available but also capable of being *legally* implemented for sale by *anyone*. If any license or royalty fees are charged for the right to implement the specification, they do not create a barrier to widespread implementation and use.

- *Maintained according to group consensus:* Loosely speaking, there is some collective support for the interface specification. The broader the consensus, the more likely a COTS product based on that specification will be accepted. We discuss the notion of consensus further in Section 6.2.3.

There are related terms mentioned in our definition of open system: component, interface specification, consensus, and implementation. These terms are defined elsewhere in the book and in the glossary.

Sometimes, the phrase *open system* is defined in terms of the expectations one has. For example, someone may say that an open system is one that *gives* portable implementations. Therefore, people immediately assume that portable products are open ("If it's portable, it's open"). Or, someone may say that if you have interoperability, you have an open system. We prefer not to take that approach. Instead, we feel that such characteristics as portability and interoperability are *consequences* of an open system approach. For example, interoperability is partly a consequence of two or more implementations that conform to the same specification, such as a standard.

The second key item we need to define is the term COTS product. We do this in the following manner.

COTS product ➡ A product that is

- Sold, leased, or licensed to the general public
- Offered by a vendor trying to profit from it
- Supported and evolved by the vendor, which retains the intellectual property rights
- Available in multiple, identical copies
- Used without internal modification by a consumer

The main ideas to keep in mind are that a COTS product is generally available, a vendor is responsible for that product, and it is used as-is.

Believe it or not, there are differing views of just what constitutes a COTS product. For example, the government has a slightly different view, which we will discuss later, in Section 7.7.

Many of the expected benefits from the use of COTS products derive from elements of the preceding definition. As the products you examine get farther away from one or more of the elements of this definition, the likelihood of enjoying the full benefits of COTS products generally diminishes.

> **Commodity Market**
>
> "The essence of *open* is that customers face a choice of vendors offering interchangeable products, so that a *commodity market* evolves." (A colleague)

As noted in the preceding quote, it is the relation between an open system and COTS products that is of fundamental importance. Taken separately, open systems and the use of COTS products have significance for acquisition. However, when these ideas are treated *together*, through a commodity market, we begin to understand the real significance of open systems and the opportunities available through the COTS marketplace.

2.2 The Promises

Some of the claimed promises of open systems and COTS products are

- Lower costs
- Less reliance on proprietary solutions
- Shorter development schedule
- Better-tested products
- Increased portability
- Increased interoperability
- More stable technology insertion

The following sections explore these promises in more detail.

Lower costs

A marketing analyst may tell you, "Cost is driving the transition to open systems. COTS products developed in an open systems marketplace, according to standards, are more likely to meet your needs. And because you can get products from multiple vendors, you will save a lot of money."

This comment introduces the notion of a standard, which we define as follows.

standard ➡ A publicly available document that defines specifications for interfaces, services, processes, protocols, or data formats and that is established and maintained by group consensus.

The analyst may advise, "If a supplier sells a COTS product that meets more than one customer's requirements, it's cheaper for you to buy that product than for you to build it yourself. It's the *standards* that allow multiple suppliers to compete, lowering costs even more."

The analyst may then explain, "Say you're building a system that requires a database. Instead of developing the database management system yourself, you can buy a COTS product that meets your needs. So the power of the marketplace fosters competition and you get a product cheaply."

A project manager from another organization may tell you, "Many of our systems have unique components. We specified them and contracted out their implementations. If we move to open systems, it has to reduce our reliance on that one contractor. We can get greater commonality with related projects."

Less reliance on proprietary solutions

A vendor representative may tell you privately, "When you develop an implementation yourself, your development schedule may slip and affect project milestones. This happens to everyone, and you know it. When you buy a COTS product, it's ready-made and ready to go, so you get a shorter schedule."

Shorter development schedule

The representative may then say, "Besides, our COTS products are key to our survival in the market. We are competitively motivated to meet schedule. We may even increase investment to deliver on time or even sooner. First to market wins! If our schedule slips, we might lose your business to a competitor. It's really competition among vendors, as much as it is competition among the COTS products they develop. We think we have good products that will meet your needs. And they're ready *now*."

A quality assurance manager may explain, "In the marketplace of open systems, there are large user bases for COTS products. The product you buy will probably be

Better-tested products

tested better than you test your own code. That's because the COTS products are tested by the marketplace—lots of real-world users."

The manager may say, "This means that well-timed purchases may bring you better-tested COTS products. Wait for the early adopters to find the problems and for vendors to fix them. When the product stabilizes, you get on the bandwagon and roll with the market."

Increased portability

A systems analyst may declare, "Open COTS products are developed to industry standards. That's what counts. This means that they are more likely to be portable, and that's important for reuse. Standards allow many vendors to develop portable products. So you can upgrade hardware and just port your software. Keep moving with the marketplace."

> **portability** ➡ The ability of software to be transferred from one environment to another [ISO 91].

Portability is measured by the degree to which the installation and operation of a product can be accomplished adequately across different environments without alteration. Software that is more likely to be portable is advantageous to both the vendor and the user.

> ### Portability Economics
>
> "Form, fit, and function, in some user-specified context, are classic measures of portability. Portability is essentially an economic issue: If the cost of porting from one system to another is sufficiently small, it becomes practical to do so. That means you can shop for price or escape a grasping vendor. And the vendor knows it." (A colleague)

Increased interoperability

A systems consultant may promise, "In an open systems marketplace, multiple vendors can produce COTS products that conform to one spec. The specs that define requirements for interoperability allow you to pick and buy COTS products. When you use COTS products in your system, you're pretty sure they'll work together. Like the Web."

interoperability ➡ The ability of two or more systems or elements to exchange information and to use the information that has been exchanged [IEEE 96].

Interoperability is important because it allows for integration of products. This integration is sometimes also referred to as *plug-and-play*. Many would argue that the desire for plug-and-play is what has driven today's computing market.

Your manager may tell your young associate, "In an open systems market, you can keep pace with current technology. You can go out and buy new products based on the latest new technology. Now you become an integrator of COTS products. And that's easier than being a developer *and* an integrator."

More stable technology insertion

Then the manager says, "A vendor has to keep pace with new technology to get a competitive edge. You benefit from the vendor's need to compete. You also benefit from vendors who collaborate on new technology to capture new segments of the market if they continue to adhere to the standard you selected."

Your manager has the young associate's attention and continues: "All systems evolve. Open systems provide a framework for system evolution. Requirements creep—the increase of requirements over time—that's life, and it's always been like that. You upgrade COTS products to get the new technology, and the key is to maintain the system with discipline. The system can be stable yet flexible. So now the battle becomes who can inject technology better, faster, and cheaper. Whoever can do that will win. Remember what I just said, and you'll understand how our company works."

Taken together, these promises seem to make a strong case for pursuing an open systems approach, especially when COTS products are the basis for implementation. When you base your purchases on standards, the promises of open systems are appealing and look profitable.

Conclusion

However, you need to consider the interests and motives of the people presenting these promises. For example, formal standards organizations are convinced that using an open systems approach and standards is the best way to conduct business. Vendors tell you that informal industry standards are really what's important. And so on. You begin to see the tension that exists among organizations in today's marketplace. A lot of it is about the struggle for economic supremacy. And survival.

2.3 The Pitfalls

Some of the claimed pitfalls of open systems and COTS are

- Higher cost
- Higher risk
- Inability to meet special requirements
- Conformance problems
- Support problems
- Increased amount of continual investment
- Requirement for a new management style

The following sections explore these pitfalls in more detail.

Higher cost
A budget analyst might say, "I think that using open systems leads to significant costs. And some of them are unexpected. You bought that COTS product from a vendor that introduced a new packaging strategy. This vendor then decided to combine the COTS product you wanted with one that you didn't need. You had no choice but to buy the new *packaged* product, even though that's not what you really wanted. So there, you just paid for something you don't want or need. And you probably paid too much."

The budget analyst may also remind you, "As if that's not bad enough, now you've got to monitor the marketplace as never before. This market analysis may involve a lot of cost and effort. Maybe the issue is ultimately about control of the product. When you use COTS products, the vendor dictates upgrades. That's a cost. Remember all those PC cards I had to order for you?"

As if you haven't heard enough, the budget person walks away, saying, "And I have no idea how you are going to plan and budget for all this. Do you have budget to maintain all this stuff? Do you?"

A software manager may comment, "When you buy COTS products, you have less control over the spec. You have no control over the quality of the COTS product. You're better off building what you want and building it right than when you buy a product. Besides, half the COTS products are probably beta test versions, anyway."

Higher risk

Then the manager says, "If you are in charge of a software implementation, you could ask a programmer to show you the source code. If there's a problem, you fix the code."

The manager seems irritated now and says, "In the open systems market, getting the source code of a vendor's COTS software isn't going to happen. The vendor protects the product's code. If the vendor's competition gets it, the company's competitive edge may be gone. Then the vendor's existence may be threatened."

Free Code?

"Even if you were to get the code, what would you do with 500,000 lines of code? It would take major, substantial effort to be able to modify such code. Don't laugh. It's no longer the case that we own the majority of the code in an embedded system. And we haven't even begun to discuss the software tools used to generate the code (ours plus theirs) in that embedded system. We are talking millions of lines of code." (A colleague)

Reading a magazine article about an expensive government acquisition, you see a quote from an unidentified official as saying: "In some of our systems, the failure of a component implementation is treated as a system failure. For example, if an airplane's systems fail, lives may be lost. In mission-critical systems, such as an avionics platform, special methods are necessary to ensure that strict performance requirements are met. Dealing with special requirements also increases our cost of testing."

Inability to meet special requirements

The article goes on to quote the official: "The open systems marketplace currently offers few standards or COTS products that meet these strict performance or security requirements. For example, you probably cannot find products tailored for high-performance avionics systems in the commercial marketplace."

"Because commercial products are developed and sold for general use," the article says, "they may not be able to provide the level of security required for certain applications. Nor can the general marketplace address the ability of COTS hardware to function under adverse environmental conditions, such as extreme temperatures. We unfortunately cannot rely on the market for all our needs. That puts us in a niche market and causes much of our cost increase. At least it's not a $700 hammer!"

Conformance problems

A quality assurance manager may point out, "In some cases, conformance tests are available. You can apply these tests to COTS products to certify the product's conformance to a standard. But in other cases—most of them, really—there are no conformance tests."

> **conformance** ➡ The condition that exists when an implementation of a component fully adheres to a given interface standard.

The manager may then warn you, "Don't assume that conformance tests are available for all standards. And if you do buy a COTS product not tested for conformance, don't be foolish and think that the product will work exactly as you expect. Even if the vendor claims that the product conforms to the standard and even *with* conformance tests, your expectations may exceed what the tests provide."

Support problems

You were having a nice conversation with your boss. But then he gets a bit worried when you start talking about your maintenance plan. The boss says, "When you buy COTS products in an open systems marketplace, you have no more control over support of that product than the man in the moon."

"So," the boss argues, "if your users come to you with a problem, you'll probably find yourself dealing with a COTS vendor that is unwilling to 'fix' the problem. You're a small fish in the vendor's pond, and the vendor picks the feeding times. And about your idea of using COTS products from multiple vendors: You'll find them pointing fingers at one another the minute an integration problem pops up. And if you think you can get on the phone and have them fix it, you're just dreaming. And, no, I don't have the budget for that high-end maintenance contract you talked about. And forget third-party maintenance; what do they know?" Your boss walks away, a bit irritated at the whole conversation.

A government manager, who was listening to this, tries to help you and says, "It's bad enough in the commercial sector. But my system is expected to have a lifetime of more than 20 years. The life cycle of typical COTS software products is about 2 years. Then there is the problem of new technologies with new products. And they want me to be able to include all of this in a program plan! And budget that far out? Want to trade jobs?" She walks away, shaking her head in frustration.

A consultant may tell you, "When you move with the pace of technology and the COTS marketplace, you need to make some continual investment. Using COTS products may force you to upgrade one or more products in your system when a new version is released. New versions have higher-quality or valuable new features, so you want to use them. If the vendor is discontinuing support for the earlier versions of the COTS product, you may have to move more quickly. And the more vendors you are dealing with, the harder things may be."

Continual investment

The consultant says, "You expect some continual investment for your system to make sure that user requirements are met. But in the open systems marketplace, you may wind up investing in upgrades that have no relationship to changes in user needs, performance, or problems. Unfortunately, this continual investment for upgrades is difficult to estimate or plan, and it is often overlooked. And don't forget, there are costs to all this, beyond just the COTS products. There are testing and integration costs, too!"

A friend whose organization decided to pursue open systems and COTS products may tell you, "Using open systems forced us to do business in a different way. When we managed the acquisition of a system in the old way, we knew where the bugs were and how to fix them."

New management style

Your friend may warn you, "Using open systems, we've encountered problems we never expected. What's more work is that we had to use new processes to find solutions to these problems. We really needed a team approach to participate in the COTS market."

Your friend will say, "Making the decision to use an open systems approach was only the first step. My boss needed to give us more support. We should have committed more time and resources. And the boss didn't seem willing to deal with the changes that made all of us feel uneasy. The boss didn't know as much as we do. Remember, *we never did it that way before."*

Conclusion   Collectively, these pitfalls seem to make a strong case for avoiding an acquisition approach based on open systems and COTS products. Most of the pitfalls listed result from the perceived loss of control experienced by managers when they move to a new approach. The result is that they may resist the move to open systems and COTS products simply because it is new and unfamiliar.

Contrasting this collection of pitfalls with the promises in Section 2.2 demonstrates why there is controversy about open systems and the use of COTS products. Many successful managers are used to dealing with controversy. It's the uncertainty due to loss of control that is a new player in this game.

Despite the pitfalls, however, it is possible to realize the promises of open systems. There is no guarantee, and it will require changes in the way you manage an acquisition project. The principles discussed throughout this book are intended to help you avoid some of the pitfalls and to achieve more of the promises.

2.4 Summary

In this chapter, we have presented promises and pitfalls identified by the supporters and opponents of open systems and COTS products. The truth probably lies somewhere between these two extremes.

Promises include

- Lower costs
- Less reliance on proprietary solutions

- Shorter development schedule
- Better-tested products
- Increased portability
- Increased interoperability
- More stable technology insertion

  Pitfalls include

- Higher cost
- Higher risk
- Inability to meet requirements
- Conformance problems
- Support problems
- Increased amount of continual investment
- Requirement for a new management style

You must decide for yourself which of these claims to accept. All have some truth to them. If you are an informed user of open systems and COTS products, you can maximize the benefits and minimize the drawbacks. With improved understanding comes informed decision making and reduced risk.

2.5 Food for Thought

1. Ask three of your colleagues to *write down* what they mean by an *open system*. Then examine our definition on page 12. How do these definitions compare?

2. Consider our definition of open system. How would you change it to define a *closed* system? What are some examples of things that meet your definition of closed?

3. For each of the promises listed in Section 2.2, do you agree or disagree? Can you detect flaws in the comments made? Would you add other promises to this list? How would you rank the promises in order of most likely to affect your acquisition?

4. Repeat question 3 for the pitfalls listed in Section 2.3.

5. A colleague buys a COTS product for use in a system and then realizes that it's not exactly what is needed. Being ingenious, your colleague contracts with the developer of the COTS product to make a "few" modifications. How do you react to this? Do you consider the result still a COTS product? Why or why not?

6. Look at the definition of interoperability on page 17. Do you agree with it? How would you test for interoperability based on this definition?

7. Your boss comes in and says, "I want you to head up an integrated product team and tell me how our corporate acquisition is using open systems and COTS products. I want to know how we're benefiting from them. I'd like an answer in ten days, but give me some ideas by Friday. Get some of the senior folks to help you with this." How would you respond?

8. Pretend that you work for a vendor of a COTS product that has its own interface and competes with another product that is based on a standard. List five reasons why this is a better approach than using standards-based COTS products. Anticipate three criticisms of your approach and develop a response.

9. You have a friend who is convinced that cost and profit drive everything. Anything to lower cost is good. Therefore, the COTS marketplace and open systems are inherently good because they lower costs. Being a bit skeptical, you want to investigate this claim of lower cost. What information would you need to investigate the claim? Where do you think you could find it? And then what would you do with it when you got it?

10. How would you respond to the following statement: "If we use COTS products, we are using an open system, as industry decides what is or is not an open system. So what's the big deal?" Who in your organization would most likely make such a statement, and why?

3

The Paradigm Shift of Open Systems and COTS Products

In both industry and government, a fundamental change has occurred in the way that organizations do business. We describe this change as a *paradigm shift*.[1] You participate in a marketplace in which you acquire products and services to help you assemble, manage, and maintain your systems. Many of the issues you face when using open systems and COTS products originate from the forces of this marketplace.

3.1 Essence of the Paradigm Shift

The essence of the paradigm shift is that you will change from a producer to a consumer. When you are a producer, you create the implementation of the component or system. You can view it from every aspect because you have control over all its features and functions. For example, you know

- The manufacturing process for making a computer chip
- The code written to implement a software component
- The testing performed on the implementation

---

1. A paradigm is an example or pattern, especially an outstandingly clear or typical example or archetype.

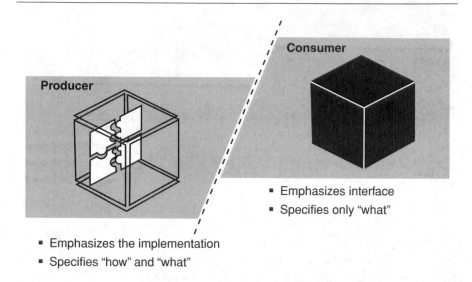

- Emphasizes interface
- Specifies only "what"

- Emphasizes the implementation
- Specifies "how" and "what"

FIGURE 3.1 Importance of the interface.

When you are a consumer, you purchase a COTS product. Most times, you can only view the product's interfaces. In fact, the product is much like a black box because you cannot see *how* the box functions, but you can see *what* it produces and/or receives. Figure 3.1 illustrates the paradigm shift in terms of your view of the product.

Differences in approach

Table 3.1 summarizes the difference between the producer (traditional) and consumer (open systems) approaches.[2]

Compare the producer and consumer approaches illustrated in Table 3.1. The most visible difference lies in stages 2 and 3. Instead of *defining* unique interface specifications, you *adopt* standard interface specifications. The specifications will be selected as a result of market research. Instead of *developing* implementations, you *procure* implementations that are based on standard interfaces. Preferably, these implementations will be standards-based COTS products. Each of these new activities is caused by participation in a larger community and marketplace.

---

2. The differences are illustrated in terms of a top-down model. However, the differences are independent of the acquisition approach and, therefore, will also be present in other approaches, such as spiral acquisition.

TABLE 3.1 Producer and Consumer Approaches

Stage	Producer Approach	Consumer Approach
1	Identify requirements.	Identify requirements.
2	Define unique interfaces.	Adopt standard interfaces based on market research.
3	Develop custom implementations.	Procure implementations based on standards.
4	Integrate custom implementations.	Integrate procured implementations.
5	Use and support system of developed implementations.	Use and support system of procured implementations.

Note that the approaches in Table 3.1 are presented as two ends of a spectrum of possibilities. These ends are characterized as pure development versus pure procurement. In reality, of course, the truth will lie somewhere in between. That is, some implementations will be procured and some will be developed for the same system. Furthermore, you can also develop an implementation that is open, in that it conforms to the associated interface standard.

The fourth and fifth stages in Table 3.1 manifest differences resulting from the shift to a consumer approach and may include the following.

- Integration of products is different, and possibly more difficult, because you have less insight into products. In some cases, a vendor may not want its products to integrate with others. The vendor may do this to retain market dominance.

- Support of products is different because you may use commercial sources to support your system.

3.2 Consequences of the Paradigm Shift

The open systems paradigm shift has significant consequences. Following are some consequences experienced by project managers.

- Interfaces become critically important to you because they specify visible aspects, such as function or data, of an associated product.

- Implementations that conform to standards become more important because standard-conforming implementations provide some assurance that the product behaves as specified.
- Because you are acting more as a consumer, you have less control over product implementation.
- If COTS products are readily available, you can insert and integrate products more quickly in an open systems environment.[3]
- You are no longer forced to rely on custom solutions, because, in the consumer world, you may have multiple product suppliers.

These pervasive changes in how you do business affect planning, selection of products and services, and the nature of your control and influence in the acquisition of systems.

Bottom-Up?

"The real issue here is of a top-down versus a bottom-up approach. Consumercentric means COTS, so bottom-up is how you'll act." (A colleague)

3.3 Marketplace Considerations

In a traditional development model, the marketplace can be simply characterized by vendors and users, as illustrated in Figure 3.2.

This figure shows individual vendors producing and selling COTS products that are then purchased by individual users. The market is characterized by *vendor-developed products*.

---

3. However, new technologies may not be readily available. For example, the real-time domain is a niche market, so it may take longer for new technologies to become available.

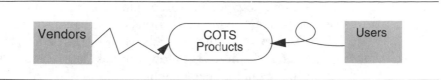

FIGURE 3.2 Product-centric marketplace.

One consequence of the paradigm shift is that you must now deal with the marketplace. In particular, we are now dealing with a *standards-based marketplace*. We show this view in Figure 3.3.

In Figure 3.3, standards bodies develop standards through the participation and influence of both users and vendors. The result is standards that are then adopted by *both* users and vendors. The vendors develop products, based on these standards, and the users make the standards part of their system specifications. As a result, the users buy the standards-based COTS products the vendors are selling.

This view of a standards-based marketplace, as shown in Figure 3.3, is an ideal model. We present it in this way to illustrate the fundamental aspects of how the paradigm shift affects project managers. Some embellishments of this model are left for you to consider in the Food for Thought at the end of the chapter.

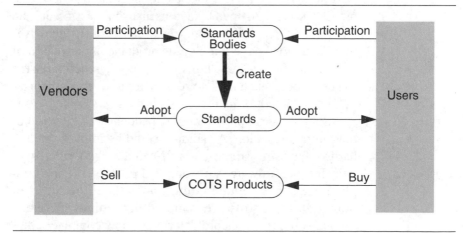

FIGURE 3.3 Standards-based marketplace.

In a marketplace in which standards exist, multiple vendors can sell implementations of the same standard. The existence of similar products usually creates competition, which in turn leads to lower prices. This is the economic argument for open systems.

Specifications

A marketplace is based on products of different types. Most products, whether open or proprietary, are based on a specification.

> **specification** ➡ A document that prescribes, in a complete, precise, and verifiable manner, the requirements, design, behavior, or characteristics of a system or system component.

Standards

The concept of open systems is based on standards.

> **standard** ➡ A publicly available document that defines specifications for interfaces, services, processes, protocols, or data formats and that is established and maintained by group consensus.

A standard is a particular type of specification. Both standards and specifications are written documents. Both describe characteristics that must exist in an implementation. However, standards are specifications that are established and maintained by a consensus process.

The term standard is sometimes used to refer to a product. For example, someone might say that "product X is an industry standard," meaning that product X is dominant in the marketplace. It does not necessarily mean that product X is maintained by a consensus process other than the marketplace, which admittedly can be a strong driver of technology. We do not include products in our notion of a standard. Sometimes, however, one may encounter the use of "product standard" to refer to a product an organization has adopted for its use.

Standards can be written independently of the form of their implementation. A standard could be implemented in hardware or software. Standards can also be written specifically for hardware, software, and processes. For example, a hardware standard determines the dimensions of floppy disks. A software standard determines file name syntax. A process standard determines how computer chips are manufactured to avoid damage from magnetic sources.

We discuss standards in further detail in Chapter 6.

Early Standards

Standards have been around in one form or another for years. Some credit Cain, from biblical times, as the standards bearer for measures. Throughout centuries, standards have been established: from the Egyptian cubit to the Greek foot to the Roman mile to the Saxon yard. Not all standards, however, were driven by consensus. Henry I found the definition of a Saxon yard inadequate and decreed that the measure for a yard equal the length of his own arm.

In modern times, the advent of science and technology revealed how important standards are. For example, a series of fatal accidents involving boilers occured in the late nineteenth century. In 1894, the Henry Clay Mine and the town of Shamokin, Pennsylvania, were destroyed when 27 boilers simultaneously exploded in the mine, killing thousands of people. By 1910, there were 1,400 boiler explosions a year. Partly as a result of these accidents, the American Society of Mechanical Engineers wrote standards for boilers; those standards were adopted by most states and practically eliminated boiler-related accidents.

3.4 Importance of the Interface

The interface specification associated with all components, especially standards-based COTS products, now assumes a central position throughout the acquisition process.

> **interface** ➡ (1) A shared boundary across which information is passed. (2) A hardware or software component that connects two or more other components for the purpose of passing information from one to the other [IEEE 96].

The term *interface* can mean different things to different people.[4] One person may think of the computer keyboard.

---

4. In the second form of the IEEE definition of interface, the term component is used. In IEEE parlance, a component is either software or hardware. In this text, however, we use the term component to denote an abstraction of something that may be later implemented. (It is interesting to note that [IEEE 96] contains 22 different definitions for the term *interface*.)

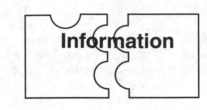

FIGURE 3.4 An interface.

Another may think of an application programming interface (API) to a database management system. Another may think of the screen display of a graphics software application. Another example of an interface is the connection between a computer and a modem. All these examples are interfaces because they all manage the transfer of information from one system or component to another and describe *what* information is produced and/or received.

Figure 3.4 is a visual definition of an interface. Note that the two elements share a boundary and that information is passed across that boundary.

The interface specifies *what* operations are performed. The implementation takes care of *how* those operations are performed. In software standards, the API defines the operations and behavior in a programming language. But the implementation defines how those operations are performed.

3.5 Product Quality Characteristics

Products can be viewed from a variety of perspectives. You can evaluate products by assessing such characteristics as reliability, usability, and efficiency, to name a few. These characteristics enable you to differentiate products from one another and provide a way to view products. As an example, Figure 3.5 illustrates several characteristics that consumers can use to evaluate an automobile.

Note that, depending on the consumers' perspective, the automobile can be evaluated and rated differently. For example, safety may be a prime concern for a family car.

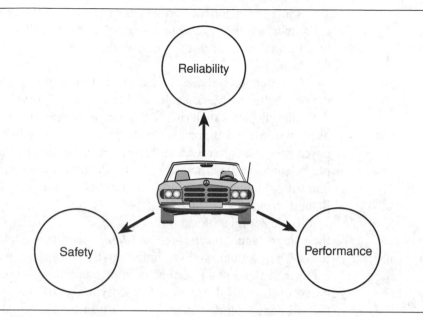

FIGURE 3.5 Examples of product quality characteristics.

As we mentioned earlier, you can view a product from a variety of perspectives: functionality, reliability, usability, efficiency, maintainability, and portability. These *product quality characteristics* are defined as follows [ISO 91].

functionality ⇒ The existence of a set of functions and their specified properties to satisfy stated or implied needs.

reliability ⇒ The capability of software to maintain its level of performance under stated conditions for a stated period of time.

usability ⇒ The effort needed for use, and the individual assessment of such use, by a stated or implied set of users.

efficiency ⇒ The relationship between the level of performance of the software and the amount of resources used, under stated conditions.

maintainability ⇒ The effort needed to make special modifications.

portability ⇒ The ability of software to be transferred from one environment to another.

Some characteristics are evaluated based on the product's interface. For example, to evaluate the usability of a word processing application, you can examine its user interface.

Other characteristics, however, require that you have the product available to evaluate. For example, to evaluate the reliability of a disk drive, you can examine materials used, workmanship, or assembly processes, or you can purchase some disk drives and test them. As another example, to evaluate the efficiency of a product, you can benchmark it, which gives you information that is not available in an interface specification.

Table 3.2 identifies product quality characteristics and their importance in *interface* and *implementation* evaluations. The product quality characteristic commonly used for each evaluation—interface or implementation—is indicated by the word *dominant*. Empty cells in Table 3.2 mean a less than dominant contribution for that quality characteristic. Note that most of the product quality characteristics are more sensitive to the implementation than to the interface.

The product quality characteristics listed in Table 3.2 are defined in an international standard [ISO 91]. Other groups have also defined product quality characteristics. For example, the MITRE *Guide to Total Software Quality Control* uses the following characteristics: efficiency, reliability, maintainability, expandability, interoperability, reusability, integrity, survivability, correctness, verifiability, flexibility, and portability [Clapp 91].

TABLE 3.2 Relative Importance of Product Quality Characteristics

Product Quality Characteristics	Interface	Implementation
Functionality	Dominant	
Reliability		Dominant
Usability	Dominant	
Efficiency		Dominant
Maintainability		Dominant
Portability		Dominant

3.6 The Loss of Control

In the producer approach, you have control over all product quality characteristics shown in Table 3.2 because you have access to and control of the interface *and* the implementation. As a consumer, you do not have control over the COTS product. And it's not just today's product but also the way that product will change over time.

> ### Change
>
> "The real shift is that in the past, we could get exactly what we wanted, and producers would bend to our will. But now the tables are turned, and we must bend our systems, and often requirements, to what the producers choose to offer, which is never exactly what we want or perhaps need." (A colleague)

Although your *control* is significantly reduced, your **Influence** choices have increased. Remember that you may evaluate and purchase multiple products in a competitive marketplace.

You can exert influence in several ways.

- You can actively participate in standards organizations to ensure that standards meet your needs.
- You can work with other consumers to increase the impact of your buying decisions.
- You can interact with producers to communicate your needs.

Finally, you can vote with your wallet!

3.7 Implications for the Government

Because of the way the government did business until about the mid-1990s, the paradigm shift for project managers in government is often a much larger and more abrupt shift than for project managers in industry. In the 1960s, the government purchased more than half of the computer equipment sold in the United States. Today, the government represents only a small percent of the overall market. The amount of influence the government has, *as a consumer*, has declined dramatically.

The Good Old Days

"The government (civil plus military) is a few percent of the market. If the government were an extremely large consumer—like it used to be—there would be no issue about persuading vendors to build exactly to government specs and needs." (A colleague)

Historically, the government as a consumer opted to build when making the build-or-buy decision. If the government did not build the products, it would contract out the work and provide detailed specifications.

Not only did the government build its own component and system implementations, but also it created a huge number of its own unique standards. Open systems presents a shift away from those unique government standards to industry standards.

During the 1990s, the federal government—from Congress on down—became committed to increased exploitation of the commercial marketplace and to acting more like businesses. Acquisition reform emphasized streamlining the procurement process and established chief information officers (CIOs) in all departments and agencies. The Department of Defense (DoD) eliminated many of its military-unique standards in favor of industry standards and performance specifications.

The shift from government standards to industry standards is only part of the change. Deciding which system components to build and which ones to buy requires careful consideration by the project staff in government. It's no longer the case that the old approach will work: The government needs to be an active participant, not a dictator, in the marketplace. Those days are gone.

Cookies, Anyone?

The story about the government buying some cookies is an example of the government as a consumer. Apparently, the government, following regulations, awarded a bid for cookies to the lowest bidder, a producer that failed to deliver a quality product. In response, to protect itself as a consumer and so that other producers would be able to compete fairly with one another, the DoD approved a military specification (MIL-SPEC) for chocolate-covered oatmeal cookies and chocolate covered brownies.

The 22-page document contains requirements for ingredients, ingredient ratios, preparation, cutting, packaging, weight, labeling, and preservation. The document includes finished-product requirements [MIL-C-44072C 90].

a. There shall be no foreign materials such as, but not limited to dirt, insect parts, hair, wood, glass, or metal.

b. There shall be no foreign odor or flavor such as, but not limited to, burnt, scorched, stale, sour, rancid, or moldy.

The document also defines the various types of defects that would cause rejection of the product, for example,

- Size not as specified
- Cookie bar interior not crisp
- Texture of brownies not hard or firm
- Coating not completely covering product

This MIL-SPEC is an example of what can happen when a government consumer and a producer have an adversarial rather than a cooperative relationship. To someone stocking or buying a package of cookies in a grocery store, this specification must seem ludicrous. To a consumer that buys millions of cookies and because of a less than honest producer, it is unfortunately a necessary part of doing business. This MIL-SPEC has not yet been canceled for procurement. But the story continues; see question 7 in Section 3.9.

Take a break and get yourself a treat!

3.8 Summary

The essence of the paradigm shift is that project managers act as consumers of COTS products rather than as producers of implementations. This change involves participation in a standards-based marketplace.

Paradigm shift

Interface   The interface to a product now assumes a central position in acquisition. Although many product characteristics are determined by the implementation, the interface specification describes visible features and behavior.

Consequences   Some of the consequences of the paradigm shift are

- Fundamental changes in the way acquisition is conducted
- Loss of control over product characteristics
- Opportunity for influence over standards and products

Government   The paradigm shift is especially challenging for government and has generated many changes.

3.9 Food for Thought

1. Consider a marketplace defined in terms of vendors, consumers, regulators, standards, and products and services.

   a. Make a drawing that shows each of these entities and how they relate to one another. (For example, what is the relation between a vendor and a product?) In what way are there cooperative and/or competitive relationships among the participants?

   b. What is the role of the regulators?

   c. How could your project participate in such a marketplace?

2. Consider the following comment: "An interface specification is a contract between the entities that exchange information. What passes through the interface is a detail. The lowly electric plug is a standardized interface, but only AC power flows, not information." Do you agree or disagree with this statement? Why or why not?

3. Go back to the discussion of Table 3.2. Do you agree with the choices that have been made for the entries in the table? If not, what would you change, and why? Do you agree with the product characteristics we have listed? If not, what would you change, and why?

4. Suppose that a standard has a lot of features your technical folks like, but it's just not perfect. If your technical folks suggest using the standard but making a few changes, which your people *need*, how do you react?

5. Assume that there may be similar products on the market for a particular function. In what way, and how, do you believe the consumer influences the *implementation* of those products? Do consumers influence the interface more or less than the implementation? Should they?

6. One of the ways the government can participate in the marketplace is as a regulator. Identify a number of ways in which this occurs. How do you feel this has changed over the past three years? What do you think will happen in the next three years? How does the government's role as a regulator affect you?

7. To continue the story about the specification of the cookie (see page 37), MIL-C-44072C is no longer valid for procurement. The reason it has not been canceled outright is that it is still included in some solicitations. It is expected that the MIL-SPEC will be replaced by a Commercial Item Description (CID). The one considered is referenced as A-A-20295, for cookies. Take a look at this CID[5] and compare it to the MIL-SPEC version.[6] How do these documents compare?

8. It is easy to laugh at the details of a specification for a cookie, as discussed on page 37. However, to what extent is it necessary to develop this level of detail in order to allow for *full and open competition?* How do you balance the need for competition with the need to avoid overspecification? Under what circumstances would you lean one way or the other?

9. Why do you suppose the government went to all the trouble of specifying the details of the cookie specification rather than just buying cookies made by a cookie manufacturer?

---

5. You can find the CID on the Web at *http://www.ams.usda.gov/fqa/aa20295.pdf.*
6. You can find this MIL-SPEC on the Web at *http://astimage.daps.dla.mil/docimages/0000\32\92\24150.PD0.*

4

Elements of an Open, COTS-Based Approach

The traditional acquisition approach is based on the custom development of a system.[1] Now we will discuss an approach based on open systems and the use of COTS products. One of the main differences between these approaches is how system architecture and design are developed. An open systems approach emphasizes the use of standards, whereas a COTS-based approach emphasizes the use of commercial products. In both cases, the approach is that of a consumer rather than of a producer. This approach applies throughout the system acquisition process, particularly in the selection of standards and implementations.

An open systems, COTS-based approach applies to more than development of new systems. You also may apply this approach in projects that

- Reengineer all or part of an existing system
- Upgrade all or part of an existing system
- Integrate existing systems

In this chapter, we provide an overview of the essential elements of the approach. We do not attempt to address all the details or complexities of the open, COTS-based approach. As you read this chapter, set aside for the moment the complexity you experience in the real world

---

1. The traditional approach is based on a producer model rather than a consumer model, as discussed in Section 3.2.

and focus on the basic steps in the process. Later chapters fill in more of the details and explore them in the context of real-world constraints.

4.1 An Overview of the Approach

The open systems, COTS-based approach, illustrated in Figure 4.1, includes seven elements and their interactions. The seven elements of the approach are as follows.

Element descriptions

- *Requirements:* baselining your current system with respect to the use of standards and COTS products, specifying system requirements and ranking requirements by priority.

- *Reference models:* defining terminology and concepts by creating a high-level model of the system.

- *Components and interfaces:* evaluating architectural approaches, identifying components, surveying technology, prototyping, and documenting the architecture.

- *Standards:* evaluating and selecting standards, establishing liaisons with standards bodies and user groups, documenting standards coordination, and resolving inconsistencies between standards.

- *Implementations:* evaluating, selecting, procuring, and testing implementations of selected standards. Special emphasis is given to the use of COTS products .

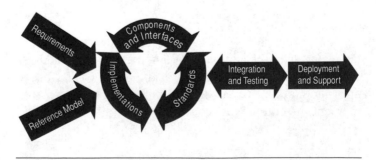

FIGURE 4.1 Elements of an open, COTS-based approach.

- *Integration and testing:* integrating component implementations and testing the integrated system.
- *Deployment and support:* distributing and maintaining the system, including all aspects of life-cycle
  maintenance.

The elements in this model are *not* executed as linear
steps. Each element affects others in the model. For example, selecting a standard might require the relaxation of a
requirement.

Element interaction

The three elements at the center of the model—*components and interfaces*, *standards*, and *implementations*—
are both interdependent and comprise an iterative subprocess.
For example, if two parts of a system cannot be integrated
as expected, you may have to change one or more of the
implementations, the standards, or the architecture. And if
that doesn't work, you may have to go back and modify
requirements.

Note that maintenance considerations are important
during all the activities. These considerations need to be
addressed as early as possible and as often as necessary.

The ability to manage and adjust, if necessary, the
amount of iteration in the approach will be a key factor to
success of a project. If there is a lot of churning in the iterative stages, it will be reflected by lack of progress, which,
unfortunately, winds up being schedule delays and/or cost
overruns. We all know the consequences of that! This is
especially true in today's environment, which pressures
managers to demonstrate success—early and often.

4.2 Elements of the Approach

In the following sections, we present details about all seven
elements of the open, COTS-based approach. For each element, we provide a list of key tasks and suggestions. Key
tasks ultimately will relate to activities in the overall
acquisition approach.

4.2.1 Requirements

Requirements must be formulated before building any system. The *requirements* element includes the following key tasks.

- Baseline your current system, if there is one.
- Specify system requirements.
- Rank requirements by priority.

Baseline the current system   If you have a current system, we assume that its requirements are specified. If you do not have a current system, skip this task and concentrate on the other two parts of the *requirements* element. However, it is important to determine the openness of each component and interface in the system. Doing so will help identify opportunities to insert open system technologies in the system. The result is a baseline of your system with respect to the use of standards and COTS products.

Specify requirements   Specify requirements for the system. This task would probably include identifying

- Functional requirements of the system
- Constraints on the system because of its environment
- Specifications of the system's interface with other external systems

We divide requirements into three general types: strategic, organizational, and technical. Examples of each for systems, implementations, and interfaces follow.

Examples of *system requirements:*

- *Strategic:* All corporate divisions shall use commercial implementations whenever possible.
- *Organizational:* The system shall conform to standards policy xxx, version 2, entitled *Standards Conformance.*
- *Technical:* All database management implementations used in the system shall provide a mean-time-to-repair of less than one hour.

Examples of *interface requirements:*

- *Strategic:* The interface specification shall be supported by at least five existing products.

- *Organizational:* The interface specification shall conform to our organization's standard policies for language bindings.
- *Technical:* The interface specification shall provide the capability to interact with a remote directory service agent.

Examples of *implementation requirements:*

- *Strategic:* The component implementation shall conform to the XYZ standard.
- *Organizational:* The component implementation shall interoperate with other, similar component implementations used in our organization.
- *Technical:* The component implementation shall perform 100K operations per second.

When we speak of ranking requirements, we are concerned with two related sets of requirements: (1) a ranking of system requirements and (2) a ranking of those requirements in the context of an interface. Clearly, some requirements are more critical than others, and you must make this determination for your system.

Rank interface requirements

Dealing with requirements is a continuing process. For example, as you move into design, you may find that some requirements may be difficult to implement, owing to lack of a standard interface specification. In this case, you might also consider eliminating or delaying requirements that are not critical, for the sake of using existing standards.

Stating Requirements

When you are in a producer mindset, specifying requirements is a fairly straightforward process. But things change when you turn to a consumer approach. This is especially difficult for government project managers. In one study that surveyed senior industry managers, their greatest complaint was that the government told them *how* to do something rather than *what* to do [DoD 93]. Acquisition reform in the government was intended, in part, to mitigate this problem.

4.2.2 Reference Models

Creating a reference model of your system provides a view of the system that focuses on its functions and features instead of its implementation. We will cover reference models in Chapter 5. In brief, a reference model is an abstract, implementation-independent description of a system in terms of entities and services. The *reference models* element includes the following key tasks.

- Define terminology and concepts.
- Identify entities and services.
- Identify relations among entities.

Define common terminology

Define common terminology and concepts through the modeling process. Although you can use other modeling methods, creating a reference model is an effective way to establish common terminology for your system. By collectively developing the reference model, your team can normalize its lexicon. This, in turn, helps clarify concepts that will apply to your system. An additional value in developing common terminology is that this same terminology can be used throughout the remainder of the project.

Identify entities and services

Identify entities and services as part of creating a reference model of the system. This process helps you to later define components of the system. The specification of services also helps in identifying relevant interface specifications later in the project. An additional benefit is that the reference model also helps to define market domains that you will need to understand later in the process.

Identify relations among entities

Identify relations among entities to integrate the entities in a reference model. Simply identifying entities and services is only part of the whole job. The integration of services establishes relations among their associated entities. The relations among entities serves as the glue that holds the reference model together.

4.2.3 Components and Interfaces

The *components and interfaces* element includes the following key tasks.

- Rank components by priority.

- Consider various architectural approaches.
- Identify components.
- Perform market research.
- Prototype critical aspects for feasibility.
- Document system architecture.

Because systems in the real world typically consist of some combination of open and closed components,[2] it is important to rank these components by priority. For example, suppose that a system has ten components, but for some reason, such as cost or time, it makes sense to migrate only five of those components toward open systems and COTS products. You need to decide which components are most important and the order in which they should be migrated. **Rank components by priority**

Likewise, there may be multiple components in your system, but standards with defined conformance tests may not exist for all of them.[3] Which ones are they, and which of them are most important? How do you account for conformance in defining your priorities?

Similarly, if an implementation of an interface is the backbone of the entire system, it might make sense to move it toward being an open system quickly. On the other hand, if an interface is for a unique piece of equipment, its priority may be lower.

Consider the various architectural approaches available to you, such as **Consider architectural approaches**

- Your organization's existing system architecture.
- General architectures, often called *architectural styles*, such as client/server, pipe and filter, or the architectural consequences of an object-oriented approach.
- Domain-specific architectures or domain-specific ideas about how to build systems. A domain-specific architecture is an architectural specification developed

---

2. An open component is one whose interface specification is open, i.e., fully defined, available to the public, and maintained according to group consensus.
3. Conformance is the condition that exists when an implementation of a component adheres to its interface specification. For more details on conformance and conformance testing, refer to Section 6.6.

for a particular application domain, such as avionics or personnel management. A key reference to work in this area is [Mettala 92]; more recent work in this area is found under the topic of product lines.

Identify components

Identify the components of the current system and of similar systems. You may find another organization that solved a problem similar to the one you have.

For example, if you are involved with a Navy avionics system, you may find someone in the Air Force is taking an open systems approach to avionics. Such cases can provide you with opportunities to share knowledge, architectures, or implementations and, later, procurement.

Market research

Market research is very important to an open, COTS-based approach. The goal of this research is to seek out information such as

- Standards related to your domain
- Standards-based implementations and their attributes, including business attributes, that can help you solve your problem
- Vendors that are market leaders and their market shares
- Technologies for which products are widely available in the marketplace and the business benefit experienced by the users of a given technology
- Which standards-based implementations work together and an assessment of how well they work

Moving Markets

"You must also survey the current markets and understand the major players' various agendas and motives, or you are sure to choose a doomed technology and/or vendor. Think of all the folks who believed that ISO-OSI would sweep away TCP/IP and the Internet protocol suite. Never happened. Cost of OSI was too high, and market leaders had already invested in TCP/IP, so the technology was already available. And cheaper."
(A colleague)

Market research must be taken seriously. Failure to properly address market considerations can have significant adverse effects on an acquisition.

Prototype critical aspects of your system for feasibility. Prototyping is a common activity in many acquisitions. However, when you use the open systems, COTS-based approach, prototyping can involve the experimental use of COTS products to determine their suitability for a system.

Prototype critical aspects

Document the architecture of your system and decisions you make about architectures, components, and interfaces. In other words, keep a current record of the vision you have for your system. You never know when you'll have to reexamine those decisions!

Document the architecture

4.2.4 Standards

The *standards* element includes the following key tasks.

- Evaluate and select standards.
- Establish liaisons with standards bodies and user groups.
- Document your standards coordination, and resolve deficiencies.

Review your market research, and evaluate and select the standards you want to use for your interfaces. Always evaluate standards against explicit criteria, including

Evaluate and select standards

- Interface requirements
- Scenarios of expected use in the intended domain
- Compatibility with other selected standards
- Availability and suitability of implementations

Establish liaisons with standards groups and user groups to ensure that you have the latest information about the standards relevant to your system. Changes in a standard could, for example, significantly limit the products available that implement the standard.

Establish liaisons

These liaisons are an important source of standards information, including status, plans, issues, and so on. You may also be able to exert influence over the development of standards. In any case, you can get first-hand feedback on what to expect from standards, and you can identify any weaknesses of the standards.

Document coordination

Document the coordination of the standards you select, and make note of any resulting deficiencies. Do not just identify the standards you want to use: Determine how you expect the standards to interoperate and where gaps exist between them. This documented coordination is called a *profile*.[4]

Changes in Government

The open systems approach may seem like a whole new way to develop systems, but government managers have dealt with standards, requirements, and iteration before. "We have always had to select standards when designing systems. More often than not, the standards were MIL-STDs but they were standards nonetheless, and we had endless debates on which were best. One thing that's changed with the advent of open systems is that we have more standards to choose from, so it's more complex to choose. The arguments are if anything more heated. But at least the gov folks have played the game." (A colleague)

4.2.5 Implementations

The *implementations* element includes the following key tasks.

- Evaluate and select implementations consistent with the selected standards.
- Procure implementations.

Evaluate and select

Evaluate and select implementations by looking for such things as

- Conformance with the standards you have chosen
- Availability on selected platform(s)
- Vendor reputation

---

4. More information on standards and profiles is provided in Chapter 6.

- Cost, performance, reliability, stability, and supportability
- Licensing information

When you decide to procure implementations, you must ask yourself questions, including the following.

Procure implementations

- Can you buy them off the shelf?
- Will you have to build the implementations you need?
- Will you customize the component implementations to fit your needs?

Although you must test an implementation's ability to fulfill requirements, such as performance and reliability, you must also test whether the implementations you have acquired meet the standards you have chosen: conformance testing.

Whenever possible, avoid modifying implementations— for example, changing the source code—that you did not produce. The more you modify, the less you will benefit from purchasing the product in the marketplace. Consider, for example, the potential difficulty of accommodating upgrades of a product that you have modified.

4.2.6 Integration and Testing

The *integration and testing* element includes the following key tasks.

- Integrate component implementations.
- Test.

Integrate the implementations you chose for your system. By integrate, we mean performing those activities that bring implementations together.

Integrate

These implementations may come from different sources. Some may be purchased from vendors, and others may be developed under contract or by your organization. Two commercial products may not integrate the way you expected them to. In that case, you may have to create "glue code" to make the two commercial products work together effectively.

Test

When you perform *integration* testing, you determine whether a set of implementations is able to meet its collective requirements. *System* testing is that form of testing to determine whether the system meets overall system requirements. This is the last place where you want to be surprised.

4.2.7 Deployment and Support

The *deployment and support* element includes the following key tasks:

- Deploy the system.
- Maintain and enhance the system.
- React to outside forces.

Deploy the system

Determine how you intend to deploy the system. You can deploy incrementally or all at once. Also, ensure that you obtain the appropriate licenses for all commercial items you plan to deploy.[5]

Maintain and enhance the system

All systems require maintenance and enhancements, such as adding new functions in an upgrade. In these cases, you will find that you may rely on sources outside your own organization for maintenance of some implementations. Drivers to maintenance and enhancements to the system can come from users as well as the marketplace. And don't forget about budget, schedules, and your boss!

React to outside forces

You may have to react to outside forces that are beyond your control. For example, if standards change, you may have to decide whether to change your implementations. If a COTS product you purchased for your system changes, you may have to decide whether to adopt the change. Or, a supplier whose product you are using may change its business plans or go out of business.

Ideally, these issues should be addressed as part of your risk-mitigation strategy. However, some events cannot be anticipated, so you must try to expect the unexpected, which also is a risk-mitigation strategy.

---

5. More information on licenses is given in Section 7.6.

4.3 Iteration

In the previous sections, we discussed the major elements of the open systems, COTS-based approach. This section covers the iteration that is fundamental to this approach. Iteration occurs in two ways:

- Iteration of the three middle elements of the approach: components and interfaces, standards, and implementations

- Iteration of all the elements in the approach

These iterations are illustrated in Figure 4.2.

4.3.1 Iteration of Components and Interfaces, Standards, and Implementations

When you select components and interfaces, standards, and implementations, you cannot select them one by one. Instead, you must consider these three elements at the same time because the choices you make about any one may affect the other two.

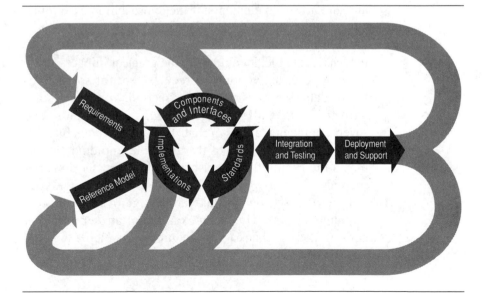

FIGURE 4.2 Iteration of elements.

This interdependence among components and interfaces, standards, and implementations is one of the defining characteristics of an open systems, COTS-based approach. For example, you might choose certain components and interfaces only to discover that no standards are available for one of the interfaces you have chosen. Or, you may find that your division of components and interfaces does not match the division that you find in the marketplace. Such a discovery might lead you to reconsider your components and interfaces and to divide components and interfaces differently to give yourself a better chance of using available standards and COTS implementations.

Likewise, once you choose components and interfaces and standards, you may look for implementations and find that there are no implementations for the standards you have chosen. This discovery might lead you to consider changing some of your standards selections so that you can find COTS products that will meet your requirements.

4.3.2 Iteration of All Seven Elements

The iterative nature of the approach applies in a larger context: You iterate not only among components and interfaces, standards, and implementations but also between any and all seven elements of the approach. For example, you might be driven by a change that forces you to change the reference model of the system. Although this may be the least probable, it could have the greatest impact.

Suppose that you have a requirement for some number of database transactions per second. You find a standard that meets all your *functional* requirements, and several implementations of that standard are available. But then you find that none of the available implementations meets the required number of database transactions per second. What do you do? One option is to change your requirement so you can take advantage of the available implementations. This is an example of an iteration that goes all the way back to the requirements element of the open systems approach.

Where to Start?

"More important, the economics of open systems have forced us from the almost pure top-down approach of yore to a largely bottom-up approach. In the old days, we paid for and got full-custom development. It was expensive, but we could get exactly what we wanted. Now, with COTS products being so much cheaper than custom, one first looks around to see what's available, then designs around this. The requirements are often bent to meet what's available. This change of approach can be disorienting to old timers, but top-down design simply does not work with systems built from COTS products; those products are what they are, and your design must bend to match. So, we may start with a very general top-down design—often called an "architecture"—but soon we do a bottom-up analysis to ensure that all requirements have been met or to identify the ones that have not been met and cannot be met at reasonable cost. Then, either the requirements are adjusted, or some custom design and implementation is undertaken." (A colleague)

4.4 Summary

In this chapter, we introduced the seven elements of an approach based on open systems and COTS products:

- Requirements
- Reference model
- Components and interfaces
- Standards
- Implementations
- Integration and testing
- Deployment and support

We stressed the highly iterative nature of the three elements at the center of the open systems approach: *components and interfaces*, *standards*, and *implementations*. Finally, we discussed the iteration and interaction of all seven elements of the open, COTS-based approach.

4.5 Food for Thought

1. Suppose that you have a legacy system, either in whole or in part, and are considering moving to an open, COTS-based approach. Can you define a process that identifies whether your current system can be mapped to an open system? What is different from developing a new system?

2. Let's be honest here. When we talked about identifying requirements, we suggested associating them with interfaces. When we talked about a reference model, we talked about identifying entities. Isn't there an architecture-like process going on here? We might think that it's top-down, but haven't we really introduced some bottom-up thinking, even early on in the process? What do you think? For example, in your experience, how many architecture-like things sneak in very early in the overall acquisition process? What causes this to happen? Is it necessarily bad?

3. One of the main benefits of developing a reference model is for project personnel to share a common concept of the system and common terminology. Does your current project have a common language? Is it written down? What are the ten most important terms to your system? Would everyone agree on their meaning and the concept behind each of them?

4. How many components are there in your current system? How many interfaces are there among these components? If you have N components, the worst-case number of interfaces would be $N(N-1)/2$. How close is your system to this value? What do you infer from this about the *coupling* between components?

5. How many standards are used in your current system? What was the rationale for choosing them? In how many instances did you have any serious choices to make, and what were they?

6. How many COTS products are used in your current system? What were some of the criteria used to select them? In particular, were the criteria the same for each COTS product?

7. We talked about changes that can be caused by the marketplace in terms of COTS products, whether new, upgrades, or dropouts. How would you address the question of changes caused by *technologies?* Sketch out the process you would use to assess technology effects on a system. How different and/or similar is your process to one for assessing standards or COTS products?

8. Much of the work associated with systems is in the area of maintenance, which may include fixes and major upgrades. Do you think that a manager's approach is necessarily different for a new development versus a system in maintenance? How would the elements of the open, COTS-based approach differ for these two situations? Do you think of the word *tailoring* when you develop your answer?

PART TWO

Understanding the
New World

One of the challenges of learning any new field is understanding the vocabulary and key concepts in that field. We will do that first, and then build on those basic ideas and develop the fundamental triad of open, COTS-based systems such as reference models and architectures, standards, and COTS products. The way in which that knowledge is applied in an acquisition is paramount to your ability to succeed. We will give you an introductory flavor of that approach by presenting some high-level roadmaps. Later in the book, we will fill in many of the details; here our concern is with foundation material and an introduction to how it can be applied.

Chapters in Part Two

5

Reference Models and Architectures

In this chapter, we cover reference models and architectures, which together form one of the key elements of the iterative process. Reference models and architectures are important in your acquisition approach because they help you identify components and interfaces. This, in turn, helps you identify opportunities for including standards and COTS products in a system.

The use of reference models can be traced to the open systems world. On the other hand, architectures have been with us for a long time. Certain aspects of architectures are unique to open systems, however. We make that connection in Chapter 8.

We must warn you that the terms reference model and architecture are used in many contexts, often without clear definition. When you encounter these terms, you should seek to understand how they are used and what meaning is intended by the speaker or the writer.

5.1 Abstraction

Both *reference models* and *architectures* are abstract representations that enable the study and development of systems.

- *Reference models* are *descriptive;* they enable you to represent systems apart from their implementations.

- *Architectures* are *prescriptive;* they enable you to represent a system with partial reference to implementations.

A fundamental characteristic of software and systems engineering over the past 30 years has been an increased emphasis on abstraction. Abstraction allows you to focus on relevant issues while minimizing the constraints associated with implementations.

For example, you can explore *what* information should be distributed to remote sites without addressing *how* the information will be distributed. The separation of *what* and *how* is extremely important. A focus on *what* emphasizes aspects of the problem space, whereas a focus on *how* emphasizes the solution space. Understanding this distinction is important because it helps you to clearly focus on either the problem side or the solution side of an overall question.

5.2 Reference Models

Using reference models, you can create a simplified view of your system. This view allows you to focus on the functions and features of the system without worrying about implementation details.

reference model ➡ An abstract description of a system in terms of entities and services.

The description of a reference model typically consists of two parts: the *graphic* part and the *textual* part. Some think of the reference model only in terms of the graphic part, or *picture,* of the system. However, without the textual description, the graphic cannot fully define a reference model.

The *graphic* part illustrates the entities and relations among the entities. The *textual* part describes the entities in terms of the services they provide and describes relations that are or are not present on a diagram.

For example, the graphic part of a reference model may have an entity labeled *communication*. However, you do not know what *communication* refers to until you read the textual specification that describes the communication services of the reference model.

5.2.1 Purposes of Reference Models

A reference model can provide a

- System-specific language for communication and reasoning
- Description of essential system functionality
- Means to manage complexity
- Framework for system evolution

A reference model provides a system-specific language for communication and reasoning. This language allows your team to begin a high-level dialogue about a system. This language also helps the team create terms that are understood by all its members, regardless of their background.

System-specific language

Reference models result in a description of essential system functionality. The team can identify the functional elements of system performance easily, without considering specific hardware or software choices. Later, the reference model can be used to help identify relevant standards.

Description of essential system functionality

Reference models are a means to manage complexity. Some of the reference models in this chapter can be used to represent very complex systems. Eliminating the implementation information allows the reference model to represent large systems more easily. In other words, the use of abstraction in the reference model means that there is less detail to deal with at this level.

Manage complexity

Reference models also establish a framework for system evolution. Because you build an abstract representation of the system, that representation can serve as a tool to plan and track enhancements and other changes over the life span of the system. Because this framework represents the system independently of the technology used to implement it, a reference model reflects only significant changes.

Framework for system evolution

5.2.2 Reference Models and Their Parts

Reference models are a type of model that consists of parts called *entities* and *services*, as illustrated in Figure 5.1. A reference model makes use of entities.

Entities and services

entity ⟹ A grouping or set of services that are part of a reference model.

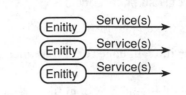

FIGURE 5.1 A reference model.

An entity is analogous to a system component. A component is to a system architecture what an entity is to a system reference model.

For example, a reference model for a communication system might have an entity called *input initiation*. The actual system—for example, a push-button telephone—might have a part called a number keypad. A reference model consists of entities, and a system consists of implementations.

> **service** ➨ A basic capability provided by an entity in a reference model.

Services[1] are provided and consumed by entities. In fact, the role of an entity is determined by the services it provides and/or consumes. In this sense, an entity provides a "home" for a service.

A service definition does not specify whether the implementation is hardware, software, or a combination of both. Service definitions are contained in the textual part of the reference model.

The following are examples of services for accessing time.

- Get the current time.
- Set the time.
- Display the time.
- Reset the time.

---

1. Instead of the term function, we use the term service because of its neutrality. Although it is also used in systems engineering, the term function has software overtones for many people.

Note that these services do not indicate the representation of time. For example, the value of time could be the number of seconds that have elapsed since some epoch, or it could be the time of day. The services apply equally well, independent of how the time is represented. The fact that services are independent of how they are implemented is a fundamental aspect of a reference model and illustrates the use of abstraction.

Reference models can be developed through a series of refinements that represent the addition of successive detail. In the case of a reference model, these refinements can take two forms:

Refinement

- Entity refinement: the process by which an entity is divided into other subordinate entities
- Service refinement: the process by which a service is divided into other services

5.2.3 Concepts Related to Reference Models

When using reference models, you may encounter discussions of domains, service classes, and attributes of service classes.

Reference models are typically associated with a domain.

Domain

domain ➡ The scope of functionality addressed by a reference model.

Examples of domains are

- Command-and-control
- Manufacturing
- Air traffic control
- Space systems
- Consumer electronics
- Telecommunications

It is often useful to collect services in groups, known as a service class.

Service class

service class ➡ A set of related services that are often present in systems of the same type or in the same domain.

An entity is described by one or more service classes. Examples of service classes are

- Operating systems
- Graphics and user interfaces
- Databases
- Communications
- Data interchange
- Multimedia

Each of these service classes contains services that allow us to develop a model of a system. For example, a reference model for a distributed database may include a communication service class. The ability to simply integrate services from the class, without worrying about implementation detail, illustrates one of the advantages of a reference model.

Design process   The development of a reference model involves a design process, just as architecture and software design are based on a design process. Frequently, the word *design* is used only in the context of a software design, but the word is much broader and must be understood in the larger context.

Suppose that you were developing a reference model for management of the pets in your house. Here are two ways you could approach the development of the reference model. First, we start with an entity called *pet management* and postulate a set of services—a service class—such as feed pet and wash pet, as illustrated in Figure 5.2. The labeled arrows in Figure 5.2 denote services.

You may then decide to refine this entity by introducing other entities depending on the type of pet. For example, you might need to deal with cats, dogs, and birds. In this

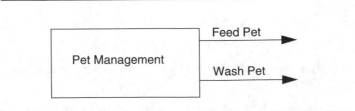

FIGURE 5.2 Basic representation of an entity.

case, you might decide to have a representation as shown in Figure 5.3. The result presented in Figure 5.3 is an entity refinement of pet management. For each possible pet, we created an entity that provides a set of similar services.

This is an example of refinement performed as part of a design process. You do a lot of design, even with a reference model, and the choices you make can have profound implications later on.

One way to characterize a service is by considering its attributes.

Attributes

> **attribute** ⇒ A qualifier or distinguishing characteristic of a service.

Examples of common attributes are

- Real time
- Security
- Fault tolerance

You may hear of *real-time secure databases* or *managed fault-tolerant networks*. Attributes address the fact that not all members of a service class are equal. For example, a *real-time operating system* is a type of operating system

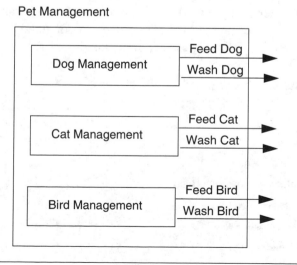

FIGURE 5.3 Refinement of representation of an entity.

that has certain features that make it useful to the real-time domain.

Service classes and attributes

Creating a table that identifies the attributes associated with service classes can help you estimate the complexity of a system, as shown in Table 5.1. To use this table, place a checkmark in each cell that applies to your system. The density of checkmarks is a simple measure of the complexity of the system. As a system's complexity increases, it may become more difficult to find a standard or a product that will satisfy the system's requirements.

5.2.4 Examples

Reference models have demonstrated their value, as illustrated by the number of successful reference models that have been developed. Their success lies in emphasis on abstraction and minimizing implementation details. Some examples of reference models follow.

- The Open Systems Interconnection (OSI) model [ISO 84] was one of the first successful reference models. It was developed for the networking domain by the International Organization for Standardization (ISO). We will discuss the OSI model in more detail later in this chapter.

- The reference model for computer-aided software engineering (CASE) environments completed by NIST (National Institute of Standards and Technology)

TABLE 5.1 Service Classes and Attributes

Service Class	Attribute		
	Real Time	Security	Fault Tolerance
Operating system	✓	✓	
Graphics and user interface		✓	
Databases	✓		✓
Communications	✓	✓	
Data interchange	✓	✓	✓
Multimedia	✓		

was originally the work of the European Computer Manufacturer's Association (ECMA) [ECMA 93] and was widely known as the *toaster model,* after the appearance of its graphic part.

- The Institute of Electrical and Electronics Engineers (IEEE) POSIX.0, representing the Open System Environment specification, is based on a reference model. This reference model was very similar to the NIST model (see following) except that the POSIX reference model was much more detailed and descriptive than that developed by NIST [IEEE 95].

- The National Institute of Standards and Technology (NIST) developed the APP (application portability profile) reference model. This reference model's graphic representation consisted of boxes, lines, and labels similar to the OSI model. The textual representation described the pieces illustrated in the graphic representation [NIST 96a].

- The TAFIM (Technical Architecture Framework for Information Management) [DoD 96] is quite extensive and consists of many volumes of information with lists of related standards. The reference model is described in one of these volumes.[2]

Reference models are usually developed in a domain that supports the work of standards groups. Such projects as Open Distributed Processing (ODP) [ISO 95], CASE Data Interchange Format (CDIF) [EIA 94], and Electronic Data Interchange Format (EDIF) [EIA 93] have also developed reference models. Reference models are also used extensively in the Joint Technical Architecture (JTA) [DoD 00c].

In the following, we provide excerpts from two reference models so that you can see how different they can be from one another:

- The OSI basic reference model for open systems interconnection [ISO 84]

---

2. The TAFIM is no longer maintained as an official document. However, it is a useful reference document, in part because of the approach taken to develop it, as well as the reference material it contains.

- The Software Engineering Institute (SEI) Open Systems Course Transition reference model

Although the two reference model differ from each other, both have the required characteristics of reference models. Figure 5.4 illustrates the OSI model, which is described in the ISO standard denoted ISO 7498[3] [ISO 84].

OSI model

Entities. In the OSI model, applications A and B communicate with each other. Associated with each application are *entities* that provide this communication, such as *presentation, session, transport,* and *network.*

Application A invokes services provided by the *presentation* entity, which in turn invokes services provided by the *session* entity, and so on through the *physical* entity. These entities use peer-to-peer protocols as an interface to the entities used by application B. Application B's entities then call each other from the *physical* entity through the *presentation* entity. Using peer-to-peer protocols, the entities enable the two applications to communicate.

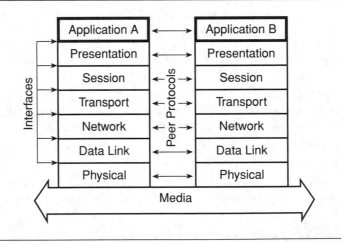

FIGURE 5.4 Graphic part of OSI reference model.

---

3. The phrase reference model is not defined in [ISO 84], which instead refers to this figure as a *layered architecture*. This variation in terminology creates potential for confusion.

Services.   Each entity in Figure 5.4 provides services to its nearest neighbor entity. For example, the *presentation* entity provides services to the *application* entity. The *presentation* entity may also use services provided by a lower-layer entity, such as the *session* entity.

The reference model is described independently of an implementation. For example, the *transport* entity provides services that could be implemented by using the Transmission Control Protocol (*TCP*) or implemented in hardware. The implementation decision to use TCP or hardware at this point is premature. The reference model specifies nothing more than the *entities* and the *services* that connect them. Later, when architecture and design specifications have been created, implementations can be chosen.

Protocols.   In Figure 5.4, the communication that takes place between applications A and B takes place in part through *peer protocols*. These protocols define how entities communicate and interoperate.

> **protocol** ⇒ A set of syntactic and semantic rules for exchanging information.

For example, data-link protocols and transport protocols in the OSI model affect communication between data-link and transport entities. Protocols must be used by two peer systems before they can achieve interoperability.

The team that developed the course from which this book was derived was composed of people from various disciplines: engineering, instructional design, marketing, and technical writing. As part of the project, the team developed a reference model for the delivery of the course. Figure 5.5 illustrates the graphic part of the reference model we used.

A course delivery reference model

Entities.   Our goal to distribute the course widely led us to define entities we called *delivery agents*. We defined a delivery agent as someone or something that delivers the course. For example, a delivery agent could be an instructor or a videotape. These two implementations have differences but perform a similar service.

Later, when discussing this problem, we decided to include the notion of a *surrogate agent,* which provided an

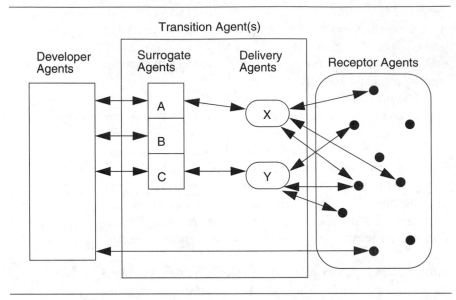

FIGURE 5.5 Graphic part for course delivery reference model.

interface between developer agents and delivery agents. The surrogate agents and delivery agent were then encapsulated as a *transition agent.* Looking at it differently, we would say that a transition agent is *refined* to consist of surrogate agents and delivery agents. The relations between entities are indicated by arrows representing required services.

Services. We then described the services that a delivery agent would provide, without specifically defining how the course would be implemented. Our reference model applied equally to the following implementations:

- Course delivery by two members of our team
- Course delivery by individuals outside our team
- Course delivery through multimedia technology

Next, we defined services that the delivery agent had to provide to a *receptor agent,* the entity receiving the course. An example of a receptor agent might be some set of course attendees, but it could also be an individual interacting with a CD-ROM version of the course at a workstation.

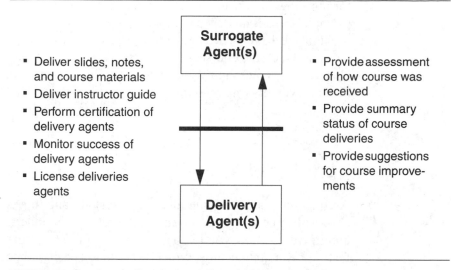

- Deliver slides, notes, and course materials
- Deliver instructor guide
- Perform certification of delivery agents
- Monitor success of delivery agents
- License deliveries agents

Surrogate Agent(s)

Delivery Agent(s)

- Provide assessment of how course was received
- Provide summary status of course deliveries
- Provide suggestions for course improvements

FIGURE 5.6 Services in the course delivery reference model.

Figure 5.6 illustrates some of the services that were defined between the surrogate agent(s) and the delivery agent(s). An important point appears in the discussion shown in Figure 5.6. The heavy line in the figure represents the *interface* between the surrogate agent(s) and the delivery agent(s). An acquisition approach based on open systems and COTS products places great emphasis on the importance of interfaces. Here, in developing the reference model, we begin to see how the interfaces arise in a natural manner as part of developing the overall model.

Benefits. The development of the course delivery reference model helped for a variety of reasons. Most important, it allowed a group of people with differing professional backgrounds to develop a common vocabulary, purpose, and vision of the work. This high-level understanding—shared by the team members—is important in the success of any project.

Another benefit of creating and using the reference model was that it established neutral ground for collaboration. The multidisciplinary team was able to use a common language and, therefore, communicate more effectively. With more multidisciplinary approaches in use today—

through the use of integrated product teams (IPTs), for example—this is an added benefit.

Finally, the reference model was used to help us identify ways in which the course could be transitioned to others. One transition mechanism—planned early in the work—is the book you now are reading!

5.3 Architectures

Architectures are fundamental to any system, and this is especially true for open systems. Like reference models, architectures allow you to focus on system function and features. But architectures typically begin to specify some implementation characteristics of the system.

The term architecture has many definitions. We prefer the following.

> **architecture** ➡ A representation of a system or a sub-system characterized by
>
> - Functionality
> - Components
> - Connectivity of components
> - Mapping of functionality onto components

An architecture must not only identify the components of a system but also define the functions of the components and their relation to one another. Just as with reference models, architectures are presented in both graphic and textual parts. Also like reference models, it is the graphic part that many people mistakenly believe contains all the important information!

Types of architectures related to computer systems include

- Hardware
- Software
- System

We define the first two architecture types as follows.

hardware architecture ⇒ A specification of the mapping of functionality and connectivity onto *hardware* components.

software architecture ⇒ A specification of the mapping of functionality and connectivity onto *software* components.

Note the symmetry of the two definitions with respect to hardware and software, as well as how each relates to the general definition of an architecture. We now apply the preceding to develop a definition for a system architecture.

system architecture ⇒ A specification of the

- Mapping of functionality onto hardware and software components
- Mapping of the software architecture onto the hardware architecture
- Representation of the human interaction with these components

To define an *open* system architecture, we take the definition of a *system architecture* and add the concept of *open*.

open system architecture ⇒ A representation of a system characterized by

- A mapping of functionality onto hardware and software components
- A mapping of the software architecture onto the hardware architecture
- A representation of the human interaction with these components
- Interface specifications of the components that are
  - fully defined
  - available to the public
  - maintained according to a consensus process

Our preference for defining things the way we have is that there is a logical relation between the various terms. Some people define an open system architecture in terms of the anticipated benefits, such as portability, but we do not prefer that approach.

5.3.1 Why Architectures Are Important

Architectures have assumed a central position in the discussion of systems. Like reference models, architectures are a way of describing a system. However, architectures provide more detailed description than do reference models. Architectures help you

- Describe a system without a lot of design detail
- Identify critical interfaces
- Map functions to components
- Manage complexity
- Evolve the system over time
- Obtain leverage

Describe a system

Using architectures, you can describe a system without a lot of detail. An architecture typically contains some implementation detail. Hiding the implementation details is a well-known principle of software engineering and applies here.

Identify interfaces

Architectures allow you to identify the interfaces that will be critical to the system. In the initial architecture development, the details of the interface semantics may not be fully specified. However, as the architecture is refined, two things can happen. First, the interfaces will be specified in greater detail. Second, you may recognize the need to add, modify, or delete an interface.

Map functions to components

A key characteristic of any architecture—hardware, software, system, or open system—is that it maps functions to components. Doing this simplifies the more detailed system development tasks.

Manage complexity

Architectures enable you to manage complexity. Because the system representation is easier to work with, you can easily see the context of component problems and their effect on other system components. You can plan the structure of the system to avoid unnecessary complexity.

Evolve

Architectures provide a framework you can use to evolve a system over time. This framework is of sufficient detail that it allows you to track and plan changes, as well as to understand the effects of these changes on system components. Two types of evolution are important to distinguish:

- The same architectural structure using different COTS products as implementations
- An architectural structure that can itself change gracefully with changes in standards and technology

In either case, the key to successful evolution is to maintain stability in the face of change.

Leverage refers to gaining advantage as a result of using some other work. Reuse of software is an example of leverage. The architectural context provides opportunities to gain leverage. One opportunity is to apply the architectural work done by others for a domain similar to yours. We will provide an example of this in the following section. Another opportunity is to participate in the development of an architecture with others who have similar interests.

Leverage

5.3.2 An Example Architecture

To be honest, to include a full example of an architecture would require many pages. A full architecture specification includes a lot of information, as can be inferred from the definition of an architecture. Do not be deluded into thinking that one piece of paper with a bunch of boxes and arrows represents a full specification of an architecture.

Instead of presenting an example of an architecture for a particular system, we will describe an example of a *generic* architecture. We will describe the Generic Open Architecture (GOA) developed by the Society of Automotive Engineers [SAE 96]. The GOA is intended to apply to airborne avionics systems, but it also applies to automotive systems, such as cars and trucks.

A generic architecture

At its highest level, the GOA is presented in terms of a layered model, as shown in Figure 5.7. Two classes of interfaces are present:

- A *logical interface* that defines a peer-to-peer relationship in the *same layer* of the architecture
- A *direct interface* that defines a service/consumer relationship between *adjacent layers* in the architecture

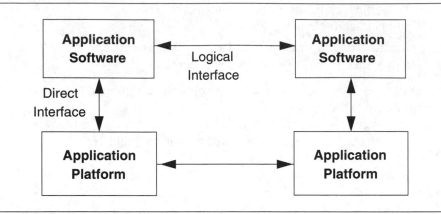

FIGURE 5.7 Basic generic open architecture.

Note that the GOA model is very similar to the OSI model discussed on page 70. Like the OSI model, the GOA model is based on layers that give it a hierarchical character. A refinement of the GOA model yields a four-layer architecture; the layers are called classes and have the following functions:

- Application software,which performs application-specific processing
- System services, such as operating system services and additional, extended operating system services
- Resource access services, which interact with physical resources
- Physical resources, such as hardware resources

A diagram of the refined model is given in Figure 5.8. The lines connecting boxes vertically in Figure 5.8 represent direct interfaces. The lines connecting boxes horizontally represent logical interfaces.

The refined Generic Open Architecture looks very much like a reference model. However, note that the refined GOA specifically accounts for software and hardware in the specification, which is not done in a (pure) reference model specification. One of the goals in developing the GOA was to be able to *minimize* implementation dependencies, which is evident in the architecture.

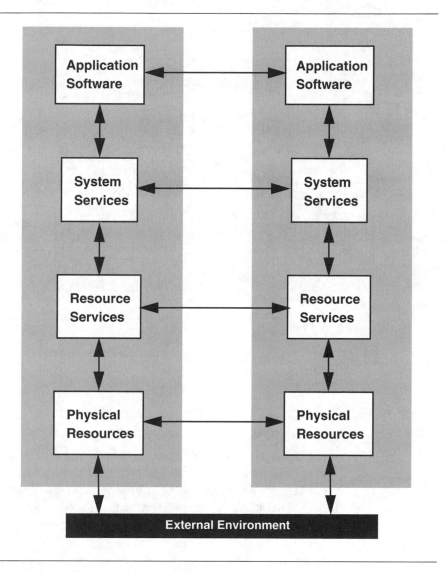

FIGURE 5.8 Refined generic open architecture.

We have noted that generic architecture specifications are useful in that they permit one to develop particular instances of the generic architecture for a particular domain. One case of this is illustrated by considering the Space Generic Open Avionics Architecture (SGOAA) developed for NASA [Wray 93]. This architecture can apply to a mission for a manned vehicle on the moon, a

Instance of the generic architecture

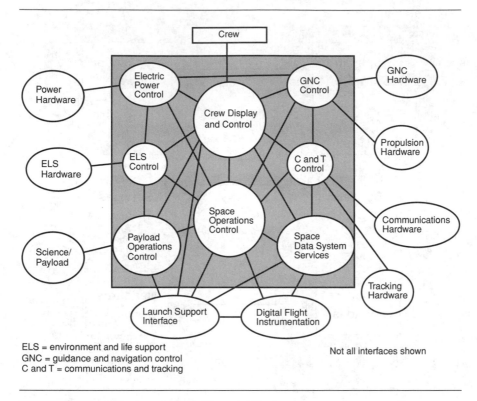

ELS = environment and life support
GNC = guidance and navigation control
C and T = communications and tracking

Not all interfaces shown

FIGURE 5.9 Example space application architecture.

robot on Mars, or a space station [Stovall 93]. This work was also used for the GOA development, described earlier.

Figure 5.9 presents a functional view of the overall SGOAA architecture. Figure 5.9 depicts the subsystems that comprise the overall system. The subsystems in the shaded area are called the space generic avionics *core*. These core subsystems are necessary for any National Aeronautics and Space Administration (NASA) space mission.

Application Viewpoint. The graphical representation of the architecture, depicted in Figure 5.9, is further refined in [Wray 93]. For example, some of the potential functions to be included as part of the environment and life support subsystem are

- Temperature and humidity control
- Fire detection and suppression control

- Atmosphere monitoring and control
- Water-recovery management
- Airlock pressure control
- Caution and warnings generation

Hardware Perspective. When applied to a particular space system, the generic architecture must be instantiated at each layer. This is necessary to ensure completeness of the architecture.

For example, when considering the hardware layer for a space system, [Wray 94] considered the representation shown in Figure 5.10. The physical layer specified in Figure 5.10 is a refinement of the top-level physical resources layer shown in Figure 5.8 in that it adds detail to the specification of the architecture. Also note how Figure 5.10 relates to our definition of a hardware architecture (see page 75). The figure includes, for example, a

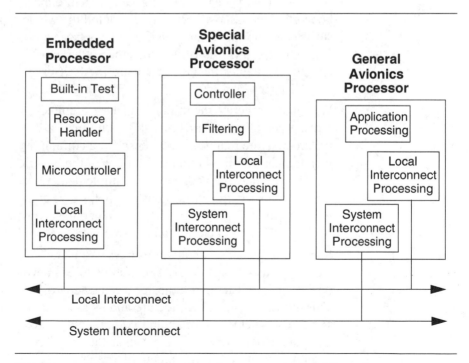

FIGURE 5.10 Physical resources layer in space system architecture.

specification of the components and how they are connected via local and system interconnects.

Manned or Unmanned. In Figure 5.9, the *crew* is placed outside the core architecture. This choice was made to allow the architecture to support manned and unmanned missions. If the architecture is applied to a manned mission, the crew would be included, as well as its interfaces to other subsystems. On the other hand, if the architecture is applied to an unmanned mission, such as a mission to Mars, the crew subsystem would not be included.

Placing the crew outside the core part of the architecture was a conscious decision that was part of developing the architecture. If the crew subsystem had been included in the core architecture, the architecture would apply only to manned missions, limiting its generality.

Some final comments

We would like to make three final comments about this example generic architecture.

- As we said in the beginning, although a picture may be worth a thousand words, it does not tell the whole story. One reason we chose to present a generic architecture is that it is less voluminous than other architecture documents; the GOA standard [SAE 96] is only 17 pages long.

- We want to reiterate the utility of generic architectures, especially standards-based ones. In that case, the architecture represents consensus of a community in a domain. Building implementations of the generic architecture may allow one to reuse implementations across a wider range of missions and helps give commonality to multiproject acquisition. When they work well, generic architectures can be a real gem.

- Sometimes, generic architectures have associated with them lists of standards. The architecture is developed to be consistent with the specified standards. This allows a generic architecture and its associated standards to help achieve greater commonality across an organization. An example of this is the Joint Technical Architecture (JTA) [DoD 00c].

5.4 A Comparison of Reference Models and Architectures

It is tempting but difficult to formally differentiate or iden- **What is the**
tify the boundary between *reference models* and *architec-* **difference?**
tures. You can think of reference models, architectures,
and implementations as artifacts resulting from a refinement approach, as illustrated in Figure 5.11.

    Reference models, having the least implementation-
specific detail, would be placed at one end. *Implementations,*
having the greatest detail, would be at the opposite end.

    Architectures would lie somewhere near the middle.
Reference models, architectures, and implementations represent steps in a refinement toward a complete system definition. A major difference between a *reference model* and

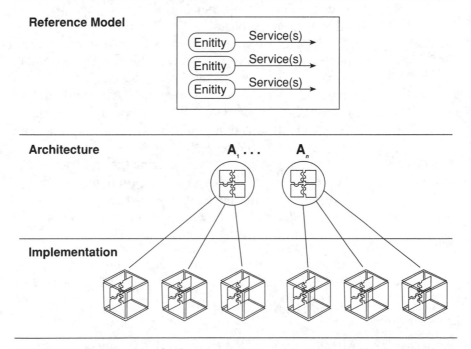

FIGURE 5.11 Relationship of reference models, architectures, and implementations.

an *architecture* is that a reference model permits *no* implementation-specific details, whereas an architecture permits some.

Filtering

As you move from reference models to architectures to implementations, you are filtering possible solutions. Each reference model can have multiple architectures, and each architecture can have multiple implementations.

As you build a system, you filter these possible solutions at each level to eliminate candidate architectures and candidate implementations. The filtering is guided, in part, by your requirements, standards, and available implementations.

5.5 Trends

It is important to understand some of the trends associated with reference models and architectures. Knowledge and understanding of these trends can help management plan and manage an acquisition.

Domain-specific notations

These days, system developers are using more domain-specific reference models and architectures. A domain architecture is an artifact that is developed in the context of a particular—application—domain. An example of this approach is the Space Generic Open Avionics Architecture (SGOAA), illustrated in Figure 5.9, which was developed for space systems [Wray 93].

Maturation of knowledge

Project managers are recognizing that generic models are useful. When a generic model for a domain is recognized by project managers, it demonstrates the maturation of knowledge and experience with systems development within domains.

5.6 Summary

Reference models

A *reference model* is an abstract description of a system in terms of entities and services. Reference models provide a high-level description of a system. They are descriptive;

they describe *what* but not *how*. They are also independent of an implementation.

Using reference models provides you with a

- System-specific language for communication and reasoning
- Description of essential system functionality
- Means to manage complexity
- Framework for system evolution

Architectures are also model representations of a system; they help you
Architectures

- Describe a system without a lot of detail
- Manage complexity
- Map functions to components
- Evolve the system over time
- Identify critical interfaces

The difference between an open system architecture and any other architecture is the increased importance of standards in the open system architecture. The interface specifications are fully defined, available to the public, and maintained according to a consensus process.
Open system architecture

5.7 Food for Thought

1. Develop a reference model for the way your project does system acquisition. What are the entities and the services? Why did you make the choices you did?

2. Earlier in the book, we discussed the marketplace. Develop a reference model for a marketplace. What are the entities and services that you included, and why?

3. To assess the reference model you developed for question 2, how well does it apply to an *electronic* marketplace? For example, when you consider an electronic marketplace, does it require modifications to your initial model or new entities and/or services?

4. Sometimes, you can reverse engineer a reference model from a product. Pick the lamp that is nearest to you, and develop a reference model for it. To assess your result, how well does it apply to a flashlight? For fun, does your result also apply to organisms that lie beneath the ocean and emit light by chemical processes?

5. The specification of services in a reference model is typically static. For example, one does not frequently hear about the *execution* of a reference model. An interesting question about the application of a reference model is to create an *operational semantics*. This is a set of services that are ordered in time. Use your reference model for a marketplace (see question 2) and develop the execution model for ordering a product, starting from a decision to obtain a product. What do you learn from this?

6. Consider the discussion of the design process for pet management. Would you say that it is functionally oriented or object oriented? What happens if you need to add a service, such as *exercise pet?* What would you change? Suppose that you were asked to continue the development of the reference model for pet management. What would you add next?

7. How would you define the term *standards-based architecture?* What do you think it means? In what ways would it materially differ from an open systems architecture?

8. How does the generic architecture described in Section 5.3.2 satisfy the items listed in Section 5.3.1 describing the importance of architectures?

9. How would you apply the generic architecture described in Section 5.3.2 to an automobile?

10. Develop a set of criteria that you would apply to determine whether an architecture is successful. Are there implications from your result? For example, do your criteria imply metrics that may be useful in an acquisition?

11. How would you allocate resources to initially develop a reference model for a system of interest? How would you then allocate resources for the life-cycle maintenance of that model? Now answer these questions for an architecture instead of a reference model. Would these activities be performed by the same person or organization? What are the implications of your results?

12. After reading this chapter, you think you have a pretty good idea of reference models, architectures, and their similarities and differences. Then you run into an old friend. When you ask her what she's working on, she says she's in the middle of developing a reference architecture. What do you think she means?

6

Standards

Standards are fundamental to an open systems–based acquisition, as noted earlier, in our discussion of the paradigm shift (see Chapter 3). Standards represent the second element in the key iteration of an acquisition approach. In this chapter, we explore a number of key standards topics, such as characteristics, organizational processes that create standards, and the concept of a profile.

From elevator cables to safety levels for gas appliances to new car tires, standards affect everyone. Some standards, such as clothing and shoe sizes, are a matter of convenience for the manufacturer and the consumer. Other standards are used in safety-critical areas, in which a failure could risk a person's life.

6.1 What Is a Standard?

Before covering standards and their role in open systems, we will look again at the definitions of *standard* and *specification*, two terms we use extensively throughout this book.

> **standard** ⇒ A publicly available document that defines specifications for interfaces, services, processes, protocols, or data formats and that is established and maintained by group consensus.

The preceding definition is in the context of computer systems. We also introduce the term specification.

Fighting Fires

In 1904, the great Baltimore fire occurred. The fire began in a wholesale dry-goods warehouse and spread so far so fast that neighboring fire departments were called to the scene. When they arrived, however, they discovered that the threads on their fire hoses would not fit the fire hydrants in Baltimore. The firefighters had to put one end of a hose in a barrel or trough pushed up against the hydrant to catch the water. After two days and 140 burned acres, the fire was extinguished. It took another fire on a much smaller scale for the problem of mismatched hoses and hydrants to be addressed.

In October of the same year, a fire broke out in the basement of the National Bureau of Standards in Washington, D.C. A night watchman, trying to extinguish the fire, discovered that the threads on the bureau's own fire hoses did not match the hydrants. The ensuing investigation revealed that 600 sizes and varieties of hose couplings were being used in the United States. By 1905, there were national standards for fire hoses, but 60 years later, some problems remained because some fire plugs still did not meet the standards [Nesmith 85].

> **specification** ➟ A document that prescribes, in a complete, precise, and verifiable manner, the requirements, design, behavior, or characteristics of a system or system component.

Note that a standard must be publicly available and also be based on some form of consensus process. These statements are not necessarily true for a specification.

Standards have merit individually, but when they are combined, their value increases. This combination is referred to as a *profile*, which itself can be a standard.

> **profile** ➟ A set of one or more base standards and, where applicable, the identification of chosen classes, subsets, options, and parameters of those standards necessary for accomplishing a particular function [IEEE 95].

Because of their importance, profiles are discussed in detail in Section 6.5.

Two other terms are relevant when we discuss the definition of a standard.

> **de jure standard** ➟ A specification created by an accredited standards development organization.

de facto standard ➡ A specification that emerges as a standard because of its product's popular use.

Note the difference between the two definitions. A de facto standard is one that is associated with a particular product. Such a standard could be, and most often is, based on a specification that is controlled by one vendor. In contrast, de jure standards are specifications produced by an organization whose purpose is to develop standards.

The types of standards development organizations can vary widely. The spectrum ranges from those that can trace their authority to ISO to standards that are developed by an industry consortium, such as the Object Management Group, which develops CORBA (the Common Object Request Broker Architecture). These various types of organizations have different goals, different processes, and different impacts on an acquirer.

A standard can begin as one kind of specification and then migrate to another type. For example, UNIX started as a particular specification of an operating system. As more people used UNIX products, it became a de facto standard. Eventually, there was a demand for standardization of the UNIX interface. It was then standardized as the Portable Operating System Interface (POSIX), a de jure standard.

It's important to understand the value of standards. When standards exist and multiple suppliers build to those standards, consumers have a chance to see benefits, such as

- Broad availability of suitable products, leading to
- Competition, resulting in
- Lower prices

Economics of Standards

"Standards exist for economic reasons. More appropriately, *successful* standards survive for economic reasons. There is an ISO Pascal standard, as well as a BASIC standard, but who cares? OSI represented a standard, and there were a number of implementations. But the nature of the marketplace—large government purchasers—kept the prices high. TCP/IP eventually eroded OSI, but it was 'just' an IETF specification. Economics works." (A colleague)

6.2 Standards Organizations and Their Processes

Standards affect the marketplace and are affected *by* the marketplace. However, many standards are not created in the marketplace. A community of standards organizations exists that develops standards according to defined processes.

Knowing about the standards community can help you understand how to deal with it and what to expect from it. Key concepts to understand are

- How standards are developed
- The differences among types of standards

In 1996, there were a total of 93,000 standards in the United States. Table 6.1 shows the division between government and nongovernment standards for the years 1992 and 1996.

Note that government and industry each supplied about half of all U.S. standards in 1992. Table 6.1 shows an important trend. That is, the number of federal government standards decreased, with a corresponding increase in the number of nongovernment standards. The trend continues, with the government adopting even more nongovernment standards.

TABLE 6.1 Standards in the United States

Organization	*Number of Standards*	
	1992 **[OTA 92]**	**1996** **[NIST 96b]**
Total Federal Government	**52,500**	**44,000**
Department of Defense	38,000	34,000
General Services Administration	6,000	2,000
Other federal agencies	8,500	8,000
Total Nongovernment	**41,500**	**49,000**
Scientific and professional societies	13,000	14,000
Trade associations	14,500	16,000
Standards-developing organizations	14,000	17,000
Developers of informal standards	NA	2,000

Going, Going . . .

The number of federal standards decreased by roughly six standards every day during the years 1992 to 1996.

However, it should be pointed out that by 1996, the government had also adopted more than 9,500 nongovernment standards. This illustrates a second aspect of the change: The government is placing increasing emphasis on nongovernment standards.

Table 6.1 shows the total number of standards for the years indicated. In reality, the number of standards that are widely used is small in relation to the total number of standards issued.

If you focus on the private sector, you will find organizations formed by member companies to create standards for many different industries. Table 6.2 lists the top ten nongovernment standards developers. For comparison, we show the results for 1992 and 1996.

TABLE 6.2 Top Ten Nongovernment U.S. Standards Developers

Organization	*Number of Standards*	
	1992 [OTA 92]	1996 [NIST 96b]
American Society for Testing and Materials (ASTM)	8,500	9,900
U.S. Pharmacopeia	4,450	5,000
Society of Automotive Engineers (SAE)	5,100	4,550
Aerospace Information Association (AIA)	3,000	3,000
Association of Official Analytical Chemists (AOAC)	1,900	2,100
American National Standards Institute (ANSI)	1,400	1,500
Association of American Railroads	1,350	1,400
Electronic Industries Association (EIA)	600	1,300
American Association of State Highway and Transportation Officials	1,100	1,100
Cosmetic, Toiletry and Fragrance Association	800	800

6.2.1 ISO and ANSI

Standards organizations can be international, regional, or national. Two influential organizations in the standards community are ISO and ANSI.

What is ISO?   ISO, a nongovernment organization established in 1947, functions as a worldwide federation of national standards bodies from approximately 90 countries. The mission of ISO is to promote the worldwide development of standards, to facilitate the international exchange of goods and services, and to develop cooperation in the spheres of intellectual, scientific, technical, and economic activity.

The work done by ISO results in many international agreements that are published as international standards.

Formation of JTC 1

The first international standards organization was the International Electrotechnical Commission (IEC). This organization began developing electrotechnical standards in 1906.

The International Federation of the National Standardising Associations, formed in 1926, developed standards in other fields, focusing mainly on mechanical engineering. Its activities ceased in 1942 because of World War II.

In 1946, delegates from 25 countries met in London and decided to create a new international organization. This organization, ISO, officially began work on February 23, 1947. The original mission of ISO was "to facilitate the international coordination and unification of industrial standards." The first ISO standard, entitled Standard Reference Temperature for Industrial Length Measurement, was published in 1951.

In 1987, ISO and IEC formed the Joint Technical Committee 1 (JTC1). Its mission is to cooperate on information technology standards.

What is ANSI?   ANSI is a privately funded, nonprofit federation of leaders representing both the private and public sectors in the United States. ANSI is also the U.S. representative to ISO [OTA 92, IEEE 95].

The purpose of ANSI is to coordinate the U.S. voluntary consensus standards community. Surprisingly, ANSI does not have any official government charter. The effectiveness of this community is attributable to the diversity and participation of its member organizations.

The stated mission of ANSI is to "enhance both the global competitiveness of U.S. business and the quality of life in the U.S." To do this, ANSI

- Promotes voluntary consensus standards
- Protects the integrity of the standards development process by requiring open consensus, including provision for due process

Although U.S. standards organizations can function independently, many choose to coordinate their activities through ANSI. Some major U.S. standards organizations, however, choose not to participate with ANSI and act independently.

Figure 6.1 [OTA 92, IEEE 95] illustrates the broad range of standards monitored by ANSI and the depth of the hierarchy of ANSI membership. ANSI membership is open to manufacturers, organizations, users, and communication carriers. More than 250 professional and technical societies and trade associations that develop standards in the United States are ANSI members. In addition, 1,000 companies and more than 25 government agencies are ANSI members. There are about 13,000 approved ANSI standards.

ANSI does not *develop* standards; its member organizations do. ANSI *coordinates* the work of its member organizations. ANSI does not *judge* the substance of standards. It *certifies* that standards organizations develop standards according to accredited procedures.

World Standards Day

ISO and the IEC designated October 14 as World Standards Day to recognize those volunteers who have worked hard to define international standards. The United States celebrated World Standards Day on October 11, Finland celebrated on October 13, and Italy celebrated on October 18 [Anderson 94].

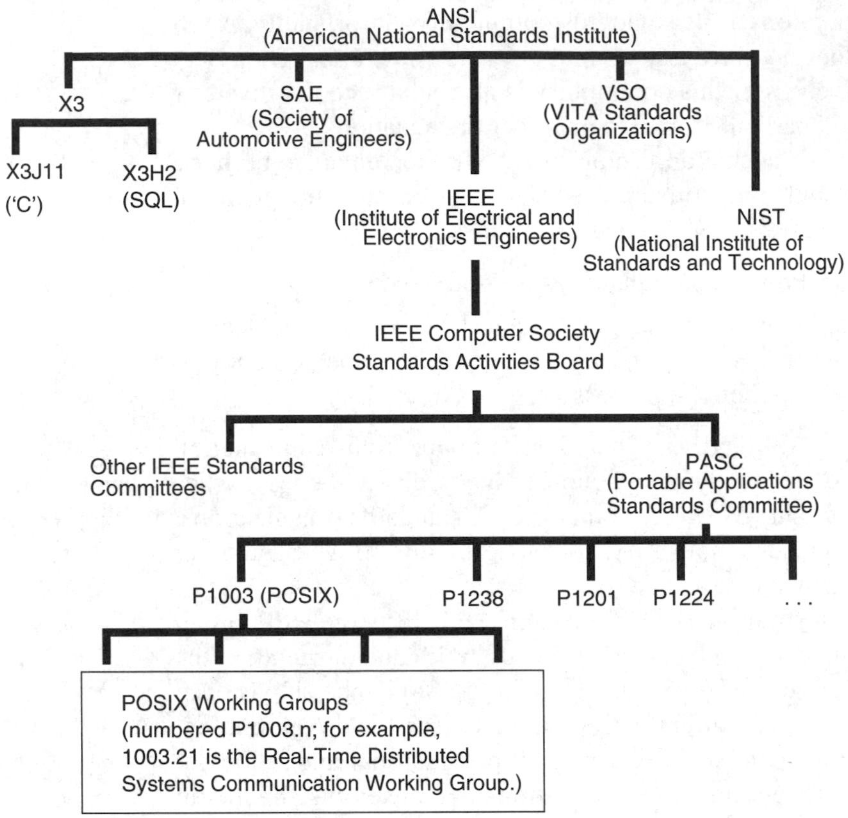

FIGURE 6.1 ANSI membership.

6.2.2 Standards Organization Categories

So far, we have presented information about two standards organizations: ISO and ANSI. Both of these organizations are accredited. However, there are many standards organizations, and not all of them are accredited.

> **accredited** ➟ The status of a standards organization when it is approved by an international standards organization or a member body of an international standards organization.

ISO is an international standards organization, and ANSI is a member body of ISO. Hence, ANSI is an accredited standards organization. Furthermore, both ISO and ANSI can accredit other standards development organizations. For example, ANSI accredits the IEEE for development of standards. The other international standards organizations are IEC (International Electrotechnical Commission) and ITU-T (International Telecommunications Union Telecommunication Standardization Bureau).

Standards organizations without a relationship to official national or international organizations, such as ANSI and ISO, are nonaccredited. Table 6.3 compares the characteristics of accredited and nonaccredited standards organizations.

Accredited standards organizations often allow people to participate as individuals if they pay the cost of attending meetings. The goal of allowing individuals to participate is to provide broad-based input to the development of standards.

Because of the cost, in some accredited standards organizations, membership fees are required for the most powerful voting privileges. Individuals representing themselves are less likely to participate in this kind of organization. Typically, individuals represent member organizations. In fact, participants at regional and international levels typically represent nations.

Figure 6.2 illustrates some internationally and nationally accredited standards organizations. Each national organization that is a member of JTC1 may accredit organizations for the development of standards. For example, an industry

Accredited versus nonaccredited

TABLE 6.3 Classifications of Standards Organizations

Accredited	Nonaccredited
Approved by official national or international bodies	Created by vendors or users, using a consensus method
Define and disseminate public standards	Define and disseminate group standards
Examples:	Examples:
▪ International, regional, national standards organizations	▪ Some industry groups
▪ Standards organizations of some professional and technical organizations	▪ Vendor consortia ▪ User groups

association may be accredited by a JTC1 member. To get a more complete perspective on how this works within the U.S. community, you can insert Figure 6.1 for ANSI in Figure 6.2. Overall, the international standards community has a complex structure, but it works rather well.

Nonaccredited groups are not approved by official national or international standards organizations. The following types of groups are usually nonaccredited.

- *Consortia* typically have defined processes for standards development and have a corporate membership.

- *Private* standards organizations are a loosely organized collection of corporations with common interests. Membership is determined by corporate sponsors and is based on the interests of the sponsors.

- *Vendor-specific* "groups" are individual vendors that develop their own specifications that are intended to be de facto standards. The consensus process is market driven and is determined when customers buy the product and make it so popular that "everyone uses it." The product's widespread use makes its specification a de facto standard.

Nonaccredited standards organizations usually have no formal connection with accredited standards organizations but may have unofficial relationships with and may even supply proposed standards to accredited standards organizations. Nonaccredited standards bodies may have

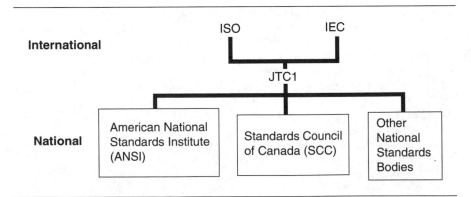

FIGURE 6.2 Accredited standards community.

significant fees for membership. Participants typically represent member companies only. In fact, nonaccredited standards organizations may not allow individuals to participate unless they represent a member company. Government participants may or may not be allowed to vote.

6.2.3 Consensus Processes

The most important distinguishing process followed by standards organizations is their consensus process. Accredited national and international standards organizations evaluate a candidate organization's consensus process to ensure that it conforms to the range of acceptable consensus processes practiced by their member standards organizations.

group consensus ⇥ An activity that includes both

- The participation of multiple people or organizations
- A process by which consensus is achieved

When approving a standard, the official standards organization requires that

- The standard's developer be an accredited member
- The consensus process used to develop the standard is acceptable

Accredited standards organizations often require elaborate processes to establish and maintain consensus. For example, in IEEE, the process includes the following steps.

Formal processes

1. Submit a project authorization request (PAR).
2. Obtain approval for the PAR.
3. Organize a working group.
4. Develop a draft standard.
5. Vote on the draft standard.
6. Approve the draft standard.
7. Publish the approved standard.
8. Forward for international standardization.

Processes also exist in accredited standards organizations for

- Making changes to a standard

- Interpreting a standard
- Periodically reviewing a standard to determine whether it should be reconfirmed or canceled

The approval process for accredited standards typically requires that a *working group* consist of a balanced mix of producers, users, and general-interest participants. Another aspect of the approval process is the *ballot group*, which may have a broader membership than the working group and which formally ballots on a standard. In IEEE, the balloting group must remain constant, and balloters have 30–60 days to respond with their votes. Approval at any level of the process requires at least a 75 percent return and, of that return, a 75 percent approval rate.

Facets of consensus

Standards organizations follow various consensus processes. These processes have three facets.

1. *Participation* determines who can be a member of the standards organization or who can participate in the development or approval of a standard.

2. A *development and approval process* defines the process that members must follow to develop standards. On completion of this process, a standard has been approved.

3. A *postapproval process* defines the process that members can follow to influence standards after they are approved.

Standards Participation

"Many organizations participate in standards groups more out of fear of what unmatched competition may do than love of standards. Follow the money, smell the fear." (A colleague)

Consensus processes

Table 6.4 presents some consensus processes used by various types of standards organizations. Note that as you move from left to right in the table, the membership involved in standards development becomes more limited.

TABLE 6.4 Standards Consensus Processes

Facet	Accredited	Nonaccredited		
		Consortium	Private	Vendor-Specific (de facto standards)
Participation	Broad; emphasis on wide consensus; anyone (often individuals) can join	Usually vendors, not individuals	Private, by invitation only	Single vendor or source

Development and Approval Process	Sequence of approvals, such as from subcommittee to highest board; requirements on balance in balloting group, percent of ballots that must be returned, percent of returned ballots that must approve, and so on.	1. Solicit proposals
		2. Either
		  a. Select a winner to which whole consortium agrees
		  b. Have proposers work together to achieve an industry consensus position
			Whatever agreement the group can reach to achieve its ends	Vendor's design and marketing processes

Postapproval Process	Mechanisms for comment, appeal, and interpretations	Mechanisms for comment; possibly limited mechanisms for appeal	Mechanisms for commenting probably available to insiders; no mechanism for appeal	Comments only through user feedback; no mechanism for appeal

6.2.4 Time, Risk, and Stability

Note how the time and risk implications also change as you move in Table 6.4 from left to right, from accredited to vendor-specific standards. For example, because of the formality and broad participation required, accredited standards usually require more time to develop than do nonaccredited standards.

The development and approval of accredited standards often take a great deal of time because many approval levels may be involved, as well as an increasing range of consensus. The risk involved in such a long process is that the standard is not available when it is needed.

As you see in Table 6.4, the development process becomes less complex as you move toward vendor-specific standards, often decreasing the amount of development

Standards development process

time required. Although there may be a risk owing to the length of time it takes to develop and approve accredited standards, the process tends to be predictable and stable. At the other extreme, everything moves quickly but at the risk of both stability and predictability.

Changes to the standard

Changes to a standard are always possible. The changes can be of two general types: (1) corrections to a standard or (2) the inclusion of new or modified functionality or clarification of existing functionality, also referred to as an interpretation. In the case of accredited standards, the process of change is relatively slow because of the formal process that must be followed to modify a standard. Many standards development organizations have a requirement for periodic review of standards, typically every five years; when the review is complete, the standard is *reaffirmed*. This means that the standard, in its current form, is still deemed relevant by the ballot group.

In the case of nonaccredited standards, changes can be handled in a relatively short time because of the reduced scale of the process. The important question is when a change should be introduced, especially for a de facto standard or an emerging standard. If the vendor of a de facto standard has a broad product base, it may be unwilling to change the product too radically. However, newly introduced products or even stable products in an evolving market are likely candidates for changes to keep pace with their market.

Fast-track process

To cope with the deliberate but slow speed of accredited processes, some accredited standards organizations are using a *fast-track* process. Instead of developing every standard itself, the accredited organization accepts and votes on standards developed by affiliated groups.

Standards and stability

An accredited standards process is usually more stable than a nonaccredited process. Typically, once the standard is approved, it changes very little. If it does change, standards organizations attempt to make the changes upwardly compatible.

If the standard is stable, implementations can be stable as well. However, the stability of a standard does not *guarantee* that implementations will also be stable.

6.3 Characteristics of Standards

Now that we have discussed how standards are developed, we can discuss some of the characteristics of standards. A typical standard consists of two types of information, as shown in Table 6.5.

> **normative** ⟶ Of, pertaining to, or prescribing a norm or standard; used in standards to indicate a portion of the text that poses requirements
>
> **informative** ⟶ Providing or disclosing information; instructive; used in standards to indicate a portion of the text that poses no requirements; the opposite of normative. [IEEE 95]

Note that the requirements in the normative portion may be *mandatory* or *optional*. The presence of different optional features of the standard in different implementations may affect interoperability.

Strictly conforming implementations are not required to include optional features. However, any optional features included in implementations must conform to the standard. It is also possible for a standard to state that some item is *implementation defined*. This means that the specification of the item is left to the discretion of the vendor developing an implementation of the standard.

6.4 Standards Maturity

One aspect of the quality of a standard is its maturity. A standard is mature if it is stable with respect to change. However, this can be difficult to evaluate.

TABLE 6.5 Typical Parts of a Standard

Typical Normative Parts	Typical Informative Parts
Specifications	Rationale
Options	Examples
Conformance statements	Guidance
	Tutorial material

Maturity is judged by a standard's

- State of development and approval
- Degree of acceptance in the marketplace; in other words, COTS products that conform to the standard exist and are being bought and used
- Age: time to work out bugs and problems

A highly mature standard is developed and approved, accepted in the marketplace, and has existed long enough for problems to be identified and fixed and for the standard to be stable. For example, structural standards for residential housing are very stable because they have been heavily used for many years.

Approval states
At any time, a standard can be in one of the following three approval states:

- Approved
- Draft: in process but not yet approved
- Canceled: approval withdrawn or revoked

Although each organization may have its own defined states or stages of development, they usually correspond to these three.

Keep in mind that a standard that is not mature today may be mature by the time your organization needs it. Also keep in mind that standards can grow old. Some go out of date very quickly as they are overtaken by newer technologies. But a number of the old ones are still with us, such as the Internet TCP/IP suite, the underlying protocols behind the World Wide Web. Seems like it's been around forever, doesn't it?

Risks versus cost and schedule
Selecting mature standards affects your system development costs and schedule. On the one hand, a desire for mature standards may require you to wait until a standard reaches maturity. On the other hand, using immature standards may be risky.

6.5 Profiles

A profile is a mechanism you can use to select and to combine standards to suit your system's needs. A profile is developed from one or more base standards. A *base standard* is an existing standard or an existing standard profile. Examples of base standards are operating system standards, network standards, or database standards.

> **profile** ➡ A set of one or more base standards and, where applicable, the identification of chosen classes, subsets, options, and parameters of those standards necessary for accomplishing a particular function [IEEE 95].

The lesson here is to recognize that your system may possibly include many standards of different types and from different sources. Furthermore, there may be competing standards that could be used to provide some required function in your system, such as the operating system or a database. Your understanding of the standards world is one of the tools that will help you to properly select standards as part of an acquisition.

Figure 6.3 illustrates how a profile is constructed using standards. Note that all the mandatory parts of the standards are included in the profile and that only the options *selected* are included in the profile.

Accredited organizations do not specify new functionality in profiles they create. Profiles can define subsets of a base standard, even a subset not sanctioned or defined in the base standard—for example, IEEE P1003.13—affectionately referred to as *slice and dice*.

One example of a profile is P1003.13, the POSIX Application Environment Profile [IEEE 98]. This standard defines four profiles for various real-time domains:

POSIX .13 Profile

- Minimal Real-time System Profile (or programming support environment, PSE 51[1])
- Real-time Controller System Profile (PSE 52)

---

1. The notation PSE is used to denote Generic Environment Profiles [IEEE 98].

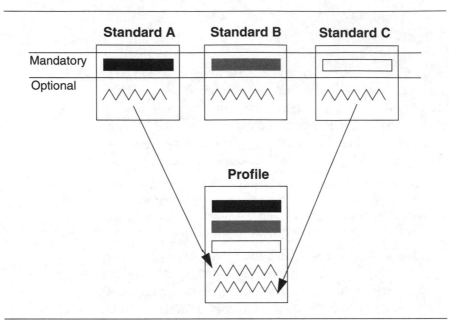

FIGURE 6.3 A profile.

- Dedicated Real-time System Profile (PSE 53)
- Multi-Purpose Real-time System Profile (PSE 54)

Each of these profiles is specified in terms of several other POSIX standards. Each profile first specifies the relevant standards used to define the profile. An example of this appears in Table 6.6. The entries in the table denote whether part (*Partial*) or all (*Mandatory*) of the indicated

TABLE 6.6 Standards in the POSIX .13 Profile

	Profile			
Standard	**PSE 51**	**PSE 52**	**PSE 53**	**PSE 54**
C Standard	Partial	Partial	Partial	Mandatory
POSIX .1	Partial	Partial	Partial	Mandatory
POSIX .1b	Partial	Partial	Partial	Mandatory
POSIX .1c	Partial	Partial	Mandatory	Mandatory
POSIX .2/2a	Partial	Partial	Partial	Partial
POSIX .5b	Optional	Optional	Optional	Optional

standard is included in the profile or whether the standard is optional for the profile.

The preceding is a high-level view of the profile in terms of the standards that comprise it. The profile specification continues by defining what particular functionality is required from each base standard included in the profile. For example, one of the standards specifies support for multiprocessing. Such functionality is called out in a profile as indicated in Table 6.7.

The terms *NRQ* and *MAN* denote not required and mandatory, respectively. We see, for example, that the minimal real-time system profile (PSE 51) does not require any of the identified functions, although the multipurpose real-time profile (PSE 54) does require the indicated functions. Table 6.7 is just a small part of the information contained in the overall profile, which contains many tables indicating what functionality is required, what is optional, the specification for conformance, and how to deal with options. Needless to say, the development of a profile is not a trivial matter! Nor is the selection of one.

TABLE 6.7 Functionality in the POSIX .13 Profile

	Profile			
Function	**PSE 51**	**PSE 52**	**PSE 53**	**PSE 54**
fork( )	NRQ	NRQ	MAN	MAN
sleep( )	NRQ	NRQ	MAN	MAN
wait( )	NRQ	NRQ	MAN	MAN

Source: From IEEE Standard for Information Technology—Standardization Application Environment Profile—POSIX Real-time Application Support P1003.13 Copyright 1983 IEEE. All rights reserved.

Profile Understanding

"You must not be lulled into thinking that selecting a profile is a trivial matter. To use a standard in a profile requires a detailed understanding of the standards. It is not enough to pick options, thinking all the work is done. Please do not let people believe this is somehow easy." (A colleague)

6.5.1 The Value of Profiles

Profiles are valuable because they provide a

- Clear method of communicating about a set of standards and the relationships among them
- Means for dealing with overlaps and gaps among the standards.

Profiles allow you to identify appropriate standards and the relations among them. Profiles also enable you to express how you expect products that conform to those standards to work together.

When you want to use more than one standard, there must be a way to integrate the standards so that they function together correctly. For example, you may put together three standards for a backplane, an operating system, and a network. When the user asks, "What time is it?" the operating system may use one measure of time, the network may use another, and the backplane may use a third. In a profile, you can identify potential overlaps and specify how implementations should deal with them.

It is difficult for industry to accommodate all the different profiles for the *same standard* because that might mean making multiple product variations, which are usually not profitable. If you try to use established profiles, you are more likely to find the products you need.

6.5.2 Profile Characteristics

Profiles are complete, allow conformance, identify gaps and incompatibilities, and allow variations.

Complete   Profiles are functionally and logically complete. To be functionally complete, profile specifications must satisfy all system requirements. To be logically complete, functions that complement each other must be included. For example, a *close* operation complements an *open* operation, and a *connect* operation complements a *disconnect* operation.

Allow conformance   Implementations can conform to profiles. A profile must be detailed and practical enough for

- Vendors to create implementations that conform to it
- Others to devise conformance tests for it

Profiles enable you to identify gaps and incompatabil-
ities among standards.

When combining several standards for a system, you
may need functionality that is not specified by any of the
standards in the profile. That missing functionality is a gap.
Filling a gap can be expensive and difficult and may require
creating "glue specifications." Identifying the gaps among
standards in your profile is useful and can be critical.

Completeness of Standards

"Most base standards are incomplete, the area of non-
consensus having been omitted, so the profile must also
be incomplete, for the same reason." (A colleague)

Gaps need not be literally *between* standards. Instead,
a gap means that there is an interface function that you
cannot find a standard to cover. For example, multicast
groups have such functions as *create* (form a group),
delete (eliminate the group), and *join* (add a new member
to the group) but perhaps not the function *union* (combine
two groups). The lack of a *union* operation may be viewed
as a gap by some applications.

If you cannot find a standard that addresses the functionality needed to bridge the gap, you need to either develop
your own specification to complete the system or find a
specification that satisfies your need. You might have to
develop the implementation as well.

Profiles and Gaps

Profiles reveal gaps between standards by comparing
the system requirements to the specification of the chosen standard(s). The same is true of overlaps. A description of a gap can be derived by using any specification
technique—requirements statement, natural language,
and so on. Similarly, the gap can be filled by developing
the glue specification that is necessary to fill the gap.

Identify incompatibilities

You may find two standards that meet your needs perfectly but that cannot work together as needed. For example, you might find two standards to use as part of a profile. One standard might accept file names with up to 32 characters, and the other might accept file names with up to 256 characters. The simplest way to resolve this incompatibility is to restrict all file names to be less than or equal to 32 characters. Such a constraint would be recorded in the profile. Figure 6.4 illustrates how standard A and standard B cannot work together without modification.

Realize too that one or more base standards may be insufficient. If these standards are combined in a profile, the resulting profile may be incomplete, because the base standards are incomplete. In such a case, you may need to add functionality, via glue specifications, to solve the problem.

Profile variations

The same standard can be combined in various ways to create different profiles. For example, Figure 6.5 represents three profiles sharing the same standards. The profiles are denoted X, Y, and Z. All three profiles tailor the standards differently, as represented by the icon in each profile.

- Profile X contains mandatory parts from standards A, B, and C and options selected from standards A and C, as shown by the arrows.

Standard A   **Standard B**

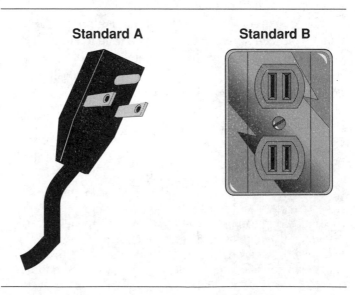

FIGURE 6.4 Incompatibilities between standards.

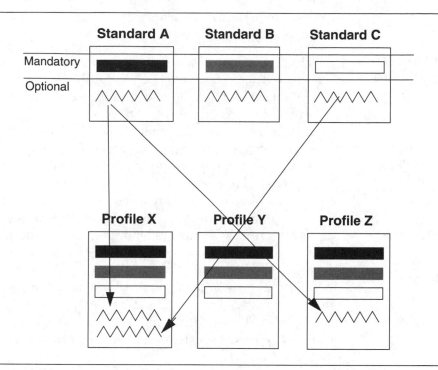

FIGURE 6.5 Profile possibilities.

- Profile Y contains mandatory parts from all three standards but does not include any options.
- Profile Z contains mandatory parts from standards A, B, and C and options only from standard A.

The preceding indicates the versatility you can gain from using the same standard in various ways.

6.5.3 Profile Issues

Some of the issues related to profiles are

- Identification of options/potential for proliferation
- Classification schemes for profiles
- Functionality specification in a profile: where to draw the line
- Achieving coherence among the standards in a profile

- Subsetting standards referenced in the profile
- Conformance

Options and proliferation

The proliferation of standard options in profiles can be a problem. After various groups select different optional parts of a standard, the result may be implementations that conform to variations of the *same* standard. Fragmentation of a standard, as specified in multiple profiles, can lead to corresponding fragmentation in the marketplace.

Classification

When you begin writing a profile, you should look at existing profiles relevant to the one you are writing. The difficult part of doing this today is the lack of a classification scheme, or taxonomy, to group profiles for this purpose.

Functionality

Profiles from accredited organizations do not specify new functionality. If you need to define new functionality and you want your profile to be recognized by an accredited standards organization, you should express it in separate specifications that can be independently realized as standards and then be incorporated into a profile. You could also propose the extension to be incorporated in an existing standard.

Coherence

Coherence specifies the relationships and interactions between the standards in a profile so that they work together. For example, if two standards in a profile contain a description of the same thing, these descriptions should be worded identically, to avoid confusion.

Coherence is difficult to achieve across a wide range of standards developed by multiple standards organizations. It is easier to achieve within a single standards organization but is often still challenging.

Subsetting

When two standards overlap a great deal, you may want to use all of one standard and part of the other. However, this strategy can cause a problem if one of the standards is defined as a *monolithic standard*—a standard with no specified options—or has few defined options.

Conformance

Conforming to each standard in a profile differs from conforming to the whole profile. If you choose to use options in the standard or if any additions to the profile are outside of the standard specifications, conformance is affected.

Subsetting Problems

An example of a subsetting problem came up when the POSIX real-time group, working on POSIX.13, intended to write a profile of POSIX.1 for real-time applications. The group's goal was to create small, medium, and large operating systems.

The small operating system would not include a file system, although a file system is mandatory in the base POSIX.1 standard. To achieve the goal of the profile, it would be necessary to "subset" the base standard, which had not previously been permitted. This subsetting problem caused serious controversy within the POSIX community. In the end, an exception was made to create a profile, called a special-purpose profile, that used only part of the base standard by allowing the omission of the file system.

6.6 Conformance

Whether you buy products or develop your own, you must determine whether an implementation is faithful to its interface standards. Recall that conformance means that a product's behavior fully adheres to the interface standard.

Note that conformance describes the *relationship* between the interface standard for a component and the implementation of the component. Conformance testing assesses the *presence* in an implementation of a feature in the standard but does not address the *quality* of the implementation.

Two primary types of conformance are

- Strict conformance

- Conformance with extensions

Types of conformance

> **strict conformance** ➟ The condition when an implementation of a component conforms to a specification and does not implement additional features.

> **conformance with extensions** ➟ The condition when an implementation of a component conforms to a specification *and* also implements additional features that are visible as part of the interface.

6.6.1 Specify and Verify

To achieve conformance, you must ensure that the standards/profiles *specify* conformance. To do so, you use such techniques as

- Conformance statements
- Test assertions
- Conformance classes

To *verify* conformance of the implementation, you use such techniques as

- Testing
- Consortium "branding"
- Reference implementations
- Conformance demonstrations

The preceding items are alternative approaches to assessing conformance of a product to a standard. The items are listed in order of decreasing quality of information provided.

Testing   Ensuring conformance of a product to its standard is obviously important. You may perform your own conformance testing or rely on vendor conformance testing. Some accredited organizations have developed conformance test suites. In other cases, such as the Ada Compiler Validation Capability (ACVC), conformance tests are developed by an organization independent of the developing organization. Whenever possible, it is best to rely on existing test suites and independent testing laboratories for conformance certification. Test suites are usually used by others and have been improved over time. Independent testing laboratories are objective and have no stake in the test results. Some products may even have been put through such testing by the vendor, so you can look for the equivalent of a "seal of approval." But realize that if there is no conformance test suite, you may have to develop one yourself; in general, that's not a trivial exercise.

Consortium branding   Some consortia determine whether implementations conform to one of their standards and "brand" them as conforming. An example of this is provided by the Open

Group, which provides a test suite that a vendor can apply to determine that a product passes the test, leading it to be branded.

Some organizations use existing implementations to test a new implementation for conformance. One implementation is selected as a reference implementation—sometimes known as a *golden sample*—and used to determine conformance of other implementations. The success of this method depends on the quality of the reference implementation. A quality reference implementation should be well specified and well tested.

Reference implementations

If you use a poor-quality reference implementation, the tested implementation may include the errors and misinterpretations present in the reference implementation.

A planned demonstration of a product witnessed by the customer or an acceptable third party can be used to test products. The results can be collected and evaluated according to factors specified by the customer.

Demonstration

Conformance demonstrations can be valuable when test suites, testing laboratories, and testing procedures do not exist. Demonstrations can also indicate where difficulties are, prompting revision of your profile to address problems. However, a demonstration is probably one of the weakest forms of conformance determination.

Ensuring Conformance

"It is very unlikely that comprehensive testing of a complex environment can be accomplished. What is gained from conformance testing is a confidence factor. What is equally important is that the vendor has committed that the product will conform to a specific version of the standard; this is a contractual commitment with implicit liability and warranty remedy. Some vendors use such words as 'implements' and 'is consistent with' to avoid the legal implications of 'conforms to.' The vendor gets to define what 'implements' means, but the standards define what 'conforms' means." (A colleague)

6.6.2 The Application View

Thus far, we have talked about conformance in the context of an implementation and an interface standard. However, another aspect of conformance is based on the application view. For example, consider Figure 6.6, which shows an interface standard and an application that uses those features, which in turn are provided by a conforming implementation. As indicated, the standard implementation and the application conform to the interface standard. However, the other path, shown at the top of Figure 6.6, shows the application using extensions to the standard implementation.

These two possibilities lead us to consider two types of application conformance.

> **strictly conforming application** ⇒ An application that uses *only* features specified in the interface standard.

> **conforming application with extensions** ⇒ An application that uses features specified in an interface standard *and* also uses additional features provided by an implementation.

The choice to develop a strictly conforming application versus an application that conforms with extensions has implications for the project. Many implementations contain additional features that are not part of a standard; in part, this allows a vendor to provide additional value. However, using such extensions clearly affects portability and may also affect interoperability. Using an implementation that

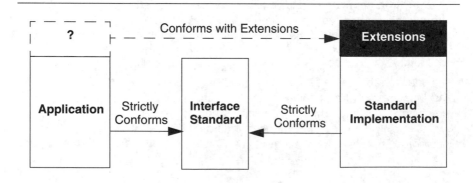

FIGURE 6.6 Conformance in the application context.

conforms with extensions also has market implications. You need to balance the desire for extra features with the requirements for portability and interoperability.

6.7 Sources of More Information

The following resource materials provide lists of standards that may help you get started finding appropriate standards for your organization.

Resources

- National Standards System Network (NSSN): *A National Resource for Global Standards* (*http:// www.nssn.org*), an on-line database of more than 250,000 standards
- IEEE POSIX.0: *IEEE Guide to the POSIX Open Systems Environment* [IEEE 95]
- The Open Group
- DODISS: *Department of Defense Index of Specifications and Standards* [DODISS 95]
- Defense Information Systems Agency *(DISA)*: *Technical Architecture Framework for Information Management* (TAFIM) [DoD 96][2]

Standards organizations also typically publish catalogs of the standards they approve. Many catalogs of standards are available on the World Wide Web.

Table 6.8 lists common service classes and some specifications that you might encounter (listed in alphabetical order). In no sense do we suggest that this list is complete! If you have heard of the items listed in the table, at least you have a basis for getting started. If you haven't heard of these items, you may need to do some homework.

Well-known specifications

Table 6.8 does not present all the specifications you will encounter or need to know about, but it should help you get started. The standards listed are both accredited

---

2. The TAFIM has been discontinued by the government. However, we list it because it still has relevant information, and other standards are based on and/or make reference to the TAFIM.

TABLE 6.8 Some Well-Known Specifications

Service Class	Specifications*
Backplanes	ISA, PCI, PiBus, VME
Data interchange	ASN.1, CALS, CDIF, CGI, CGM, EDIF, GIF, HTML, IGES, JPEG, MP3, ODA/ODIF, PDES/STEP, SGML, XDR, XML
Data management	RDA, SQL
Graphical user interfaces	X Window System
Graphics	Open-GL
Interconnections	Firewire, NTDS, RS-232, SCSI, USB
Networks	ATM, Ethernet, FDDI, Fibre Channel, FTAM, FTP, ISDN, OSI†,SMTP, SNMP, TCP/IP, TELNET, X.25
Objects	CORBA, COM
Operating systems	POSIX, Windows (variants, such as NT)
Programming languages	Ada, C, C++, FORTRAN, Java, Visual Basic

*.See Appendix B for a listing of acronyms cited here.

†.The reference to OSI here is general in the context of the OSI Basic Reference Model (see further [ISO 95]). That is, a number of standards are associated with the OSI model, such as for presentation and transport services.

and nonaccredited. Some were developed by formal standards development organizations; some were developed by industry consortia; others are de facto standards.

6.8 Standards in Government

Over the past few years, the U.S. government has decreased its efforts in standards work. For example, in the DoD, the number of military specifications and standards has decreased considerably, as indicated in Table 6.1. The decrease has been driven by acquisition reform. However, the government has not abandoned development of specifications and standards altogether.

Government standards

Table 6.9 lists some sources of government standards you may hear about. Unlike the non-government organizations we have covered thus far, some government organizations, such as the Defense Information Systems Agency (DISA) and the Open Systems Joint Task Force (OSJTF), have missions related to standards and other forms of

TABLE 6.9 Some Sources of Government Standards

Item	Name
FIPS	Federal Information Processing Standards
DODISS	Department of Defense Index of Specifications and Standards
JTA	Joint Technical Architecture [DoD 00c]
CALS	Continuous Acquisition and Life-Cycle Support
ITSG	Information Technology Standards Guidance [DoD 97]

guidance and assistance. Although standards are used in the private sector, the public sector generally uses standards more extensively and more strictly.

In the 1990s, government acquisition changed significantly, and new trends emerged, as illustrated in Figure 6.7. The trends toward the top of Figure 6.7 are certain or nearly certain. The trend at the bottom of the figure, moving from accredited standards toward consortium standards, is still uncertain.

Government trends

The trend from accredited standards to consortium standards is caused mainly by the slow response of accredited processes for standards development. Consortia standards have emerged from industry as a means to provide standards in a more timely fashion. Sometimes, consortia are formed to counter the dominance of a particular de facto standard.

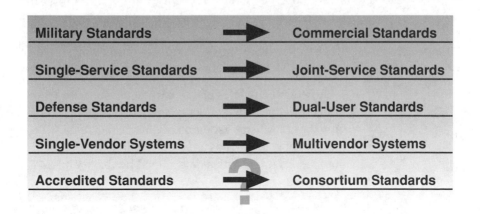

FIGURE 6.7 Trends in government acquisition.

Order of preference

When selecting standards, government managers need to be aware of certain hierarchies. For many years, the primary policy within the DoD was defined by MIL-STD-970 [MIL-STD-970], which delineated an order of precedence. MIL-STD-970 was canceled, however, and in its place the Defense Standardization Program [DoD 00a] specifies the use of standards in the following general descending order of preference:

1. International standardization agreements
2. Nongovernment standards
3. Commercial Item Descriptions (CIDs)
4. Federal specifications
5. Federal standards
6. Federal Information Processing Standards (FIPS)
7. Defense specifications
8. Guide specifications, such as Contractor Performance Assessments [DoD 99]
9. Defense standards
10. Defense handbooks
11. Consortium standards
12. De facto standards
13. Company standards

However, other documents are considered discretionary and may be used if relevant. One such document is the guide to best practices for evaluating contractor past performance [DoD 00b].

Government policy

The government position on standards was stated in Public Law 104-113 (the National Technology Transfer Act):

> All Federal agencies and departments shall use technical standards that are developed or adopted by voluntary consensus standards bodies, using such technical standards as a means to carry out policy objectives or activities determined by the agencies and departments.

Note the use of the term *voluntary consensus standards bodies*. There had been movement in this direction, and use of voluntary standards was selected "in the interests of greater economy and efficiency." This and other related information was specified in the OMB Circular A-119 [OMB 93].

Although the use of nongovernment standards has been part of DoD policy for years, the DoD culture and practice have only recently started to shift to open systems and the use of COTS products. Prevailing policies have long encouraged the government to give preference to nongovernment standards and Commercial Item Descriptions whenever practical. In 1986, the Packard Commission report [Packard 86] recommended avoidance of overspecified military standards and urged the harmonization of the standards selected with the commercial marketplace when choosing products to buy. The Perry memo [Perry 94] changed the default and burden of proof to favor solutions using commercial products instead of military specifications. The Kaminski memo [Kaminski 94] took this a step further for the DoD, including the establishment of the OSJTF.

Culture Change

"I encourage you and your leadership teams to be active participants in establishing the environment essential for implementing this cultural change" [Perry 94].

The combination of the Perry and Kaminski memos indicated the future thrust of the DoD, setting the stage for the use of open systems and alignment with industry, implicitly through the use of more COTS products. The government was effectively giving up *control in the large*. The results are still being felt today.

6.9 Summary

In this chapter, we explained what standards are, how they are developed, their characteristics, and who develops them.

We also covered profiles and their benefits, limitations, and issues surrounding them.

Definition of standard

A *standard* is a publicly available document defining specifications for interfaces, services, processes, protocols, or data formats and is established and maintained by group consensus.

Benefits

Using standards provides such benefits as

- Broad availability of suitable products, leading to
- Competition, resulting in
- Lower prices

ISO and ANSI

ISO is the worldwide federation of national standards bodies that promotes the development of standards. ANSI is the self-designated national coordinating body for U.S. standards development organizations.

Types of standards organizations

Standards organizations can be categorized into four types:

- Accredited
- Consortium
- Private
- Vendor specific

Consensus processes

Standards organizations follow various consensus processes in their approach to

- Participation
- Development process
- Postapproval process

Information in a standard

A typical standard consists of two kinds of information:

- Normative: required material, including options
- Informative material that poses no requirements; non-normative

Profiles

Profiles provide a way to select and combine standards to suit your organization's needs. We presented information about profiles, including their

- Characteristics
- Value
- Issues

Conformance is the condition that exists when an   **Conformance**
implementation of a component adheres to its interface
specification.

6.10 Food for Thought

1. We have defined a standard as a document. Some people would define a standard in terms of a product. What
are the pros and cons of each of these approaches?

2. Some people use such terms as *open standard* or *open
system standard.* How would you interpret these
terms?

3. In Chapter 2, we gave our definition of open system on
page 12. Suppose that instead of the phrase "maintained
according to group consensus," we had used "maintained according to an accredited standards body."
What difference would that have made? Can you think
of specifications that would fit one definition, but not
the other? Under what circumstances would the second form of the definition be more desirable?

4. If you were developing policy for your organization,
what general criteria for standards selection would you
use? Weight each requirement. For example, how
important is the type of consensus process or stability
of the standard?

5. A colleague commented: "Maybe 10 percent of standards are ever used, and 1 percent are widely used."
Do you agree with this statement? If it is true, why do
you think there are so many standards?

6. You need to develop policy for your project about
whether to use vendor extensions to a product that
conforms to an interface standard. Some of your technical folks say they want and need these extensions;
others are wary. What will you write as policy and
why? How did you deal with market considerations
when developing your policy?

7. What are the ways in which you can influence a standards body? How much will you budget for it?

8. You get a promotion to manage multiple projects. Now go back and answer question 7 again.

9. An old friend has become the chief information officer for a state government and is charged with developing an information architecture for the state. Your friend always had a lot of respect for you and asks for the three most important recommendations you can provide about standards and open systems. What are they?

10. According to the Federal Acquisition Regulations [FAR] section 6.302-1(b)(4), the use of standards can be justified for "other than full and open competition" if only specified makes and models of technical equipment and parts will satisfy the need for additional units or replacement items and only one source is available. How would you expect this to affect your acquisition?

11. The following text is from the Federal Acquisition Regulations, Subpart 11.101 (c): "In accordance with OMB Circular A-119, *Federal Participation in the Development and Use of Voluntary Consensus Standards and in Conformity Assessment Activities,* agencies must use voluntary consensus standards, when they exist, in lieu of Government-unique standards, except where inconsistent with law or otherwise impractical. The private sector manages and administers voluntary consensus standards. Such standards are not mandated by law (e.g., industry standards such as ISO 9000)." Can you develop some general guidelines that would indicate when a voluntary consensus standard is "otherwise impractical?"

7

Commercial Off-the-Shelf (COTS) Products

The third part of the key iteration in the overall approach is to acquire implementations. In this chapter, we particularly focus on COTS implementations. We also discuss several other kinds of off-the-shelf implementations. We then cover interacting with the marketplace and why the adage, caveat emptor, or buyer beware, still applies.

7.1 COTS and Open Systems

Part of the motivation for moving to open systems is to take advantage of the commercial marketplace. It is possible to implement an open system without using commercial off-the-shelf (COTS) products; many advantages of open systems would still be realized. In fact, people sometimes confuse the use of COTS products with the idea of open systems. Think back to our definition of open systems: Nothing in that definition *requires* that the implementations be obtained commercially. If you develop an implementation that conforms to a standard, it is open but not a COTS product. In Table 7.1, the entries under the heading Standard Interface emphasize the role of COTS products in an open systems approach.

Although open systems and the use of COTS products are not the same thing, both have contributions to make to

TABLE 7.1 Interface and Implementation Choices

	Standard Interfaces	Nonstandard Interfaces
COTS Products	Standards-based COTS	Other COTS
Developmental Items	Standards-based new development	Everything else

an acquisition effort. Used together, their value multiplies. Another way to think of it is that through the use of standards, open systems provide a means for taming the chaos of the marketplace.

But COTS products may not be appropriate for all systems or all components within a system. The use of COTS products must be carefully considered. It is a nontrivial decision and process to get the most you can from using COTS products and technology.

7.2 Kinds of Off-the-Shelf Components

COTS products

As with open systems, there are many different ideas of what "commercial off-the-shelf product" means. In Chapter 2, we introduced the definition we use throughout this book.

COTS product ➡ A product that is

- Sold, leased, or licensed to the general public
- Offered by a vendor trying to profit from it
- Supported and evolved by the vendor, which retains the intellectual property rights
- Available in multiple, identical copies
- Used without internal modification by a consumer

An important term—vendor—is introduced in this definition. A closely related term is supplier.

vendor ➡ A company that creates and supports a COTS product.

supplier ➡ A provider of an off-the-shelf item.

For COTS products, the terms vendor and supplier are synonymous. However, the term supplier rather than vendor is used to denote providers of non-COTS products, such as shareware. As we will see, the provider of a product can be as important as the product itself.

Another term used in the definition of a COTS product is modification.

> **modification** ⟿ Changes that alter the internal makeup of a product; for example, changing the source code of a software product.

It may be tempting to modify a COTS product, but in doing so, you are on dangerous ground. In particular, a modification may introduce errors in the product or may break conformance of that product to a standard. In any case, modifying a COTS product is likely to break any license agreement or warranty.

Our definition of a COTS product is somewhat idealized. A number of off-the-shelf (OTS) items do not quite fit the definition but are of interest. For example, "freeware" is off-the-shelf software, but no one is looking to profit from it directly. Similarly, in some market niches, such as device drivers, consumer modification is standard practice for some vendors, which include consumer modifications as part of a future release of the product. This illustrates how consumers can help to develop products. It's like having your cake and eating it too.

Other off-the-shelf items

Other terms stray even farther from our definition. A term often used, especially by government, is nondevelopmental item (NDI) [FAR, Part 2]. An NDI is an off-the-shelf item typically available from sources other than vendors. Figure 7.1 illustrates a taxonomy of off-the-shelf items.

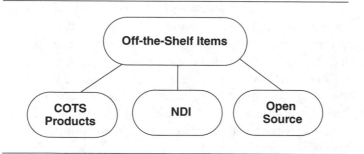

FIGURE 7.1 A taxonomy of off-the-shelf items.

Another term you may encounter is *open source software*. This refers to software that is made available in source code form to others under license that includes a proviso that modifications that are made are shared with the community. Be aware: Open source is not the same thing as open system!

Figure 7.1 should not be interpreted literally; it is intended to illustrate high-level distinctions among OTS items. The definition of a COTS product is based, in part, on expectations of both the buyer and the provider. The result is a certain latitude in what constitutes a COTS product.

But whether they are COTS products or other off-the-shelf items, what all of them have in common is that they exist before you acquire them and that someone else is responsible for and controls them. Although we focus here on *commercial* off-the-shelf items and the differences generated by competition in the marketplace, most of what we discuss applies, to varying degrees, to any off-the-shelf item.

7.3 Key Characteristics of COTS Products

COTS products have a number of key characteristics that distinguish them from one another and thus affect your decisions about using them.

Market segment
One such characteristic is the market segment to which they belong. COTS products can usually be categorized by the kind of functionality they provide. Thus, the market segment for operating systems is different from that for financial management systems. If you can identify the market segments that are of interest to your system, it will provide a start for your market research and reduce the complexity of finding competitive products. Your reference model can be of great help here. As you delve into various parts of your system, you may find whole worlds you never knew existed out there in the marketplace!

Technology
COTS products also differ with regard to the technology they implement. Even though you may know the market

segment that is of interest, more than one technology may be represented by the products in that segment. For example, your system may need the services of a database management system. For this market segment, several available technologies, including relational and object-oriented, are embodied in products. If one of these technologies can be determined to provide services that are more appropriate than the other for your system, you have narrowed your search and its complexity or at least reduced the number and variety of products you will need to examine.

Another important distinguishing characteristic of COTS products is the standards they implement. Even products that are in the same market segment and that implement the same technology may conform to different standards. It is in this characteristic that open systems and COTS-based systems come together to provide the greatest benefit. Ultimately, it will be the integration of COTS products that will be of paramount importance; standards-based integration helps ensure the integration of conforming COTS products. **Standards implemented**

Performance is another characteristic that distinguishes COTS products from one another. Some people contend that COTS products will not work in their system because the products will not meet stringent performance requirements, such as safety, security, or hard real time. For example, a few programs have developed their own operating system executives because of the developers' conviction that no existing executive would have the efficiency needed to meet hard real-time deadlines. The developers were convinced that only an executive tailor-made for their particular system and circumstance would meet the requirement. **Performance characteristics**

By specifying the performance requirements of a system, we set up the basis for identifying the set of products having acceptable performance. For example, for certain environmental conditions, implementations that fit the requirements may be available from a number of different sources. You may find items you could use that are

- Ruggedized: modifications made to a COTS product to make it suitable for special use, such as for a military environment

- Militarized: designed and manufactured from the outset to meet a military specification
- "Normal": COTS products with no special engineering that nevertheless meet the requirements

In this case, the performance characteristics also determine the size of population from which you may be able to choose, as pictured in Figure 7.2. If the performance characteristic is fairly common, such as the need for even normal COTS products to withstand being dropped, many COTS products will have the required performance characteristic. However, the number of available products decreases as the stringency of the requirements increases. So in Figure 7.2, we see that there are fewer ruggedized than COTS products and even fewer militarized ones, but the ones that are there meet very stringent requirements.

Product availability

Another distinguishing characteristic is the availability of a COTS product. Although our definition asserts that COTS products need to be available—in multiple, identical copies—sometimes a new version with features you want has not made it to market yet. Or perhaps not enough copies are available to suit your needs. For example, computer manufacturers have often found that they have underestimated the demand for an item and are without the manufacturing capacity or parts necessary to meet the demand.

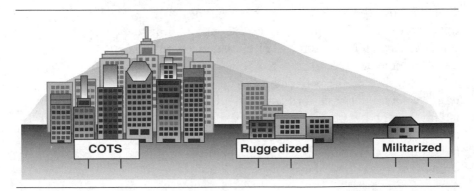

FIGURE 7.2 Relative number of product types.

Product maturity is another characteristic that distinguishes COTS products. Two products in the same market segment that implement the same technology and exhibit the same performance characteristics might be best distinguished by their maturity.

COTS product maturity

There are two considerations in product maturity. One is the length of time the product has been around and its history during that time. For example, has the product historically changed radically from one release to the next? How frequently are new releases made available by the vendor? How reliable are new releases? See Appendix C, Sample Questions, for more ideas.

The other aspect of product maturity is vendor maturity. Has the vendor been around a long time? Does it have a solid history of reliability and responsiveness with both this and other products? Is the vendor on a stable financial footing, or is it still funded by venture capital? All other things being equal, the maturity of both a COTS product *and* its vendor can make a significant difference in your system's success.

Vendor maturity

7.4 Deciding to Use COTS Products

The decision to use COTS products to implement components in a system should be a conscious one. That is, it should be carefully reasoned, based on a study of what is available and the overall—both immediate and long-term—needs of the particular project. Even though it is common policy in both the government and private enterprise to use COTS items whenever possible, it is still important to decide when this makes sense and to know when it does not. It is a business decision.

COTS business case analysis is the mechanism for determining the long-term desirability of using—or choosing not to use—COTS products to implement a system. A business case develops and communicates the relative costs—based on results of cost modeling—and benefits of all the

COTS business case analysis

alternatives worthy of serious consideration, both "build" and "buy." A business case can be used at the levels of

- A whole system: "Should I take a COTS-based approach overall?"
- An individual component: "Should I use a COTS product here?"

A business case is dependent on the articulation of the key success factors for the project. Without knowledge of the success factors for the project, there is no basis for deciding the relative merits of one alternative over another.

The business case usually makes use of feasibility studies to explore how well a given product will meet the needs of the system. The business case then goes on to articulate a complete cost/benefit analysis and recommended course of action. It is not always the case that the argument for using COTS products will come down literally to cost savings. In some cases, you may find that a COTS-based system will cost about the same as another approach but that a great deal more functionality or performance can be realized, or perhaps the system can be fielded more quickly, all for the same number of dollars.

7.5 Negotiating between Requirements and the Marketplace

One of the biggest challenges in using COTS products or any OTS item is to realize that they are created on the basis of the developer's assumptions about the environment in which they will be deployed. Among those are assumptions about architecture and requirements, especially built-in notions of what processes the user will use and how the user will use the product in support of those processes. This is the main reason that you need to maintain flexibility in the system requirements: A rigid, top-down approach to requirements may make it impossible to find COTS products that can fulfill the need.

Process Mismatch

On June 9,1999, the *Wall Street Journal* carried a story about two large waste management companies that had put a great deal of effort and money—$103 million in one case and $45 million of a projected $250 million investment in the other—into the adoption of SAP's enterprise resource planning product, only to abandon it before getting any real use. The product is described as "elegant though extremely complex software that can monitor and help manage a company's every move." The comment from one waste management executive was, "They expect you to change your business to go with the way the software works." Although the SAP executive quoted did not dispute that SAP R/3 customers often have to change their businesses to use the software, he said that the cost and the change are worth it because the software allows companies to operate more efficiently. Perhaps that depends on understanding and appreciating at the outset what is involved. As this executive said, "The most important thing is executive commitment. It's not an [information technology] project—it's a business transformation." On the other hand, your project may have a good reason for pursuing such a change, as reflected by the comments of an executive from another company: "Your processes have to change. As a company that acquired so many companies, [we] didn't have uniform processes. Part of our challenge was to get 500 places using standard procedures."

Ranking requirements

From the beginning, it is important to understand the relative importance of various requirements. Although the word *requirement* usually refers to a trait or a capability the system *must* have, not all requirements are of equal priority. Most sets of requirements can, in fact, be divided into those that are essential, those that are highly desirable but can be traded off, and those that are just "nice to have." A clear understanding of all these levels is important, or you will not be able to determine what can be traded off and what cannot be compromised.

Products influence requirements

A prudent approach to the use of open systems and COTS products will start with a general, tentative specification of the requirements; it is tentative pending discovery of what the marketplace has to offer. Market research will reveal a great deal about what functionality and behavior are provided by products in the market segment of interest. This information can then be used to revisit the initial requirements and refine them to make them more conducive to fulfillment by the marketplace.

You will find that the marketplace has a great deal to say about the requirements you finally settle on. The requirements will determine the types of products you look at, but the capabilities of the available products will in turn have a strong influence on the final requirements. The capabilities may indicate requirements that need to be scaled back or eliminated, but they may also suggest more extensive requirements that you had not realized were feasible. Realize there may be essential requirements that simply cannot be satisfied by any COTS product.

Negotiating requirements

It will be necessary to negotiate your set of requirements. Users often embark on a new system, expecting it to look and behave exactly like the existing system. Their perception of the requirements is based on the process they use—which has probably evolved over a number of years, influenced by many different circumstances—and how their current system supports that process. The users may well perceive *all* requirements to be hard and fast and be unwilling to consider negotiation or trade-offs. Extensive user education may be necessary before the users are comfortable with the mindset of flexibility that is necessary for effective use of COTS products.

The negotiation may require a lot of patience and dialogue, as well as a clear understanding of who all the stakeholders are. Those who have a say in the system requirements may extend far beyond the end users, particularly if anything the system does is subject to laws, regulatory agencies, policies, or congressional or corporate mandates. In addition to the end users and the acquisition team, including the integration contractor, the stakeholders include the customer—the one funding the acquisition—executives at a higher level in the acquiring organization, and those whose systems must interface with your system. Stakeholders also include those whose processes interact with the ones supported by your system, even if their systems do not directly interact with yours.

It is up to you, as the acquirer, to facilitate the negotiation among all these stakeholders and the marketplace. *You* must help to turn the original set of notional requirements

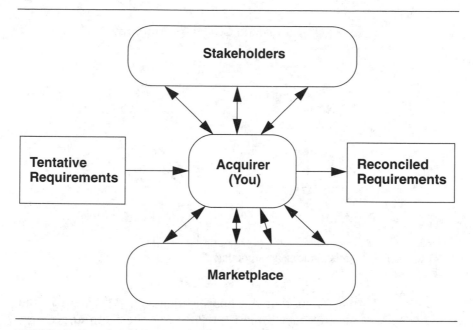

FIGURE 7.3 Requirements negotiation.

into the set of requirements that can be fulfilled by the
marketplace, as pictured in Figure 7.3.

7.6 Buyer Beware

The phrase caveat emptor is well worn but just as applicable today as ever. Even the best-intentioned vendors may
be given to hype; nothing can protect you against that
except your own effort. Knowing the relevant marketplace
is your best defense, and market research is the first line in
that defense; see Section 11.2 for more information.

Market research may look at more than just standards
or products. It is often important to examine competing
technologies before considering competing products.

**Products and
technologies**

A COTS product implements a particular technology.
Similarly, a given technology is realized through the products that implement it. For example, as pictured in Figure 7.4,
a technology, such as distributed object technology, may

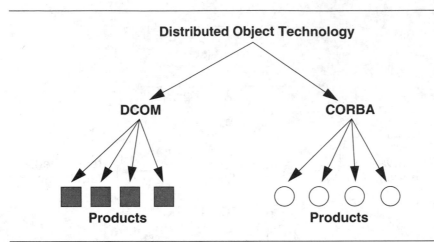

FIGURE 7.4 Relating technology and products.

have more than one approach, such as Distributed Common Object Model (DCOM) or the Common Object Request Broker Architecture (CORBA). Each of these, in turn, is implemented by a number of products from various, competing vendors.

Selection criteria

Criteria are needed to provide the basis for making a technology or product selection decision. Criteria will typically be derived from the requirements for the system in general and for the component for which the COTS product is being considered in particular.

Although it might be tempting to define and to evaluate against all possible requirements, that can be counterproductive. It is expensive to do deep evaluations either on too many products or with respect to too many criteria. Instead, it is more useful to determine those criteria that will best distinguish among similar products. In addition to the distinguishing characteristics mentioned in Section 7.3, consider such things as

- Completeness of functionality
- Compatibility with user processes
- Compatibility with system architecture and other COTS products already selected
- Reliability

- Life-cycle support requirements
- Cost
- Complexity

Note that many of these criteria, such as reliability, performance, and cost, are implementation characteristics; many are characteristics controlled by the product's developer, so techniques must be found and used for evaluating them. We alluded to this in our earlier discussion of the consequences of the paradigm shift; see Table 3.2. Other criteria have to do with the vendor, a particularly important criterion if many products are available. A reasonable set of criteria may be determined by considering the requirements that would pose the greatest risk to the system if they were not satisfied.

Many different techniques can be used to evaluate COTS products and their vendors. Their selection and use will depend on the nature of the decision being made. Some examples of techniques are

Evaluation techniques

- Literature analysis, including such diverse resources as references from other users, market segment analyses from companies like the Gartner Group, and Standard and Poor's reports for vendor financial information
- Gap analysis, a determination of both the requirements that are or are not met by the product and the product features that go beyond current requirements
- Vendor demonstrations
- Exercising the product in a testbed
- Model problems, which are small experiments that focus on specific design questions and product behaviors
- Benchmarks
- Prototypes of a large subset of system functionality, incorporating the COTS product being evaluated

More than one technique may be used as part of the same decision-making process.

Besides variation in techniques, there may also be variation in the amount of effort expended on different

Levels of effort

A Hellish Experience

A systems manager died recently and was met at heaven's gate by St. Peter. St. Peter said that the manager's life was such that he could go to either heaven or hell. The manager thought it over and asked whether he could see both before he made a decision. St. Peter agreed, and the two of them floated down through the clouds, past earth, into hell. The manager was amazed to see people eating, drinking, dancing, laughing, and generally having a great time. Plenty of food and wine were fueling the party.

St. Peter and the manager then floated up, past earth, through the clouds, and into heaven. Everyone there was dressed in white robes, peacefully sitting around, not doing much of anything except reading, drinking tea, and quietly chatting. The manager decided that this was way too boring for him, so he asked to go to hell.

A few weeks later, St. Peter was passing through hell on another tour and saw the manager, chained to a wall, being whipped and prodded with glowing red-hot pokers. The manager called out to St. Peter, "What happened? This isn't the hell that you showed me!" To which St. Peter replied, "That was the demo." (From www.netfunny.com/rhf, author unknown)

product selections. Some decisions are so far removed from the ultimate success of the system that it would not make sense to expend much effort making the choice; they are almost suited to the proverbial coin toss.

On the other hand, some selections are vital to the system in question. They typically deal with components that are critical to the main mission, or objective, of the system. These are the choices that will make or break the system, so they demand careful consideration and extensive investigation.

License negotiation

In most cases, it will be necessary to secure licenses for the COTS products that will be used. The licenses of interest here are not the kind that come with shrink-wrapped software; there is no room for negotiation with those. The licenses of concern here will need to be negotiated with the vendors to find the terms that best suit the needs of both the project and the vendor.

There are many different kinds of licenses and can be many different bases for licenses, such as per seat, per process, or enterprisewide. The choices among these and other factors will affect cost and may affect other important aspects of the system, such as the architecture.

Licensing Matters

In one highly distributed system project, the first round of market research identified one candidate whose licensing structure assumed a single, centralized instance of the product. The cost to procure the number of licenses that would have been needed for the program's architecture would have been prohibitive. So the project rejected that product and chose another. A couple of years later, when dissatisfaction with the chosen product led the project members to investigate the marketplace again, they found that the vendor whose product had been rejected before had changed its license fee structure. The vendor had realized that its licensing structure needed to accommodate distributed architectures, and this time the vendor's product won.

Other licensing considerations are

- Development versus maintenance licenses
- Whether the licenses can be "passed-through," as from the developer to the maintainer
- What kind of support the vendor will provide
- Agreements on caps on the fees and the terms under which product functionality can be separated out into another product

License agreements can also establish escrow accounts. These specify the terms and conditions, such as vendor demise or abandonment of a product, under which the acquirer gains full rights to the COTS product, including source code and design information.

The approach to licensing options needs to be carefully considered and then negotiated with each vendor. Although it may seem an innocuous part of business, licensing considerations have forced more than one project team to consider alternatives.

The license agreement becomes the basis for the whole relationship between a project and each of its vendors. There is no longer a place for an adversarial relationship with one's vendors; nor is this typically a situation in which the buyer takes the product and has no further interaction with the vendors. With COTS products, it is important to recognize your vendors as your partners, organizations

Vendor relationships

with which you share a common interest: success, both theirs and yours.

This common interest does not mean that the vendor makes concessions to your project. The vendor's success still lies in the profitable satisfaction of as large a market share as can be attained. The new relationship is built on the development of mutual trust and respect, and it may be fostered through regular meetings and interactions during which you and your vendor share information on plans and goals. Only by knowing your needs can the vendor take them into account; through knowledge of the vendor's plans, you will be better able to make your plans and to influence the vendor's. Other things you can do to create such a relationship are joining vendor user groups, volunteering to be an alpha or beta test site, and working collaboratively to create a product that not only satisfies your needs but also enables the vendor to sell more widely.

Data rights   When you build implementations, you have access to all the technical data necessary for creating and maintaining those implementations. However, when you buy products, you generally do not have access to data rights. Getting data rights that are outside of the vendor's typical license agreements will in general cost you. In some cases, data rights cannot be obtained at all, at any cost. Before attempting to negotiate for extraordinary data rights, be very sure that you that really need them. And you have the resources to follow through.

7.7 Government Policy Implications

Because of the promise of benefit from exploiting the marketplace—not to mention the downside of public disclosure of $700 hammers—there has been a continual move in both industry and government to make more use of commercial technologies and COTS products. In fact, the government has built on and reasserted past policies that have directed increasing use of what the marketplace has to offer.

For all the talk about COTS products in government circles, there is no definition or use of the term in the Federal Acquisition Regulations (FAR). Instead, the FAR defines "commercial item" [FAR, Part 2], which differs in four essential ways from our definition. A commercial item

Commercial Items

- Includes services *and* products
- Does not distinguish between items that have a commercial vendor behind them and items that are developed primarily for a company's in-house use but may also be available for sale
- Does not require that the item presently exist
- Allows for modification, which the FAR text goes on to constrain

Federal government policy states that government agencies and departments should acquire commercial items and use commercial distribution systems whenever these adequately satisfy the needs of government [FAR]. If you are a project manager working in the government, you are most likely required to follow these guidelines, which include

The policy

- Defining requirements in terms that enable and encourage offerors to supply commercial items
- Modifying requirements in appropriate cases to ensure that the requirements can be met by commercial items

The rules have changed in recent years to reflect new policies. The FARs affirm the federal government's preference for the acquisition of commercial items "by establishing acquisition policies more closely resembling those of the commercial marketplace and encouraging the acquisition of commercial items and components" [FAR, Part 12.000]. To this end, the FAR policy, dated 23 November 1999, states:

Agencies shall—

(a) Conduct market research to determine whether commercial items or nondevelopmental items are available that could meet the agency's requirements;

(b) Acquire commercial items or nondevelopmental items when they are available to meet the needs of the agency; and

(c) Require prime contractors and subcontractors at all tiers to incorporate, to the maximum extent practicable, commercial items or nondevelopmental items as components of items supplied to the agency.

Although the government regulations use the term commercial item, we will continue to use the term COTS product because of its broader acceptance in the wider community.[1]

COTS business cases

Business cases for the use of COTS products and open systems are very useful decision-making tools. A business case is not unlike the economic analysis the DoD already uses, and other government agencies already use various forms of business case analysis. The main difference is that an economic analysis usually reflects a detailed analysis of a single "leading" alternative, whereas a COTS business case is the mechanism for developing and communicating the costs and benefits of several competing alternatives. People must be educated about working in the context of COTS products and the paradigm shift, described in Chapter 3, but unfortunately, little training is available in this area. One of the goals in developing this book was to help fill this gap.

Buy instead of build

The ultimate goal now is to improve systems—making them "faster, better, cheaper"—by buying their parts instead of building them. This change entails a great deal of culture shock, which seldom gets the same attention as the potential for saving money and fielding superior systems. The *use* of COTS products is a significant change that goes beyond the products themselves. To acquire COTS products effectively, project managers in the government must know about the COTS marketplace and the regulations that apply to the use of COTS products.

Software

Specifically with regard to software, the FAR states that COTS software and its documentation should be used under the licenses commonly available to the public, provided that those licenses are consistent with federal law and otherwise satisfy the government's needs. The FAR

---

1. Also, the FAR does not define the term component; it appears clear, however, that it is intended to mean an implementation, either hardware or software.

specifically says that the government shall *not* require a contractor or a vendor to furnish technical information that is not customarily provided to the public or to provide the government "rights to use, modify, reproduce, release, perform, display, or disclose commercial computer software or commercial computer software documentation except as mutually agreed to by the parties" [FAR].

The FAR goes on to say that licenses should be included as addenda to contracts when appropriate. These policies ensure both that the government is operating as closely as possible to the way the commercial marketplace works and that both the government and the vendor are protected.

With regard to technical data, the FAR says that the government shall acquire only the technical data and the data rights customarily provided to the public (see FAR Part 27 or agency FAR supplements). That way, the government does not incur the additional expenses for the vendor to create government-unique materials.

Technical data

7.8 Summary

In this chapter, we discussed various kinds of off-the-shelf items:

- COTS products
- Items that differ slightly from the COTS product definition

We then discussed business case analysis, which provides a way to make decisions about using COTS products.

The key characteristics of COTS products are

- Market segment they are part of
- Technology they implement
- Standards they conform to
- Performance characteristics
- Availability
- Maturity

The discussion of negotiating between requirements and the marketplace reminded us of why this is necessary and gave the essential ideas as

- Ranking requirements
- Understanding the influence products have on the requirements
- Learning how to negotiate between the many kinds of stakeholders and the marketplace

The adage "buyer beware" requires you to think carefully about

- Relation between products and technologies
- Product selection criteria
- Evaluation techniques you will use
- Level of effort it makes sense to expend on various COTS product decisions
- Challenges of license negotiation
- Management of relationships with your vendors
- Data rights you really need

We closed with a discussion of government policies. Note that the government definition of a commercial item differs from our definition of a COTS product.

7.9 Food for Thought

1. Think about the kinds of component implementations in your system right now or the ones you are thinking about using. Are any of them COTS products, according to the definition given in Section 7.2? For other kinds of off-the-shelf items, how far are they from the elements of this definition? Based on where and how much they differ from the elements of the definition, can you predict how these differences will affect the benefits and liabilities you should expect?

2. What would be important elements for a COTS business case for your system? What would you need to

know to compare the advantages and disadvantages of custom and COTS-based approaches?

3. How does your system architecture influence the business case analysis for a COTS product?

4. How will you go about deciding whether COTS products are appropriate for your system? What are your "success factors"—those criteria that must be satisfied for your system to fulfill your stakeholders' expectations?

5. As you are probably aware, most systems contain spare capacity requirements for hardware; for example, at least 50 percent of memory must be unused on initial delivery. Does this concept apply to COTS products in the following sense: If you have a choice between two COTS products and one has more additional features, which you could use in an evolution of your system, is that COTS product necessarily better? Discuss the COTS product *feature capacity* as part of product selection.

6. How might licensing agreements affect your system architecture? What kinds of licenses would be most beneficial for your situation? Do they differ for various components of your system? If so, how do they differ?

7. Consider Figure 7.3 and identify any changes to the figure to accommodate the case of a transition of a legacy system to an open, COTS-based system.

8. If an implementation you purchase is a COTS product, does that make it open? Cite several examples to support your answer.

9. Are there any circumstances that would prompt you to consider modifying a COTS product? What skills would be required to attempt such modification? What would be the long-term consequences of taking such an approach? Are there any modifications that are okay?

10. On your project, is there any risk of a vendor's going out of business or being bought by another vendor? Would you use an escrow account if there were? How would you decide whether the risk was great enough,

in light of the resources you would need to be prepared to allocate if you were to exercise the escrow? Can you think of any other ways to mitigate this risk?

11. Despite the best efforts of those in charge, there are still often problems implementing good COTS-related policies. One of these is the budget cycle. How do you suppose your organization's budget practices affect your ability to be successful using COTS products?

12. If you were doing an evaluation of the maturity of a COTS product, how would you weight product maturity versus vendor maturity?

8

Acquisition Roadmaps

In this chapter, we consider the larger context of reference models, architectures, standards, and COTS products. We also consider some aspects of integration.

We use the term *roadmap* to mean a set of acquisition activities that result from key choices made as part of an overall acquisition process. The roadmaps we present illustrate key strategies you can use to develop and to maintain your open, COTS-based system.

8.1 A General Approach

In Chapter 4, we described the iterative nature of the acquisition approach. That approach is shown in Figure 8.1.

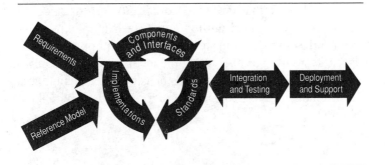

FIGURE 8.1 Elements of an acquisition approach.

Iteration
Do not be lulled into thinking that the general approach is a purely top-down process. It's not; it contains iteration in various areas, and it also contains a very distinct bottom-up perspective. Thus, the general approach is really a combination of top-down and bottom-up approaches. Success is determined by your ability to align those approaches.

The activities in the center wheel involve the most iteration in the open systems, COTS-based approach:

- Identifying *components and interfaces*
- Selecting *standards*
- Selecting *implementations*

The critical iteration present is in the context of an open, COTS-based approach. This approach is radically different from one in which you define all the system components and develop implementations yourself.

Associated with the iterative nature of the process are a myriad of decisions that must be made. For example, you may find a standard that meets all your requirements, but the COTS implementations may not be available for three years. Waiting three years for an implementation of a standard is risky. You may consider contracting out for development of an implementation because you need one sooner. Or, you may decide to use another standard until COTS implementations are available for the standard you want. In all cases, there are consequences not just for the initial deployment of the implementation but for the evolution of the system as well.

Although the primary iteration is in the center of Figure 8.1, note that there is also iteration with respect to other aspects included in the figure. For example, requirements are seldom cast in stone, especially for open, COTS-based systems, because of the need to negotiate requirements with the marketplace. It is possible for a change to a requirement to propagate through other activities in Figure 8.1.

8.2 Open Systems Highway

The approach shown in Figure 8.1 is based on open systems. A more general approach is shown in Figure 8.2, which illustrates both an open and a closed system roadmap.[1]

If you begin at the top of Figure 8.2, you can follow the steps of the open systems approach and better understand the relations between them. But don't interpret Figure 8.2 too literally: Our purpose is to illustrate ideas rather than define a process.

After developing a concept of the system and the requirements the system must satisfy, a reference model is developed that consists of entities and services. Once the reference model is complete, one or more architectures can be developed. From an architecture, an iterative process begins that identifies components and selects standards, implementations, and/or standards-based implementations. Take a look back at the discussion of Figure 5.11, where we also discussed this point.

The emphasis of an open systems roadmap is on the use of standards. Often, the standards-based implementations will be COTS products, but it is not required.

Note that the view of the system is most concrete at the bottom of Figure 8.2 and most abstract at the top. As the system develops, the developers take it from an abstract idea to a physical system that can then be used. This is an example of a *refinement process*.

---

1. Figure 8.2 shows two different types of relations. One relation is *part of* and is represented by the circle near the top of the roadmap that links *entities* and *services* together and is labeled *reference model*. For example, an *entity* is part of a *reference model*. The second type of relation is that of *derived from* and is represented by the rectangle that links *implementations, components, standards,* and *standards-based implementations* together. For example, a *standards-based implementation* is derived from a *standard*.

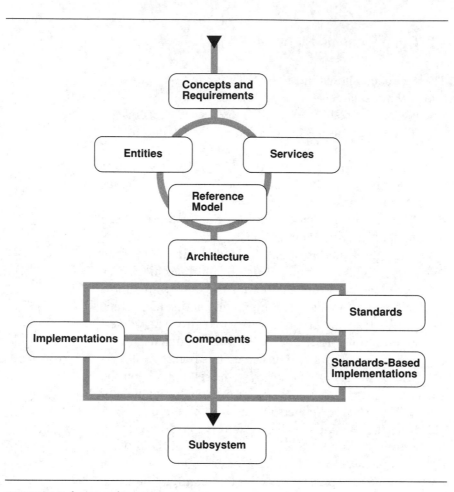

FIGURE 8.2 A general systems roadmap.

8.3 Upgrades

Sources of
upgrade

Upgrades are a matter of course when dealing with systems. The degree to which a system can change and the time and effort to make that change are important for several crucial reasons. Some *general* sources of change, with which you are probably familiar, are

- Customer changes in requirements, such as for increased functionality or performance
- Opportunities for technology insertion, such as moving to object-oriented technology

In the context of open systems and COTS products, however, you may now need to deal with upgrades from new sources, such as the need to keep up with changes in

- Standards
- Products or the marketplace

Figure 8.3 illustrates possible sources of change in the overall acquisition approach, with arrows pointing to the boxes that are involved in possible upgrades.

These kinds of changes almost always cause a ripple effect. For example, a new requirement might be that the system must have an interface with another system. Following are some of the ripples that might result. **Ripple effects**

- The reference model may need additional services to accommodate data transfer to external entities.
- The system architecture now must account for the new interface.
- A new standard may be associated with the new interface, and it must be accommodated in the existing system.
- A new COTS product might be sought that will support the new data exchange interface.
- Introduction of a change to one COTS product may force upgrades to other COTS products.

The preceding potential changes are typical of a change to integrate with another system. And we have not even talked about overall implications for attributes of the system, such as performance, security, or fault tolerance.

The ability to isolate sources of change is very important. The more extensive a ripple effect is, the more difficult it is to handle the changes.

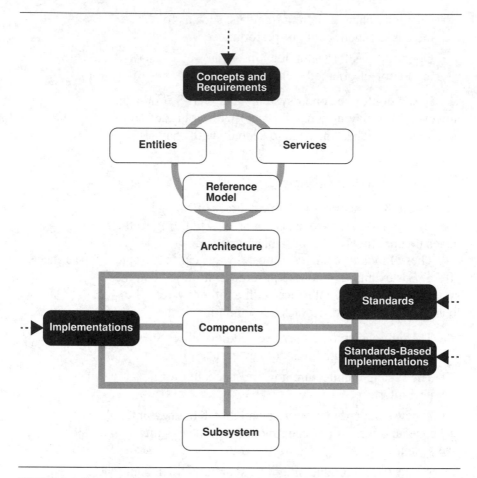

FIGURE 8.3 Sources of upgrades.

8.4 The Open, COTS-Based Path

Figure 8.4 represents the two main paths that lead to the development of a system or a subsystem. One path, the gray line, follows the left-hand side of the rectangle, and the other path, the black line, follows the right-hand side.

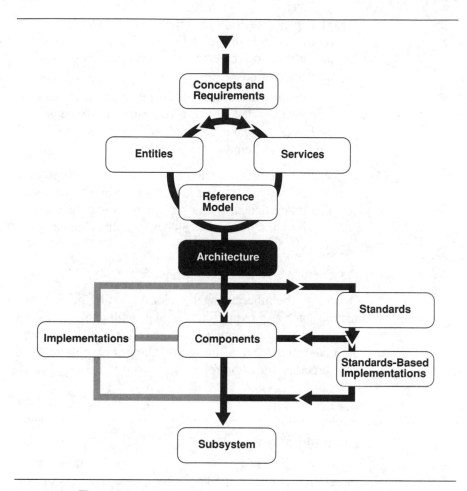

FIGURE 8.4 The open systems path.

However, the importance of standards is unique to open systems, and using standards affects the way the roadmap is viewed.

Alternative paths

- The *closed path* is the one that follows the left-hand side of the roadmap. Choosing this path means that you buy or build implementations not based on standards.

- The *open systems path* is the one that follows the right-hand side of the rectangle. Choosing this path means that you select standards and standards-based implementations.

- *Architecture* is emphasized in the center of the road-map because that is where you can achieve the greatest leverage from using an open systems approach with your system.

When we emphasize an open, COTS-based approach, it changes the focus we place on possible sources of upgrades. In particular, we must pay attention to the changes introduced by the marketplace—specifically, changes to

- Standards
- Standards-based COTS products

Of course, the other changes we discussed in the previous section, such as a requirement change, still apply here. But the reason we give emphasis to the changes introduced by the marketplace is that these are changes over which you have precious little control.

8.5 Integration

Integration is one of the key activities for success in systems development and evolution. Unfortunately, it is not enough to select standards and COTS products. There remains the problem of integrating these implementations in order to successfully meet the project goals. The road-map we presented is useful in discussing the integration of subsystems. Integration can take place at various levels:

- Implementations
- Standards
- Architectures

This list has been presented in a bottom-up manner. We will examine each of these approaches.

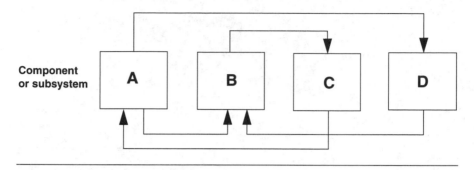

FIGURE 8.5 Integration through implementations.

Figure 8.5 illustrates the integration of four subsystems through implementations. This is also called *point-to-point* integration. This illustration can apply to the integration of subsystems within the same system or between different systems. Point-to-point integration is useful when dissimilar subsystems must interact. Point-to-point integration can help overcome architectural differences between the systems. Ultimately, all integration is achieved through implementations. However, if you integrate several subsystems by using point-to-point integration, the integration can be complex and difficult to maintain. The result can be the familiar spaghetti-like connectivity, as indicated in Figure 8.5.

Integration through implementations

For example, if you wanted to integrate two systems, one for billing customers and the other for tracking contacts with customers, you might integrate them by using point-to-point integration. This involves using an implementation that enables the two systems to work together, like a translator product that converts the format of data it passes between them.

Figure 8.6 illustrates the integration of implementations by using standards as the integration mechanism. In this illustration, each of the four subsystems uses the same interface standard. This illustration also can apply to the integration of subsystems within the same system or between different systems.

Integration through standards

To integrate two implementations by using standards, the implementations must conform to the standard that

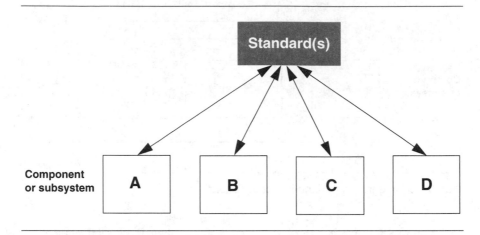

FIGURE 8.6 Integration through standards.

serves as the basis for the integration. Note that if an implementation conforms with extensions, this can introduce challenges for successful integration.

Note that this type of mechanism raises integration up a level. Integration is achieved by first selecting standards *and then* selecting conforming implementations. But remember, the iteration of selecting standards and implementations still applies.

To integrate the billing and contacts systems by using standards, you select a standard that enables the systems to work together. For example, sharing a standard data format for passing data between the systems may be sufficient to integrate the two systems.

Integration through architectures

Figure 8.7 illustrates the integration of implementations, using architecture as the integration mechanism. The implementations work together because they are based on the same architecture.

This may be an idealistic view of integration, but when it is achieved, it has tremendous benefits. This illustration also can apply to the integration of subsystems within the same system or between different systems. An example of this is the benefit gained from the use of a generic architecture, such as in the Generic Open Architecture discussed in Section 5.3.2.

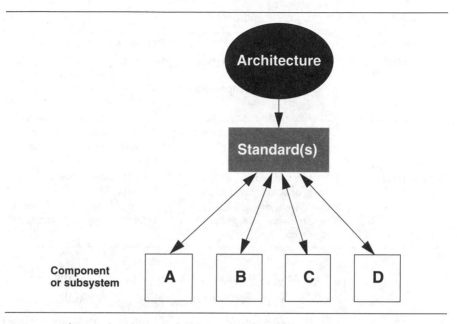

FIGURE 8.7 Integration through architectures.

Architectural integration constrains how the components of the system are connected even more than point-to-point or standards-based integration do. However, if you are in a high-performance domain, you may encounter problems, such as integrating two networks that have different bandwidths.

Follow the requirements of the system architecture when selecting or developing a subsystem's architecture. With a flexible architecture, the implementations will likely be more successfully integrated and could be changed without compromising the integrity of the architecture. In other words, it is important to create architectures that are flexible enough that they (1) allow the system to evolve and (2) evolve themselves.

Table 8.1 summarizes the relative merits of these various integration approaches. Another way to characterize integration approaches is shown in Figure 8.8. As you move to the top of the diagram, the following trends begin to emerge.

Summary of integration approaches

- Greater integration is possible.

TABLE 8.1 Comparing Integration Approaches

Approach	Strengths	Concerns
Architectural	• Performed in overall, defined context • Provides framework for evolution	• Dealing with special requirements, such as security, may cause problems later in development
Standards-Based	• Availability of conforming implementations simplifies integration and evolution	• May need to develop project-specific profile • Appropriate standards may not exist
Point-to-point	• Localized in scope • Fairly easy to change locally • Can handle special cases or requirements, such as fault tolerance	• Can become uncontrolled and spaghetti-like • Can break architectural model • Upgrades may be more difficult

- More opportunities for evolution are possible.
- More approaches to integration are available.

Each higher level in Figure 8.8 subsumes the technique of the lower level and adds its own characteristics. Successful integration at the architectural level requires considerable care and can have far-reaching effects. For example, the ability to accomplish the proverbial "plug-and-play" capabilities is increased by successful architectural integration.

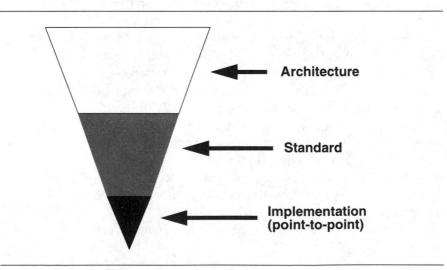

FIGURE 8.8 Integration leverage.

8.6 Summary

In this chapter, we introduced a roadmap for open, COTS-based systems, as illustrated in Figure 8.9. The open systems approach is based on the right-hand side of this figure.

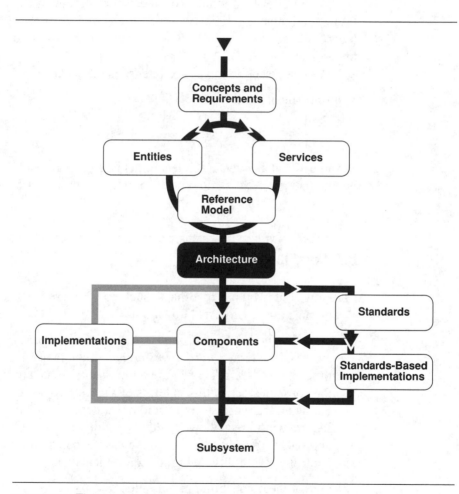

FIGURE 8.9 The open systems path.

We identified typical sources of upgrades:

- New system requirements
- Changes to a standard
- Changes to a product that is based on a standard
- Changes to a product that is not based on a standard

When deciding where to take your system in the future, you must determine whether to use *standards*. You must also decide whether to *build* or *buy* standards-based implementations.

We discussed three types of integration mechanisms:

- Implementations
- Standards
- Architectures

We argued that architectural integration has greater potential benefit to a project than do other integration approaches.

8.7 Food for Thought

1. How could you use roadmaps (such as in Figure 8.4) in managing a project? How might they help?

2. Anyone who has been around a real system is all too aware of the term *requirements creep,* although at times it must seem like requirements *sprint!* What are the consequences of this in terms of Figure 8.2? Knowing that your system could be susceptible to requirements creep, how would you modify the overall approach? To what extent does the roadmap help you control the volatility owing to requirements creep?

3. One of the points brought out in the discussion of Table 7.1 was that you could build your own implementation of a standard interface or buy a COTS product. Under what circumstances would you believe building your own implementation to be the preferred approach? How would you defend such an approach to your boss?

4. A fellow manager comes to you and says, "I'm stuck in integrating my system with Harriet's. The boss wants it done quickly to get the product out. Both Harriet and I would like to go back to the architectures, but it seems we could get it faster by tweaking implementations. That's what we did last year and the year before that. Got any ideas to help?" How do you answer this?

5. Is it necessarily true that, if an implementation changes, the architecture changes? In contrast, is it necessarily true that, if the architecture changes, it means a change to the implementation(s)?

6. Under what circumstances would point-to-point integration be preferred in a development effort? How about standards-based integration?

7. Discuss whether and how you can achieve architecture-based integration using COTS products.

8. Suppose that your system is expected to have a lot of COTS products. Consider the various integration approaches in the context of upgrades to products. For example, is point-to-point integration easier than architecture integration if upgrades to COTS products are expected?

9. How does reuse affect the various approaches to integration?

10. Suppose that you find out that your system has to integrate with a system about which you and your staff know very little. To what extent would you see value in an integration through reference models? Describe the strengths and concerns of such an approach.

11. How does the use of (a) strictly conforming standards-based implementations or (b) conforming implementations with extensions affect integration approaches?

12. In Figure 8.6, we illustrated integration via a standard. In reality, the components in your system will be integrated through the use of a profile. How would you change Figure 8.6 to illustrate integration through the use of a profile?

13. Referring to Table 8.1, consider the case of a new technology. If you wanted to evolve your system to a new technology, what are the strengths and concerns about integrating a new technology with a legacy implementation?

14. Consider the model in Figure 8.10 for point-to-point integration. In this example, some glue code is used to *wrap* Implementation-1 in order to integrate it with another implementation. Describe the strengths and concerns about using glue code as a wrapper to achieve the integration. What are the long-term consequences of this approach?

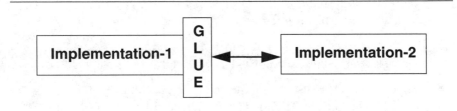

FIGURE 8.10 Model for point-to-point integration.

PART THREE

Managing the Transition

One basic truth of the paradigm shift is that the transition to open, COTS-based systems is more than an engineering concern. It will change much of what you do daily. It will also present some special concerns and challenges for those in management positions. Your understanding of the engineering changes will provide the basis for understanding the impact on other aspects of acquisition, such as on procurement.

Chapters in Part Three

9

How Open Systems and COTS Products Can Change Your Business

This chapter explains how using open systems and COTS products affects acquisition and other aspects of how you conduct business. These changes happen because the COTS and open systems approach influences processes, costs, and schedules. The following sections identify the changes caused by open systems and the use of COTS products and compares this approach to the traditional, custom development approach.

9.1 Kinds of Changes

Using an open, COTS-based systems approach can change

- *What* is done
- *Who* does it
- *When* it is done
- *How* it is done

What, who, when, and how

    Regardless of the kind of change, changes initiated by an open, COTS-based approach can provide advantages, including more alternatives, over a traditional approach. Such changes can also help you achieve the goals you have for your system more effectively and efficiently, provided that you can adequately handle the challenges you must meet, on almost a daily basis.

Causes and effects

Figure 9.1 illustrates the multiple COTS- or open systems–related causes of change and the multiple effects of these changes on the way you do business. The amount and the nature of the change your organization experiences from using open systems and COTS products depends on the nature of your organization and how closely its approach to acquisition already resembles that required for open, COTS-based systems.

For example, on average, government organizations may experience dramatic change when adopting an open, COTS-based approach. The reason is that they are accustomed to a producer model, whereby they contract out development or develop systems themselves according to their own detailed specifications. The use of standards is not new in government; historically, there have been a large number of government standards, such as military standards. However, in the past, many government managers were trained to tailor the government standards rather than to use nongovernment ones. Such tailoring does not apply in the new world of COTS products and open systems.

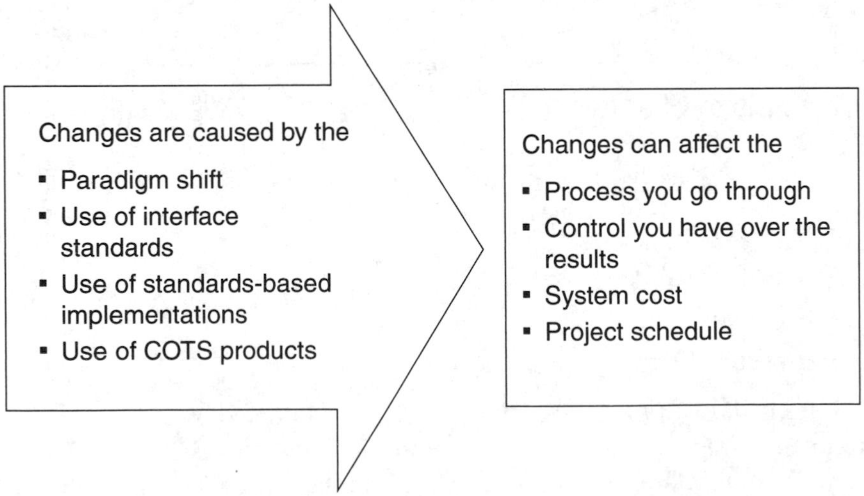

Changes are caused by the

- Paradigm shift
- Use of interface standards
- Use of standards-based implementations
- Use of COTS products

Changes can affect the

- Process you go through
- Control you have over the results
- System cost
- Project schedule

FIGURE 9.1 Causes and effects of changes.

9.2 Potential Changes

In the following sections, we list potential changes that can be caused by the use of standards or standards-based COTS implementations. Table 9.1 provides an overview of which elements of an open, COTS-based approach affect each of the activities in the overall acquisition process. Note that the element *Standards* affects nearly all acquisition activities.

An X in a table cell means that that element significantly affects the activity to its left. If no X is in a table cell, the effect is less significant.

The discussion in this chapter addresses specific changes we've identified. These changes are organized according to the activities listed in the table.

Acquisition planning covers both the decision to acquire a new system and the decision whether to use an open, COTS-based systems approach. Some probable changes to acquisition planning follow. **Acquisition planning**

- An open systems or COTS-based approach can require new *acquisition strategies*. Some government regulations have not caught up with the spirit of the open systems and COTS initiatives. Similarly, corporations with outdated policies that don't acknowledge the value of standards or incorporate their use may have some catching up to do.

- Using open systems fosters *competition* because standards enable multiple vendors to create and to sell standards-based COTS products. You can capitalize on the marketplace because these vendors compete with one another for your business. Getting this advantage, however, requires you to take a new, more robust, and thorough approach to market research.

- *Architecture component decisions* are affected by the use of open systems. Using standards limits the choices that the developer has for the components of the architecture and thus limits the variety of COTS products available in the marketplace. Conversely, the use of COTS products can heavily influence architectural features and decisions.

TABLE 9.1 Effects of Open Systems and COTS Products on Acquisition Activities

Activities	Requirements and Reference Models	Architecture, Components, and Interfaces	Standards	Implementations	Integration	Test	Deployment	Support
				Elements				
Acquisition planning			X	X				
Business management and contracts			X	X				
Risk management		X	X	X				
Requirements management	X	X	X	X				
Engineering and manufacturing	X	X	X	X	X			
Test and evaluation			X	X	X	X		
System support			X	X			X	X
Configuration and data management					X	X	X	
Continuous planning and review			X	X				

- Planning for *systems evolution* is both easier and more difficult when using open systems. Open systems promote modular system design, which is essential to an evolutionary architecture. When using COTS products in your system, systems evolution involves selecting new products or upgrades to existing products instead of developing new implementations. On the other hand, the marketplace will force some component changes, owing to product upgrades that would otherwise not be necessary.

- The overall *cost profile* of a system changes with the use of open systems and COTS products. Early design and feasibility costs are more likely to increase; however, the system life-cycle costs may decrease.

All these changes will affect how you plan the acquisition.

Business management and contracts involve ensuring that the system meets the business needs of the organization and that the contracts used to develop and maintain the system include language that satisfies the goals of the organization. Some probable changes to business management and contracts follow.

Business management and contracts

- The *"build or buy" decisions* made when developing or modifying an open, COTS-based system will probably be different from those for closed systems. With open systems, you must decide whether to build or buy every system component; however, your decision to build it may be based on the availability or maturity of a standard or the products that conform to it.

- Using open systems might make it possible to increase the accuracy of *cost estimates*. The reason is that standards and standards-based implementations—whether custom-developed or conforming COTS products—promote a more predictable cost of development. However, the uncertainties of the COTS marketplace will require a good deal of contingency planning. In reality, this increased accuracy will not occur until estimators gain experience with the open systems and COTS-based approach. Before that time, estimates are likely to be less, not more, accurate.

An open, COTS-based approach changes where costs are incurred during system development and maintenance. Development costs may go down, and, if you are buying products, your maintenance costs may go up.

- *Contracts* must have a new flexibility. In reality, neither standards nor COTS products fit together exactly; nor are they likely to completely cover any system. How you deal with additions and changes is important, but it can be difficult. The contracts you use must be able to respond to the variations and unexpected events engendered by an open systems and COTS-based approach.

- Using open systems can create new elements and evaluation factors in a *request for proposal* (RFP).

Risk management

Risk management involves identifying the risks of acquiring a system within the context of the stakeholder organizations and formulating strategies to track, mitigate, and manage those risks. Using open systems and COTS products decreases some risks and increases others. Some probable considerations for COTS and open system risk management follow.

- Standards provide a *ready-made specification* that reduces risk at the interface level.

- COTS products may need less *testing*, but the integrated system could need more testing.

- COTS products may have commercial *support* available, but coordinating multiple sources could complicate maintenance and support of the integrated system.

- *Protecting and controlling technology* is difficult, if not impossible, when your system is open, as standards and COTS products are by definition available to anyone willing to pay for them. This could be a problem for organizations that have a critical need to control technology export.

- Rapid *prototyping* to test the system's concept and usability is easier with open systems and COTS products. Because prototyping can use existing products, it can be done early in the development cycle. The ease and reduced cost when using existing implementations allows you to try several approaches instead of only one.

Requirements management involves investigating exactly what is required in terms of form, fit, and function—without specifically naming implementations—and defining the system boundaries, purpose, and performance needed for a system. Some probable impacts on requirements management follow.

Requirements management

- Some desired *system characteristics*, such as interconnectivity, are easier to achieve because many standards support and encourage the development of implementations that have these characteristics.

- Open systems and COTS products make it easier to *find alternatives* to the traditional approaches used in concept development. Standards can be a factor in concept feasibility and risk reduction because some standards integrate well and others do not. COTS products can help with these, as well as suggesting alternative approaches to the fulfillment of requirements.

- Some cost, schedule, and performance *trade-offs* favor an open, COTS-based approach. Standards can save you time and effort when defining the interface, and COTS products used without modification are faster and cheaper to buy than build because of economies of scale and competition. Together, standards and COTS products help focus trade-offs that are necessary for requirements management.

Engineering involves determining what is necessary to produce the system, including architecture, design, integration, and system test. Some probable impacts on engineering follow.

Engineering

- Open systems can introduce new considerations in the development of *design specifications* from requirements. For example, using standards can reduce designers' control because they must use the standards to develop features of the system, but doing so can increase designers' ability to concentrate on the best design for the necessarily unique aspects of the system.

- *Systems engineering responsibilities* change with a move to open systems and COTS products. System engineers need to understand open system acquisition strategies and business case analysis and to assess the marketplace to keep abreast of changing products and technologies.

- Open systems with the use of COTS products result in less implementation *development* effort and more system *integration* risk. On the one hand, standards provide ready-made interface specifications, and standards-based COTS products provide the building blocks for initial prototypes as well as ultimate system implementation. On the other hand, without direct control of interfaces and product market cycles, system integration risk can be high. COTS products can have hidden incompatibilities. Sometimes, in fact, it may be impossible to make them work together.

- *Reliability, maintainability, and availability* can be affected by the use of open systems. These three characteristics are driven by the implementation, not by the interface (see Table 3.2), so the vendors developing the COTS products control these characteristics.

Forces Affecting Maintainability

The following list identifies some system aspects that can be affected by COTS products and so affect maintainability:

- How and when the system must be upgraded
- What preventive and corrective maintenance is necessary
- How much downtime or turnaround time is possible
- How many personnel are required for system operation or maintenance
- What level of skills is required of users, operators, and maintainers
- Which special tools are needed for system operation and maintenance
- What equipment is needed for testing
- Which diagnostic capabilities are needed and available

- Using open, COTS-based systems can reduce *costs and shorten the project development schedule*. COTS products are usually immediately available, thus shortening the schedule and decreasing the cost of acquisition. In addition, standards-based implementations allow costs to be prorated across the entire user community, saving money over user-specific development.

- *System producibility* can be affected by using open systems. In fact, using standards can result in simplified design that is often better for production. On the other hand, although standards-based COTS products are immediately available in the marketplace, they can make system integration more difficult because even standards aren't enough to ensure that COTS products will always integrate easily.

- Using open, COTS-based systems can affect *quality* both positively and negatively. Standards-based implementations can provide information about attributes and design elements earlier than non-standards-based implementations. Because the implementations are based on standards, you may have information available to you in the standard itself and from others who have tested the quality of conformant implementations. This is an example of how interacting with the marketplace allows you to gain leverage through knowledge of product quality. COTS products can, however, be of lower quality because of possible "rush-to-market" pressures.

Testing and evaluation involve determining whether and how well the implementations and the overall system serve their purpose and satisfy requirements. Some probable changes to testing and evaluation follow.

Testing and evaluation

- Using open systems, your approach to *testing and evaluation* may change, but the need for testing and evaluation is not eliminated. For example, standards and standards-based implementations can make unit—for example, a single COTS product—testing easier, but integration testing may be more difficult.

  Although testing is usually limited to black-box testing when COTS products are involved, you should create and maintain an ongoing test capability, and you may need to design new open systems tests for interoperability, portability, and scalability.

- The *cost* of your project and the project's *schedule* can be affected both positively and negatively by open systems and COTS-based testing. On the positive side, conformance tests may already be available for standards and standards-based implementations, saving both time and money. In fact, standards-based implementations may have already been tested, particularly for conformance, thus saving time and money.

  On the negative side, long-term testing costs may increase. For example, a new product release can require testing the whole system again. Regression testing of interfaces between developed code and upgrades to COTS products may increase overall testing effort.

- Another concern about testing is *test certification* and how the tests are developed and administered. When you use commercial laboratories and test agencies to certify products, you should know who certified these organizations and whether the certifying organization is objective about the standard and conformance of implementations.

Buyer and Tester Beware

Some vendors of COTS hardware to the military and aerospace community are suppressing publication of comparative test results of their products by threatening lawsuits. This is what happened with a DC-DC converter. A government aerospace organization tested several such products from various vendors and planned to publish the results on the World Wide Web. The vendors stepped in and threatened to sue them if they proceeded and effectively stopped the results from being published.

This example highlights a concern about using COTS products. Although the testing performed by manufacturers is valid, it may not cover all aspects of performance. If vendors can block the publication of independent test results, the only way for users to discover a potentially vital gap in performance will be to perform their own tests—if they can afford to. Although they need to be prepared to test COTS products, buyers also have to consider the policies of the vendors they are dealing with, how their leverage changes depending on the size of their purchase, and workarounds to offset the possible drawbacks of using COTS products [Dizard 96].

System support involves considering the practical **System support**
aspects of providing system access to users and distributing the necessary materials, training, and so on, to those
operating and maintaining the system. Some probable
changes to system support follow.

- Using open systems and COTS products will result in
  changes in the amount of *control* you have. The
  implementation of a product can be changed in any
  way the vendor sees fit, without notice to the customer. When you use standards and COTS products,
  you can neither dominate the market nor control the
  development of products.

- *Maintenance planning* can change for you because
  standards may change as a result of standards organization processes and COTS products change at the
  discretion of the vendor.[1] In fact, using COTS products can sometimes *prevent* bugs from being fixed
  immediately if that fix does not benefit the majority of
  the vendor's customers. Usually, vendors offer little or
  no continued support for old versions of products, so
  sooner or later, you may be forced to make maintenance changes you would not otherwise have made.

- *Supply support* can be affected by using open systems
  and COTS products. Coordination of multiple vendors
  can be a new challenge. Routine market assessments
  to keep abreast of upgrade opportunities and shifts in
  the marketplace should help you manage the continual turnover in the marketplace.

- *Training and training support* needs can be affected
  by a move to open systems and COTS products. You
  may select commercial training, or you may require
  less training because users are already familiar with
  the common look and feel of COTS products.

---

1. Although both of these changes will affect maintenance planning,
they do not have the same frequency. The rate at which most standards
change is much slower than the rate at which most products change. So
it is more likely that product changes will affect you.

Configuration and data management

Configuration and data management involve maintaining accurate information on the configuration of the system and its data. Some probable changes to configuration and data management follow.

- Open systems support an *interface-based approach* to system architecture. In fact, standards and profiles provide readily available interface descriptions and information vital for configuration management. Configuration management is dependent on interface identification and management.

- Using COTS products forces you to cope with vendors' *special features*. The special features added to a product reflect a vendor's need to make up for deficiencies in a standard or to differentiate its product from those of other vendors. If your system becomes dependent on vendor extensions, moving to another product may be extremely difficult.

- *Backward compatibility* can present a new issue that affects the productivity of system users or results in other problems. If you consider and address backward compatibility, you can use the data in your system continuously and avoid delays or problems accessing data. But your configuration and data management capabilities must provide information to assist in determining backward compatibility problems.

- The *rate of change* and *causes of change* for open systems and COTS products are different from those for custom-developed implementations and systems. Standards and products change at their own pace and can affect your development and maintenance schedules. Sometimes, your schedule can, and probably will, be driven by changes in a vendor's product. All these factors place heavier burdens on the configuration management capability.

- New concerns about *data rights and warranties* can emerge with open systems and use of COTS products. When you buy COTS products, full disclosure of the products' design is unlikely.

data rights ➞ The ownership of design information required to create or to modify a product.

warranties ➞ Legal contracts that define how a product is expected to perform and the responsibility of the product vendor to address problems.

Continuous planning and review involve monitoring the overall system development and maintenance process. Some probable changes to planning and review follow.

Continuous planning and review

- *Trade-offs* on cost, schedule, and performance can be affected by using open systems. If you use standards-based COTS products, they are likely to be less expensive and available sooner than anything you develop yourself.

  Performance requirements can be one focus of trade-off studies. Performance of implementations is determined primarily by the developers. Although system performance is dependent on implementations, it is also determined by your ability to integrate a host of different implementations effectively.

Heed a Cost and Schedule Warning

"Staying on schedule and budget is more a matter of realism and avoidance of adverse selection of vendors than any one technology or technology approach. If you ask people to exceed the speed of light, you will always find someone willing to promise it. Ask for a demo first." (A colleague)

- Using open systems and COTS products can affect many aspects of *planning*, such as planning for resources, system engineering, testing, evaluation, and maintenance. Open systems and COTS products also require that you plan for multiple generations of hardware and software to keep them synchronized. But the farther out in time, the more difficult it is to predict the directions the market will take.

9.3 Summary

Four
perspectives

Open systems can change your systems development approach by affecting

- *What* is done
- *Who* does it
- *When* it is done
- *How* it is done

Probable
changes

Probable changes are summarized in Table 9.2.

9.4 Food for Thought

1. One key skill is the ability to seek out appropriate standards for your system. What are the traits of people who will deal successfully with the standards community? Has your contractor ever participated on a standards committee?

2. Develop a policy document that addresses the use of vendor-dependent features for your organization. Give that document to a junior colleague to critique. Then give it to a senior colleague. Do you get the same results? Explain any differences.

3. We noted that prototyping is easier when using open systems and COTS products. Are there issues associated with this capability, especially from a customer perspective? If you create a prototype and show it to a customer who wants to deploy it, what do you say?

4. You are part of a team performing a large acquisition that is expected to incorporate many COTS products from multiple vendors. Develop a process for resolution of integration issues for various products. Give this process to a colleague and see whether your colleague can find any holes in it.

TABLE 9.2 Comparing Aspects of Traditional and Open, COTS-Based Systems Acquisition

Aspect	Traditional	Open, COTS-Based Systems
Ability to see "inside" the system	You can see "inside" the system because you create it or use a contractor who follows your specifications.	You will not see "inside" the implementations you purchase.
Systems engineering	You create the entire system, using unique interfaces.	You create the system, using standard interfaces and products from multiple sources.
System integration	You integrate your system as part of the system development process.	You integrate your system, using a more complex process to accommodate standards-based implementations from multiple sources.
Interoperability	You achieve interoperability only if it is designed in from the start.	Although interoperability still needs to be designed in from the start, you may achieve interoperability more easily when you use standards that include interoperability in their specifications.
Sources of component implementations	You have limited choices and typically contract out the development to a single source.	You have more choices, resulting from a standards-based commercial marketplace.
Testing	You test the whole system at all levels, including unit test.	You emphasize interface, functional, and integration testing.
Configuration management	You can control the configuration of the system and must understand configuration management concepts.	You have less control over the configuration of the system, and the configuration management process is more complex.
System changes	Changes are generated mainly by the user base and can be managed.	Changes are generated by the user base and by external forces, including vendor upgrades and market forces.
Support	You create, staff, and fund support for your system.	You typically outsource at least some support to vendors and third-party providers.
Control	You have direct control over your system.	You have indirect control over your system through vendors and consultants.
Risks	You encounter many familiar risks.	You reduce and eliminate some risks but encounter new risks, some old risks, and old risks that have changed.
Cost and schedule estimates	You use traditional methods that may result in inaccurate estimates.	You may be able to increase the accuracy of cost estimates because standards and standards-based implementations promote a more predictable cost of development.
Actual cost and schedule	You may experience cost and schedule overruns.	You have opportunities to reduce costs and stay on schedule, but they are *not* guaranteed.

5. We have noted that there will be many unexpected events; the watchword of open and COTS-based systems is: "Expect the unexpected." But how do you write a contract for that?

10

Special Concerns for Managers

In Chapter 4, we told you about the basic elements of an open, COTS-based system approach, but we asked your indulgence in that we ignored, for the time being, the realities and constraints that impinge on any system development today. In this chapter, we now focus on major areas of concern with which managers will be confronted when using an open, COTS-based approach. We discuss various ways to think about these concerns. First we look at what the manager is trying to accomplish in the transition to open, COTS-based systems. Then, we discuss these concerns for the major areas of cost, schedule, performance, and people.

10.1 The Manager's Quest for Control

In their quest for control over the elements that make up a system, managers have to be willing to make trade-offs when dealing with the changes that come from using an open, COTS-based approach. Managers must also be willing to continue to improve their planning processes and to actively manage risks.

In part, the changes in how managers must do business are driven by new realities, such as decreasing budgets and shortened schedules, and new initiatives, such as the acquisition-reform effort in the federal government. But some of the changes are driven by shifts caused by the various forces that affect how much control the manager has over the system.

The conflict

These forces are represented by four groups of players: managers, the marketplace, standards groups, and the organization—corporation or government agency. These four groups can become engaged in a struggle for control over what goes into the creation of new systems and upgrades of existing systems.

- *Managers* focus on strategic and tactical issues in an attempt to produce the best system they can to fit the need within financial, contractual, legal, schedule, and technological constraints.

- The *marketplace* often has a mind of its own, driven by pursuit of market share and profit. Financial considerations—some short term and some long term—dominate this viewpoint.

- *Standards groups* work to achieve consensus with as many people as possible in their affected community. The specific needs or interests of any single system are not of concern for them, although they may be of concern for individual participants in a standards group.

- The *organization* focuses on large-scale trade-offs and economies of scale.

Managers need to deal with conflicting goals, competition, and cooperative relationships because of the contentions among these groups. Each group is working to optimize its own objectives. Cooperation cannot be assumed. But your chance of success is greater if you understand the motives and operating methods of the others. For example, you should not join a consensus-based standards group and expect it to always give you the features that you think are best for your system.

Keeping your eye on the prize

When faced with these conflicts, remember how you got in the middle and why. Yes, there are liabilities and constraints associated with the move to COTS products and open systems, as illustrated in Figure 10.1. But keep in mind what it is you are trying to achieve—the benefits pictured

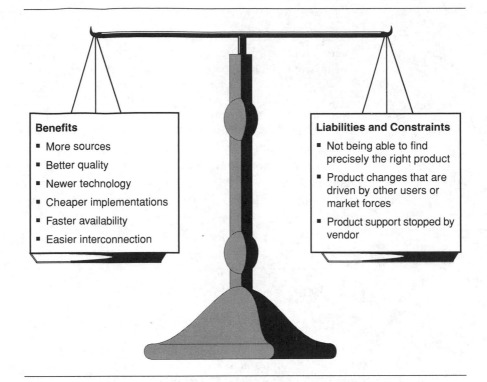

FIGURE 10.1 Benefits, liabilities, and constraints of COTS products.

in the figure. Nothing comes for free, so the importance of the goals you are trying to achieve will determine how many of the liabilities you can tolerate and how far you are willing and able to go into open systems and the use of COTS products. One of your challenges as a manager is to find the right balance for your system between the benefits and the liabilities.

Following are new sources of change that present challenges:

Sources of change

- Updates to standards
- New standards
- Abandoned standards
- New versions of COTS products
- Abandoned COTS products
- New COTS products

- New technologies
- Ripple effects, for example, operating system upgrades may force application software upgrades, or discontinuation of a hardware product may affect other hardware products, related software implementations, and even the design.

These changes extend beyond system performance and will affect cost and schedule as well.

Next, we look at some special concerns that arise from pursuing an open, COTS-based approach. These management concerns fall into four categories: cost, schedule, performance, and people.

10.2 Cost

One of your major concerns as a manager is cost. Most managers will ask, "How will my costs change by using an open systems approach?" This question has spurred activity toward developing a cost model for open, COTS-based systems, although no complete models exist as yet. Today, most of the data to answer the question of cost is anecdotal, but it should not necessarily be discounted.

We cannot tell you exactly how your costs will change, but we can just about guarantee you that the distribution of your costs—your *cost profile*—will change. Initial development investment costs could increase, but life-cycle costs could decrease.

10.2.1 Cost Considerations

Cost increases   Examples of areas in which costs could increase are

- Training for open systems and use of COTS products
- Market research
- Selection of standards
- Standards profile development
- Evaluation and selection of COTS products

Some life-cycle costs, such as testing, could increase; testing becomes a continuous process driven by product upgrades and changes in the marketplace, in addition to the normal, user-driven system upgrade pressures. Because of the frequent turnover in the marketplace, there will also be continuous market research and product selection activities.

The savings you may achieve depend on, among other things, **Cost savings**

- The breadth of application—how common an application is across systems, for example, a word processing application is very common
- The time interval over which costs are amortized
- The number of shared instances over which costs are amortized

Although cost amortizations improve over a longer period of time, this must be balanced with the shorter time periods that accompany technology insertion and the length of time a given item will be available and used.

Managers may realize cost savings in design and support, but it may require initial investments to achieve long-term savings. The major savings may arise when it is time to upgrade a system. A properly implemented open system is an evolvable system, but it takes development investment to reap long-term savings. An example of life-cycle costs that could decrease are those associated with maintenance organizations that are no longer needed or at least can be significantly scaled back because of a reduced need for in-house maintenance.

You also need to consider the costs and potential savings associated with specific techniques, although they are going to be more difficult to factor in reliably. Cost factors associated with open, COTS-based systems and that may contribute to a cost decrease are **Other cost factors**

- Software portability
- Software reuse
- Marketplace participation
- Commonality—yielding cost/quantity improvements

One Program's Cost Experience

The Army's Intelligence and Electronic Warfare Common Sensor (IEWCS) program is an example of making an initial investment to reap long-term benefits. After the contract for IEWCS had been awarded, it was decided that the program needed to take an open, COTS-based approach. At the cost of $10 million and an 18-month schedule slip, the program team selected a set of standards and started development, using standards-conformant COTS products. After nearly ten years, including one technology refresh cycle and with projections in hand for the anticipated costs and benefits of a second one, a cost case study was conducted. This study found a total IEWCS life-cycle cost avoidance of $856.6 million, broken down as follows:

- Total R&D cost avoidance: $35.0 million
- Total production cost avoidance: $388.4 million
- Total operations and support cost avoidance: $436.0 million
- Total administrative cost avoidance: $6.2 million

As with many programs, IEWCS introduced many other innovations at the same time it decided to take an open, COTS-based approach, so not all this cost avoidance is attributable to COTS and open systems. But certainly the bulk of the R&D and production cost avoidance stemmed from the use of COTS products and open systems, and it clearly outpaces the initial $10 million investment. In addition, IEWCS got more for its money from this approach than it had originally anticipated. Not only did the COTS technology and products give it a better coverage of the communications spectrum than the predecessor systems had provided, but also each technology refresh saw immense savings in size, weight, and processing power of the system [IEWCS 96].

Each of these factors represents either a class of techniques (those available to increase software portability or reuse), a result of taking advantage of competing products or technologies (marketplace competition), or the result of a technology-smart policy (increasing common use of a particular technology and associated products). Done correctly, each has the potential for reducing your costs over a broad range of estimation factors.

Technology insertion

A technology cost factor that may contribute to a cost increase is the proliferation of technology insertion. This can happen when a program gets carried away with new technologies or when too many new technologies are tried.

Technology insertion might also increase configuration management efforts and reduce commonality savings.

Faster technology insertion may also result from backward compatibility and interoperability and the use of contractor independent research and development (IR&D), as well as standards. The ability to keep up with technology may be critical for some domains, although it must be balanced against the liability of "churning" by changing the system too frequently. The increased speed of system upgrade may reduce costs—after all, "time is money"— but it may also have noneconomic advantages if keeping up with technology is necessary for keeping up with the competition or threat. Of course, each upgrade will still cost money, so, if they come too frequently, upgrades may have an overall effect of increasing costs.

Cost savings from reductions in maintenance—facili-   **Maintenance**
ties and personnel—come from

- Fewer repairs at more detailed levels, as COTS products are more commodity-like; for example, it may be more cost-effective to throw away broken products— because of greater portability, reduced unit costs, or higher reliability—than to repair them at a low level
- Increased reliance on commercial support

Reduced costs spent on spares and parts might result from

- Competition
- Cost/quantity improvements
- Amortization of nonrecurring costs
- Software commonality and reuse

10.2.2 Costs versus Benefits

Managers need to understand cumulative cost versus cumulative benefit. These are the costs and benefits accrued and achieved over the lifetime of a system. In coming up with total costs to compare, managers must be sure to compare the same cost categories when analyzing the traditional approach versus an open or COTS-based systems approach. Of course, "the same cost categories" are in some cases analogies. For example, costs of programmers for custom development may be compared to costs of product evaluation, licenses, and vendor relationships for COTS-based development, as they are both part of the costs of obtaining software. The point is that you cannot make a realistic comparison if you leave out some of the true costs of either alternative.

Compare total system costs by comparing initial (development) and life-cycle (recurring) costs for the use of standards versus unique interfaces and for in-house or contractor development versus COTS products. The results will vary for each system. Just as with the traditional approach, managers need to predict costs as accurately as possible and to make trade-offs when using an open, COTS-based systems approach.

Development cost factors

Among the development cost factors that managers need to compare for open, COTS-based systems versus a traditional approach are

- Hardware and software
- Nonrecurring production
- Allowing for change
- Technical data
- Documentation
- Contractor services
- Support
- Training, including equipment
- Initial spares
- Facility construction
- Research, development, test, and evaluation (RDT&E)

These cost factors are likely to involve both personnel and other resources.

Life-cycle cost factors

Life-cycle costs that managers need to be concerned with are summarized in Table 10.1. Life-cycle costs could decrease because of the use of standards-based COTS products. These items are cheaper and available sooner than are custom-developed ones. Replacement parts may be available from competitive sources; the need to sustain

TABLE 10.1 Categories of Life-Cycle Cost Factors

Cost Categories	Life-Cycle Cost Factors
Personnel	Operators and maintainers
Maintenance and continuing investment	Overhaul, repair, replenishment spares, preplanned upgrades, software support and maintenance
Training	Instructors and material, students
Operations and support	Documentation maintenance, supply system management, disposal

current in-house training or maintenance capabilities may be reduced; some tests may already be available; and products may already have been tested to some extent. However, there will still be integration costs, as well as the new life-cycle costs involved with finding replacement products and new technologies as the system evolves.

10.2.3 Budget Adjustments

Taking an open, COTS-based systems approach will have budget implications when you are planning. Among general budget considerations are

- Training for open systems and COTS product acquisition
- Continuous market research
- Selection of technologies
- Selection of standards and profiles
- Selection of products
- Licenses, warranties, and vendor negotiations
- Flexibility in procuring and integrating product upgrades
- Ongoing test and evaluation

If managers are committed to provide training in open and COTS-based systems acquisition, they need to adjust the workload of their staff. Managers need to consider how turnover may impact their organization's ability to retain knowledge. Also, managers need to plan to continually update their staff's knowledge of technology, standards,

Training

COTS products, the marketplace, and, for the government, acquisition reform.

Market research and product/ standard selection

You need to budget for a market research group whose job is to stay on top of the standards, technologies, and products that are relevant to your system. At the least, you will need someone to conduct the surveys and analyses that are necessary to choose the right standards and products for your situation. These services may be provided by your staff or from such organizations as the Gartner Group, DataQuest, or Ovum.

Licenses, warranties, and vendor negotiations

Licenses are a necessity with just about any COTS product. Even freeware, shareware, and open-source software entail licenses. Licenses are a budget item because they have associated costs, but these costs can vary radically, depending on the negotiations you conduct with the vendor. License options range from an enterprise-wide to a per seat basis. Other variations include development versus maintenance versus end user licenses and the level of support to be provided by the vendor.

All these variations are negotiable with most vendors. Therefore, it pays to train buyers and engineers in these differences and to take the negotiations seriously as an aspect that can affect design and engineering as well as cost.

Sound software warranties are a rarity, but they may be worth consideration. Warranties are a budget issue first because they will cost the buyer. In addition, a warranty can expire before the system is ready to be retired. Managers need to budget for extended warranties or other ways of handling expired warranties. Additional costs are associated with purchasing an extended warranty or trying to make repairs without one. Warranties can become a legal issue when they are not upheld by vendors; then you must take legal steps to rectify the situation. Warranties have broader implications, however, because project staff need to read and understand them and plan for their expiration.

Other potential legal issues are data and intellectual property rights and certification liabilities. For managers in the government, government policy mandates and changes in Congress and the administration are potential legal issues.

Flexibility

Nothing is constant but change, and one key to success with open, COTS-based systems will be a mind-set and a plan that demonstrate flexibility. If your system has many COTS products, you may be faced with a product upgrade monthly. Every few years, you may be faced with technology upgrades. In between, there will be changes in the marketplace, such as withdrawal of a product, entry of a new product, or demise of a vendor, to which you will have to react. Having both the frame of mind to be proactive and the contingency plans—and budget—to support your flexibility will be a real advantage.

If the march of the marketplace is constant, so too is the testing that you will have to do in response to that march. New products will need to be tested, upgrades will have to be confirmed, and the resulting system will have to be regression tested, at the very least.

Ongoing test and evaluation

10.2.4 Special Government Concerns

Government managers have additional considerations, such as basic ordering and original equipment manufacturer agreements, and color-of-money issues. Changes in the administration, Congress, or the office of the secretary for the particular federal department, such as the Secretary of Transportation, can influence budgeting decisions.

The phrase "color-of-money" is well understood in both the government and the business world. It means that available funds are typically divided into various expenditure categories. For example, in the DoD, these categories run from basic research (6.1) to maintenance (6.5). Rules stipulate which categories of money can be spent on which activities, including restrictions on funds if they are for RDT&E as opposed to maintenance.

Color-of-money

Managers must figure out which kind of money will pay for each activity with open, COTS-based systems. The distribution of money and colors-of-money will change, as illustrated in Figure 10.2.

For example, consider the following kinds of questions.

- Do continual technology insertion and upgrades constitute 6.1, 6.2, or 6.3 activities?
- Is this kind of technology insertion and upgrade a legitimate use of operations and maintenance money,

Traditional Approach

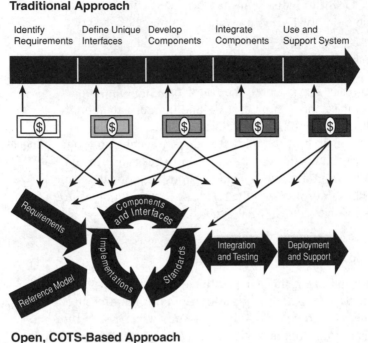

Open, COTS-Based Approach

FIGURE 10.2 Implications of the color-of-money.

or is it something that can be supported only with RDT&E funds?

- Could integration now be considered research and development (R&D)?
- Should test and evaluation (T&E) be considered an operations and maintenance (O&M) cost?
- Can you set up early maintenance contracts using 6.1 or 6.2 dollars?

These questions are as important as changes to regulations, laws, and organizational policies. Unfortunately, there are not yet any definitive answers, and different decision makers seem to be taking different approaches. It will take a while for all the rules and regulations to catch up with the move to open, COTS-based systems.

10.3 Schedule

Managers can expect schedule changes owing to an open systems or COTS-based approach. Many of the schedule factors parallel the cost factors we just discussed; for example, initial system activities are likely to require more money *and* more time.

When you are planning, be aware of how decisions early in the process affect milestones later in the process. Expect that initial system activities will likely be slower, system design may be faster, getting component implementations may be much faster, and taking supportability into account may slow down the early schedule.

For government managers, acquisition is governed by many laws and regulations, some of which have not caught up with the paradigm shift. Regulations, especially those dealing with the use of COTS products, are still changing and can create an unstable situation that contributes to the frustrations and schedule delays you may experience.

Although the use of open, COTS-based systems is spreading rapidly, it is not yet universally accepted. Even if it were, not everyone knows how to function and to succeed in the new context. (This is particularly true in the government—after all, government contractors are as accustomed to being told what to do as government managers are to telling them what to do!) Some possible schedule concerns follow.

Broader schedule concerns

- No single, coherent marketplace provides products for all the technologies that are of interest to you. Instead, the overall marketplace is really a union of several separate market segments. Schedule impacts include market research activities and possible longer integration time.

- There are not necessarily standards or standards-based COTS products for all the things you might need. Examples of robust marketplaces for standards-based products include POSIX-conformant operating systems and TCP/IP-conformant network components, but other specialties are not so well supported.

All these conditions may have schedule impacts, as it may take longer and be more difficult to achieve certain program goals.

Taking these conditions into account may seem overwhelming at first. But the good news is that most project managers have had to use standards in the past, and many are probably using some COTS products right now: compilers, commercial hardware, text editors and publishing software, spreadsheets, and so on. Approaching systems from an open, COTS-based systems perspective may not be so foreign to you, even though you may not feel prepared for the sheer magnitude of the effort when standards and COTS products are the primary elements of the system.

Industry managers have been using COTS products for years and have also participated in standards organizations or have experience using de facto standards. In some respects, using an open, COTS-based approach is something that industry managers have more experience doing than most government managers do. In both cases, they may tend to confuse a COTS-based approach with an open systems one (see Table 7.1).

10.4 Performance

A question managers need to ask themselves is whether they can buy a product that satisfies their requirements. This is especially a consideration for real-time, fault-tolerant, secure, or high-availability systems. If the product's performance is not going to fulfill the requirements, this may be an instance when you should not buy a COTS product but instead should either build an implementation or relax a requirement. There is a broad spectrum between build and buy, and the use of open systems does not limit that spectrum. With open, COTS-based systems, you may not see performance benefits immediately, but if you are moving with the marketplace, performance may tend to improve over time because of technology insertion and product maturation.

Standards play a role in performance, too, although this is not often recognized. You must determine whether COTS products based on standards meet performance requirements. It may be advantageous for an organization to define a preferred set of standards to limit choices and thereby achieve greater interoperability. **Standards**

Standards-based COTS products provide opportunities for adopting technological advances almost as they occur. But you must resist the temptation to chase the latest gadgets and performance capabilities. Stick to your standards, and make sure that changes make sense in the face of all trade-offs.

When assessing the performance of a COTS product, it is important to identify those components that are performance critical and to understand those components as part of the evaluation process. Refer back to the discussion of quality characteristics, especially Table 3.2. Consider the environment in which the COTS product needs to perform, and then build a test suite to evaluate candidate COTS products. Components can be rated by the importance of the purpose they serve within the system. If a system fails to perform in, for example, a hard real-time situation, the system's mission may fail. **COTS products**

10.5 People

The paradigm shift is not just a technical change but also a sociological and organizational change. You need to be aware of the people issues surrounding an open, COTS-based systems approach and to be committed to dealing with them.

10.5.1 People Issues

Issues that managers need to take into account and deal with before they become problems are

- People's jobs and job security
- Staff's comfort and stress level
- Training and education

- Performance evaluation and incentives
- Organizational changes
- Bases of managerial power and influence

Job security

People need to understand that evolving to an open, COTS-based acquisition approach does not necessarily mean that their jobs are in jeopardy. But people may be asked to perform tasks that are unfamiliar, break old habits to form new ones, or gain new responsibilities or be asked to relinquish previous ones.

For example, someone who is used to working alone may see being asked to work on a team as a sign that he or she has not been doing a good job. That person may also resent the interference or have had bad experiences working on teams. These experiences are not unique to an open, COTS-based systems. However, effective teaming is very important to success.

It is important to look for opportunities that provide "skill portability" whenever possible. For example, a person who has done testing for an in-house development team has important skills, but they may need to be augmented with new skills for black-box testing of COTS products.

The stress of change

When people are asked to change the way they do business, it is natural that they may become stressed or uncomfortable. Managers need to recognize these tendencies and create a nonthreatening work environment.

Think of a person, sitting alone at their desk, who has not had to interact with others, happy in the world of development. In the open systems world, this person is told to look up and look around. The person does so and realizes that this new world cannot be controlled in the way that the earlier environment was. With time and familiarity, not to mention training and management support, this person's stress should start to abate. This situation presents a prime opportunity for managers to demonstrate real leadership.

Training and education

Training and education are vital for a successful transition to open, COTS-based systems. Managers need to provide or point out opportunities for learning terminology and concepts and how to complete certain tasks. For example, a few courses teach the basics of open, COTS-based systems, and organizations provide information about standards (see Section 6.7) and COTS products and vendors.

Managers also need to devise ways to evaluate staff performance and to provide incentives for a job well done. This is a challenge because using open, COTS-based systems is a new way of doing business; old measures may not apply. For example, how do you rate someone's ability to evaluate alternative standards and to select one?

Performance and incentives

Organizational changes resulting from the change to COTS products and open systems are another issue that managers need to consider. Someone may be promoted to management and inherit problems from a previous manager. This person may have to report to someone who has no understanding of open or COTS-based systems and their importance or who may be lagging on the learning curve. Downsizing, budget constraints, and shortened schedules can all result in or be the result of organizational changes. Examples are the elimination of a maintenance group or the initiation of a market research group.

Organizational change

Bases of managerial power and influence should not be downplayed, and they too can be the victim of organizational changes. You need to lead by example, knowing that others look to you to set the vision and the tone. The people networks on which you depend may change with the corresponding changes for open, COTS-based systems, so power structures and relationships change. You need to be prepared for this and make appropriate plans.

Bases of power

As if this degree of change were not enough, the change to open, COTS-based systems usually does not occur in isolation; other disciplines are likely to be introduced and used at the same time. Examples of these other disciplines are reuse, reverse engineering, reengineering, process improvement, and concurrent engineering. These disciplines are mostly synergistic, not in conflict, with an open, COTS-based approach. Rather, an open, COTS-based approach can be viewed as another improvement in tandem with some of these examples. But this introduction of additional new disciplines increases the stress of change.

Other disciplines

Up to this point, you have been reading about all the new information you will have to know before you can take advantage of open or COTS-based systems. You are

Remember: evolution, not revolution

already equipped to deal with a large number of open systems and COTS product issues. We cannot emphasize enough that the transition to open, COTS-based systems is an evolution, not one big change. Ask yourself whether you are ready to make judgments—or to oversee others who are making those judgments—about the maturity of standards and COTS products. Are you prepared to take a team approach, including your contractors, when you are planning and scheduling the use of an open, COTS-based approach? Your affinity for flexibility and willingness to deal with change will be important attributes you want to foster in both yourself and your staff.

10.5.2 Addressing the People Issues

There are general ways to alleviate some of the concerns resulting from the change to open, COTS-based systems. Ensure that everyone involved in the effort understands open, COTS-based systems; they need training in these areas. Use a team-based approach with explicit, open, and honest communication.

Resistance to change is a natural human response, and managers need to deal with it. Resistance indicates that a

---

Management Style

The magazine *Inc.* surveyed top executives and asked them to identify films that influenced their management style. The top ten films were

- *Twelve O'Clock High*
- *12 Angry Men*
- *Apollo 13*
- *It's a Wonderful Life*
- *Dead Poets Society*
- *Norma Rae*
- *Bridge on the River Kwai*
- *Glengarry Glen Ross*
- *Elizabeth*
- *One Flew Over the Cuckoo's Nest*

person either disagrees with or is uncomfortable with a situation. Managers need to recognize that everyone has a personal frame of reference, based on experiences. Once again, explicit communication is necessary to dissolve resistance and to promote cooperation and enthusiasm.

10.6 Transition Strategies

In this section, we identify transition strategies that can help you integrate an open, COTS-based systems approach into your current systems acquisition practices. Use these strategies as a guide for the development of your transition plan.

Before you can make the transition to open, COTS-based systems, you must identify your current situation. This should include examining your existing system, staff, and contractors. Your readiness to make the transition can be evaluated by your answers to a set of questions. These questions assess the qualities of your system, components, and organization that make your project a good (or poor) candidate for open, COTS-based systems. Appendix C, Sample Questions, contains questions you can start with to make your assessment. You may want to add other questions to those suggested by this list, but these are probably the minimum for getting insight into your readiness.

Self-assessment

The results of your assessment may indicate that it will be difficult to move aggressively toward open, COTS-based systems. Instead, you may decide to move more slowly, starting with the barriers your assessment revealed. You may not be able to start on an open, COTS-based systems approach immediately, but perhaps you will be able to put some changes in place in the near furure to give you a better prospect for success. Whether you are ready to create a transition plan today or will have to wait for full realization some time in the future, you will need such a plan to see you through the transition. Remember, however, that planning is a continuous process and that the sooner you start, the sooner you will initiate the change in direction of your project.

Planning   The first group of transition strategies develops an overall transition strategy and plan. The strategy covers your approach to every aspect of the transition to open, COTS-based systems. The plan identifies revenue sources and contracting strategies. Recruit knowledgeable team members and develop the plan collaboratively.

Government agencies can ask such organizations as the OSJTF for help in planning their transition to open systems. Fewer organizations are available to assist with COTS-based systems questions; look for information from your peers who are succeeding in this new world.

People   The second group of transition strategies prepares the people in your organization for open, COTS-based systems. Educate your people about open systems and the COTS marketplace in general and about your specific open systems and COTS product plans if any have been formulated. Introduce your people to your approach and to the changes that will affect their jobs.

This preparation also includes identifying a champion for open systems and the use of COTS products. This champion must be a person who understands and supports the move to open, COTS-based systems and has the peer respect and influence to promote the success of the effort. This person (or set of people) need not be in a position of authority; sometimes, a grassroots champion can be more effective than one who has been "crowned" by upper management.

Process   The last group of transition strategies addresses the processes to assist your transition to open, COTS-based systems. In particular, this should include strategies for easing the transition to processes that are new or changed for open, COTS-based systems, such as

- Identifying and managing your new risks
- Starting a market research effort
- Beginning with a pilot project

Other process elements will be suggested by the new approach you adopt.

When you identify your new open, COTS-based risks and plan for them, you can make the transition more easily. Make risk management a defined part of your transition process.

The results of market research provide information about relevant standards, standards-based COTS products, and the historical activities of the major participants in the marketplace. Market research may also be used to keep an eye on technology evolution and new breakthroughs, alerting the project when it looks as though a new technology is ready for serious consideration. The sooner you start your people doing market research, the better positioned you will be to take advantage of the marketplace.

Pilot projects are an effective way to learn about new things without significant risk to your project. Start small, learn from the experience, and then take on greater challenges. In particular, find a small project that is not on the critical path and assign a core group of people to it. Through their experiences, you can better determine how open, COTS-based systems affect your current processes. You can make the necessary changes to those processes and then take on a larger effort with more of your people.

10.7 Summary

In this chapter, we discussed the direction of your organization and the forces that are vying with you for control over how your system develops and evolves in the face of a changing acquisition environment.

We presented the four main areas of concern for managers:

- Cost
- Schedule
- People
- Performance

We also included some additional concerns, particularly for government managers.

The transition strategies you can use include the following.

- Prepare the people in your organization for the acquisition of open, COTS-based systems.

- Define the processes to assist your transition to open, COTS-based systems.
- Develop an overall transition strategy and plan.

Estimates, Anyone?

Let us leave you with something to think about. We emphasized the importance of planning and estimating cost and schedule and provided some rationale for possible schedule slippages and cost overruns. Managers often accept that, no matter how well they plan, cost and schedule will change. Keep in mind that the existence of cost and schedule overruns is relative to some projected value. What you may categorize time and again as overruns may actually be an estimate that is converging on the true number. As you hone your skills for dealing with the cost, schedule, people, and performance concerns presented by an open, COTS-based acquisition approach, learn from your experiences so that each time your estimates and methods for dealing with the concerns improve.

10.8 Food for Thought

1. Who are the stakeholders vying for control on your project? Do you foresee, or are you experiencing, conflicts among these various stakeholders' goals? If so, how will you engage the relevant stakeholders in addressing the conflict?

2. How can you strike the balance you need on your project between the liabilities and the benefits of an open, COTS-based approach? Are there aspects of your system that are not amenable to this new approach?

3. How do you currently estimate your costs? If you use a work-breakdown structure (WBS), think about how open systems and the use of COTS products affect that WBS. Are some activities unchanged? Are others new? For the activities that you've done before but will be somehow changed by the use of COTS products and an open systems approach, how will they change? What do you expect to be your primary cost factors?

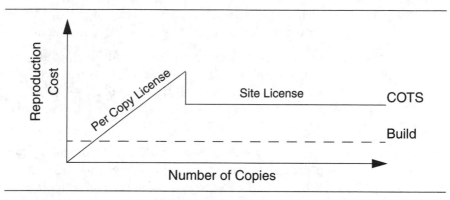

FIGURE 10.3 Comparison of unit reproduction costs.

4. You are talking to a new acquaintance about the potential cost savings of COTS-based and open systems. He argues: "But if I build it, I'll bet my unit reproduction costs are less than with COTS products, where you pay N times the cost of one, unless you get a site license." And he neatly draws the diagram shown in Figure 10.3. How do you respond? What factors and considerations might he be missing? (*Hint:* There's more to life than copying costs.)

5. Next, you and this acquaintance discuss rates of change associated with product upgrades. He draws the diagram shown in Figure 10.4. Do you agree with his

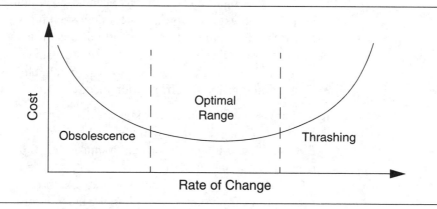

FIGURE 10.4 Comparison of rates of change.

argument that there is an optimal rate of change? What do you think the optimal range is for your system?

6. What do you think the potential is for finding other projects with similar needs and interests with which you can share responsibilities and costs? What approaches can you use to convince people on those projects to work with you?

7. Creating source code is very different from taking the products of others and making them work together. What is the difference in the mindset and temperament required? Do you have people with the skills and the inclination to take a "black-box" approach to integration?

8. How would you seek out a contracting officer who is capable of taking a progressive approach? If you don't have any who are known for this in your organization now, how could you go about "creating" one?

9. An open, COTS-based approach is new for most people. What kinds of incentives do you have in place now for your own personnel and for your contractors or consultants, if you use any, to encourage them to take on this new challenge successfully? If you already have a contract in place, what techniques can you devise to motivate the contractor to change to an open, COTS-based approach within the terms of the existing contract?

10. The need for market research has been noted at many points. But must *every* program conduct such market research? If so, duplication of effort will result in significant costs. Develop a strategy for your organization to share costs associated with market research. How would you grade yourself on your success at this?

11. You are told to decrease your staff by 10 percent. From what job categories will you make the cuts? Suppose that you are told instead to make the 10 percent cut but to increase the use of open systems and COTS products by 25 percent over the next three years. How does your answer change? Do you think

you can get the cuts reversed to achieve the 25 percent increase?

12. You manage an acquisition project and have been told to transition to considerably greater use of open systems and COTS products. Develop a *transition* plan for a new organization to support this new approach. What's the new organization look like? What are your cost and schedule estimates for completing the transition? How will you manage ongoing work during the transition?

13. What changes would you make in your organization to handle the standards and COTS product acquisition activities more efficiently? What criteria do you look for in the leadership position(s)?

14. Develop a psychological profile that can identify a successful manager for a COTS-based, open system acquisition project. How would the profile differ if you were looking for a manager for a traditional development effort?

15. You are in charge of a division that has several projects doing open, COTS-based acquisition. Does this change how individual projects are normally staffed? For example, do you take some staff from each project to put on a corporate COTS product IPT (integrated product team) that is a resource for all the projects? What are the pros and cons of this approach? Has power changed in the organization?

16. Are you surprised that the movie *Gandhi* is not on the list of top ten films influencing management style (page 198)? Why or why not?

17. Think about your management and sponsors, too. What if they want you to use open, COTS-based systems when it's not appropriate? How will you convince them? Conversely, what if you want to use an open, COTS-based approach and they are resistant? What could you do to reassure them?

11

Engineering Practices

In Chapter 4, we introduced an overall open, COTS-based systems approach, which we illustrated as in Figure 11.1. We now develop details of the engineering practices for the overall approach. Note that each of these steps may be executed by you, by a contractor, or by a joint acquirer/ contractor integrated product team (IPT).

11.1 Determine Concepts, Requirements, and Reference Models

When determining concepts, requirements, and reference models, ensure that the following are accomplished.

Your current system is baselined. If the current system, assuming there is one, is not understood thoroughly,

**Baseline
current system**

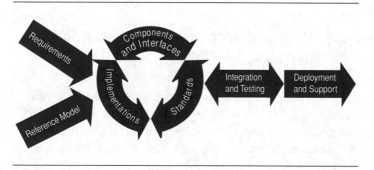

FIGURE 11.1 Elements of an open, COTS-based approach.

migrating it to any new approach or technology will be difficult and unpredictable. It is particularly important to understand your current system from the point of view of its current openness and how it exploits the marketplace.

Unify terminology and concepts

The terminology and concepts are defined and used consistently across the project team and harmonized with those in the marketplace. The development of a reference model (see Chapter 5) makes an excellent approach to this goal, as it encourages the team to discuss the fundamentals of the system independently of any architectural or implementation details.

A reference model may be adopted or created. The reference model establishes a basis for understanding the domain of the system and its possible components.

This work may then be carried over into other important foundational documents, such as domain-specific architectures and data and information models. Data element standardization is also becoming increasingly important in all enterprises, public and private. Harmonizing the terminology and concepts with the marketplace makes it easier to see where standards and standards-based COTS products can be applied.

Consider the future

The system is considered a part of a larger future system. One of the hopes for open, COTS-based systems is that through their use, we can anticipate future requirements for interoperation and integration and be ready for those requirements as the system evolves. However, our ability to create this future depends on standards and the way they are used to achieve interoperability.

11.2 Define Architectures, Components, and Interfaces

When defining architectures, components, and interfaces, ensure that the following are accomplished. Although they are presented linearly here, keep in mind that the process for developing the system architecture goes hand-in-hand with the selection of the corresponding standards and the selection of COTS products.

Market research is conducted for standards-based COTS products. It provides the starting point for standards and product selections. It normally covers standards and standards-based implementations. Standards profiles that meet the stated needs of your system—or at least come very close—may also exist. These profiles should be included in the market research as well.

Market research is composed of two separate activities: *market survey* and *market analysis.* In a market survey, the goal is to determine what is available and what the features and characteristics of each product and vendor are. Market analysis then looks at these results collectively to determine which are the feasible candidates for the job at hand.

You may have done market research in the past. Now, you may need to apply more effort to address open, COTS-based systems. The research must be thorough; the information provided by market research is the lifeblood of your acquisition.

Market research should identify the major participants, their agenda, and their motivation. Market research reduces your risk when you address the iterative elements of the approach: components and interfaces, standards, and implementations. Hence, one goal of market research is to make sure that you do not select a doomed technology or vendor. Sometimes, avoiding a potential wrong choice is just as important as making the right choice. In some instances, technologies that appeared to be quite promising fizzled out in a relatively short time. Identifying such technologies, especially in the early stages, can be extremely difficult; it helps to be lucky sometimes!

Market research must be broad in its scope, in terms of both the range of things it considers and the resources it draws on. You need to learn about the qualities of the products. But you also need to learn about the marketplace in general: who the players are and how they interact. As a consumer, you need to learn how to "shop" for standards and COTS products. Some ideas for qualities to look for in your market survey are

- Availability
- Maturity of the standards, technologies, and products

Perform market research

- Existence of multiple product sources
- Market acceptance
- Member of a product-line family
- Thoroughness of test and evaluation
- Availability of technical data
- License options
- Performance benchmark results
- Warranty restrictions
- Quality assurance

As time progresses, the research should be updated as necessary. Although it provides a great deal of information, your research can become outdated quickly, sometimes in a matter of months. It must be kept current because it will be needed again later in the process. Be circumspect, and don't get lost in the richness of what may be available. Only standards that apply to your system and the products that implement them should be included.

The information you need might already have been documented by someone else. But even then, you may need to collect some additional market research information directly, especially if the existing work is more than a few months old. It may also be that an existing survey fails to discover all the information that is important for your system decisions.

Market research will help you determine the suitability and availability of appropriate standards and products before beginning a development effort. It will help the architects and designers know what products are available and how they will impact the system. Preliminary architectures, particularly open system architectures, will constrain your choice of products. But the architects and designers must also appreciate that the capabilities and features of the standards and products available in the marketplace will also constrain and influence the architecture and design, just as they do the requirements. This is an example of the iteration we described earlier; see Section 4.3.

Collaborate   *Other organizations that are moving to open systems in your domain are approached as potential collaborators.* Some ideas might be gained from talking to those organizations. The more common the actions of the members of a domain, the greater the influence the domain will have in the marketplace. Investment in such features as high availability or survivability might be affordable when pursued as a group.

Prototyping is done using existing capabilities, such as COTS products, to help answer feasibility questions. Prototypes based on quickly obtainable COTS products may help with questions about the ability of standards-based implementations to meet a need, even if those COTS products may not be used in that way in the finished system. Prototyping can also help refine system requirements as a risk-mitigation approach. However, as with any prototype, you must resist the pressure to field a prototype prematurely: no prototype before its time!

Prototype

System architecture concepts are harmonized with

Harmonize concepts

- General architectures supported by the marketplace
- Architectures used by similar organizations
- Domain-specific architectures

Examples of general architectural approaches that are available in the community are

- OSI (open systems interconnection)
- Client/server
- Database management with transactions

The system's interface and component requirements are understood, documented, and prioritized. Requirements on the interfaces are essential elements in the evaluation and selection of appropriate standards.

Determine interface requirements

Requirements are not always completely stable. In fact, when trying to take advantage of the marketplace, remaining flexible about requirements is a necessity. But documenting and prioritizing the current requirements can help you decide whether to add an expensive requirement that may be requested or proposed later.

The architecture is initiated and evolved. As you consider the architecture, it is essential that knowledge of the marketplace—both technologies and products—be taken into account. Standards will have a profound influence on

Create and evolve the architecture

the system architecture, dictating some important characteristics. Technologies and individual COTS products may also have the same effect. Conversely, certain architectural decisions will constrain the field of candidate standards, technologies, and products, as some may not be usable in the context of chosen architecture features.

Document the desired architecture

The desired open systems architecture is documented, including its components, interfaces, and rationale. This architecture represents the desired "final" architecture. The rationale is needed for architecture decisions because the target architecture will evolve, too. If the process and basis for decision making is documented, it will be easier to reconsider the decisions in the future.

Prioritize components

The system's components are prioritized to help concentrate on those that best match an open, COTS-based systems approach and to eliminate those not worth moving to open systems or COTS products. To support such decisions, you perform a cost-benefit analysis. Prioritizing components and their interfaces also helps when choosing the scope for a pilot project.

Some considerations that may help you to prioritize components and their implementations, especially for legacy systems, are provided in Table 11.1. Note that some of the items in the table suggest giving the component a high priority for migration, whereas others suggest giving it a low one. Components that are heavily used or very modular may have the biggest payoff. Components that are unique or deeply embedded may not be worth making more open.

Some implementations may have be to changed anyway. For example, component implementations that no longer meet performance requirements, need major reengineering, are not supportable, or are implemented on inadequate

TABLE 11.1 Component and Implementation Priorities

Component-Specific Considerations	Implementation-Specific Considerations
▪ Frequency of use by other components	▪ Still meet performance requirements or need severe reengineering
▪ Modularity	
▪ Uniqueness	▪ No longer supported by the vendor
▪ Embedded	▪ Implemented on inadequate hardware
▪ Maintenance required	▪ Seldom used or even actively avoided

hardware may be good candidates for migration. Component implementations that require low maintenance or that are unused may not be worth the trouble to change them to open interfaces or COTS products.

11.3 Select Standards

When selecting standards, ensure that the following are accomplished.

Market research on standards and standards profiles is continued, and the information is kept current.

Continue market research

A set of high-level criteria is used to narrow the candidate standards to a manageable number, such as

Screen with high-level criteria

- Level of consensus ("pedigree")
- Product availability
- Completeness
- Maturity
- Stability
- Problems/limitations

High-level criteria like these[1] are helpful for narrowing the pool of candidate standards to a manageable number but not for making a final decision.

Candidate standards are evaluated and selected. An evaluation method and criteria for selecting standards are established and followed.

Make the selection

There is no set evaluation method for selecting standards. However, you can derive the evaluation criteria from your prioritized requirements. The scheme in Table 11.2 is an example criterion that corresponds to a requirement that a standard have wide commercial acceptance. To establish effective requirements and evaluation criteria, you should gather ideas from a variety of sources, including Appendix C.

To minimize personal biases, a variety of people participate in the evaluations. The evaluation process may be

---

1. These high-level criteria are from [NIST 96a].

TABLE 11.2 Example Standards Evaluation Scheme

Requirement	Weight (1–10)	Criteria Definitions	Raw Score	Weighted Score
Commercial acceptance	10	▪ 10: wide acceptance ▪ 5: partial acceptance ▪ 0: not accepted	5	50

approached, at least in part, by mapping standards onto requirements or by adjusting requirements to more closely match the standards. Either way, compromises are common.

A Real Experience

The evaluation scheme illustrated in Table 11.2 was used by the Next Generation Computer Resources (NGCR) Operating Systems Standards Working Group (OSSWG). At least three people reviewed the specifications for each class of criteria, and many classes had up to seven reviewers. Analyses were done to ensure that one score or reviewer could not dominate the results. In the end, the technically stronger specification was not selected, owing to its lack of market support. In hindsight, this was the right choice.

The standards with the highest *technical* evaluation scores may not be the best choices if *nontechnical* scores, such as for pedigree, are low. So an equitable way of aggregating all these scores and determining a final selection—perhaps through a voting process—must be established.

Create standards liaisons

Involvement with the standards organizations that support the system's chosen standards is established. This is how influence over the standards' characteristics can be exercised.

Without at least liaison contact, it is difficult to track a standard and anticipate changes that might affect your system. There are various ways of maintaining liaisons with standards bodies. You can stay in touch through publications and mailing lists, the World Wide Web, or attendance and participation at meetings. It will not make sense to pursue the same kind of liaison with all standards groups that are relevant to your system. For a standard that is still under development or evolution, a member of the project team should, if possible, be in the standard's balloting group. For stable, mature standards, it might be sufficient to receive a monthly or quarterly newsletter that reports on status and plans.

Project management creates and maintains liaisons with other acquisition organizations that are similar in scope or interest. Other organizations can sometimes share standards liaison information with you. Or, cooperation with another organization or project group that has similar interests can be arranged, so that one project "watches" one standard while the other "watches" another, and both projects share the information.

Form other acquirer liaisons

If possible, *an existing profile that appropriately integrates the selected standards is found.* If no suitable profile exists, one can be created by doing the following.

Document the standards profile

- List the standards.
- Select options, parameter value ranges, and so on.
- Record the relations among the standards, options, and so on.
- Address gaps for all missing functionality without developing your own specification, if possible.
- Decide whether and how conformance will be ascertained.
- Document the profile.

It may be possible to find a profile that meets the system's needs or one that comes very close. If a close match is found, the preceding list should be reviewed to evaluate the profile further.

If only one standard is chosen, this profiling step may not be necessary. *Only if* there is willingness to take the standard exactly as is, with no limitation on options or other alterable aspects of that standard, can the standard serve as the profile with no further work.

Completion of the profile is an iterative process that typically requires the help of experts. See the *New Attack Submarine Open System Implementation, Specification and Guidance* [NUWC 95] for a detailed example of what can be involved.

Sometimes, you will find that you have gaps in your profile, as illustrated in Figure 11.2.

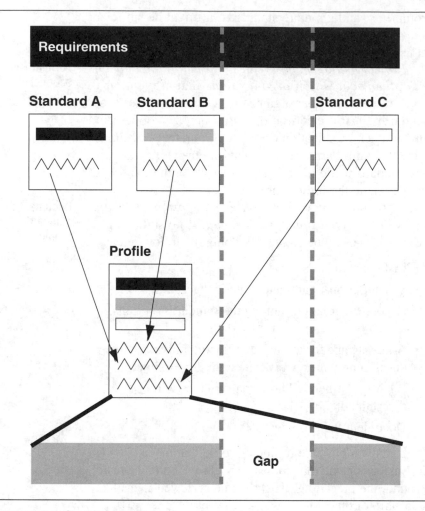

FIGURE 11.2 Gaps in a profile.

The profile in Figure 11.2 is based on three standards and their specified options. The selection and development of the profile are based on the requirements. However, not all requirements are satisfied by the profile, resulting in the gap shown at the bottom of the figure. Hence, the profile does not cover all the requirements.

There are several ways to deal with gaps in a profile.

- Accept the deficiency.
- Suggest changes to a standard.

- Search for additional or alternative standards or specifications.
- Develop your own specification for the missing functionality.

Whatever the course of action, it is helpful to the standards community if the requirements that describe the gaps between standards are documented and communicated to the appropriate standards organizations. Also keep in mind that a gap in a profile will need an implementation later.

11.4 Select Implementations

When selecting implementations, ensure that the following are accomplished.

Market research about candidate products is continued, and the information is kept current. These candidates can be narrowed down to a manageable number before applying full evaluation criteria.

Continue market research

An evaluation method and criteria for selecting implementations and their vendors are used. The evaluation method and criteria prepared will also guide the development of component implementations that must be built instead of bought.

Evaluate and select

For the evaluation, sources such as the following can be used:

- Product documentation and manuals, such as user and maintenance guides
- "Hands-on" trial use or prototyping
- Information about the vendor
- Information from other customers of the COTS product
- Information from "evaluation" agencies

Also, some commercial resources provide useful information on various COTS products and their vendors, including such organizations as the Gartner Group, DataQuest, or Ovum and published reviews in various magazines and on the Web. Some ideas for the selection of criteria are given in Appendix C.

Ensure conformance

A mechanism to establish or ensure conformance of standards-based implementations is defined and used. To ensure conformance, make sure that

- Conformance is discussed in the profile.
- Proof of conformance is sought when selecting implementations.
- Any implementation you build conforms to the profile.

To benefit from using an interface standard, the implementation must fully adhere, or conform, to the interface standard, *and* other implementations must use, or conform to, it properly.

If an implementation provides a service differently from the specification in the standard, the implementation does not conform to the specification. If the implementation adds services not found in the standard and other implementations take advantage of these, you may find it impossible to replace that implementation with others that strictly conform to the same standard. You also just got locked into the extensions and add-ons of a particular product and vendor.

11.5 Acquire Implementations

When acquiring implementations, you have four choices: purchase existing products, choose different standards, convince a vendor to "fix" a product, or obtain a custom implementation.

Purchase

Purchasing COTS products is relatively easy. The difficult part is finding products that both conform to the standards *and* meet your other requirements.

Choose different standards

When "shopping" for implementations, you may find that products are simply unavailable for some standards. In those cases, *choosing different standards* may change things so that existing COTS products can be purchased. This is part of the normal open systems iteration emphasized in Chapter 4.

If an implementation "almost" fits the system's needs, you may *work with the vendor* to provide what is needed. This may involve "convincing" the vendor to make the changes you need by offering to pay for development. This strategy, however, is usually very costly, and the change may not arrive in time for the current project. Besides, vendors are sometimes unwilling to make special versions, no matter how much you may be willing to pay.

Convince

What's "Close"?

Remember the adage: "Close only counts in horseshoes and hand grenades." An implementation that "almost" fits could turn out to be more expensive than a custom development! Your business case analysis should help decide what to do.

If a required implementation cannot be found, *the implementation may be developed* by the acquiring organization or a contractor. Although developing may be the most expensive choice, it may be your only choice for continuing with an open systems approach.

Develop or contract

When dealing with COTS products, *escrow accounts for the designs or software code of critical system components are considered*. This ensures that you have access to the product's source code or designs if the vendor's business plans change or the vendor goes out of business. Be sure, however, that you do so with full knowledge of what you are undertaking: If you exercise the escrow option, you must be prepared to maintain someone else's legacy code or design for the rest of the life of the system or at least the life of that product in the system. Escrow accounts are not always a good answer but are an option that may be worth considering.

Consider escrow accounts

Test suites are used to test the conformance of implementations to their interface standards. This applies to all implementations, whether they are COTS products or custom-developed implementations. In most situations, however, there are more interfaces without conformance test suites than with them. The conformance of all interfaces

Test conformance

must be addressed; if some conformance tests are not available, they need to be developed.

11.6 Integrate and Test

When integrating and testing the system, ensure that the following are accomplished.

Limit customizations

Customization is carefully limited. Customization ranges from simply setting installation parameters to making source code changes to a COTS product. The range of such types of changes is indicated in Figure 11.3.

The essence of the distinction between modification and tailoring deals with how an implementation is changed. A modification causes a change to the internals of the implementation, but adapting an implementation for a particular environment does not change the internals.

The extent of customization should be limited because it

- May mean that part of the implementation will not conform to applicable standards
- Takes effort that will have to be repeated every time the vendor upgrades the product
- May, in the case of source code modification, void licenses, warranties, or support agreements
- Reduces the extent to which you might be able to take advantage of the marketplace as it advances

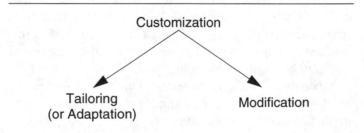

Customization

Tailoring
(or Adaptation)

Modification

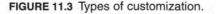

FIGURE 11.3 Types of customization.

Potentially, consumers can be locked into using one product from one vendor. Some customization, however, may be the most viable option because of system requirements that have no corresponding standards or products available. Where feasible, use of a strictly conforming implementation helps avoid the risk of being locked into using one product or supplier.

Customization is risky. Table 11.3, adapted from *The COTS Book* [USAF 89],[2] contains an analysis of the probable results of various kinds of customization done by vendors, prime integration contractors, and you. Note the warnings for the most risky customizations.

If the risk is too high, COTS products that must be customized should not be purchased. If COTS products are customized, consider isolating the customized functions from the standards-based functions so that the customized part of the implementation can be eliminated, if necessary.

Tailoring is controled.   Tailor

> **tailoring** ➡ Using mechanisms that a supplier builds
> into a product to allow it to meet the specific needs of a
> particular system. Tailoring does *not* involve changes to
> the internal aspects, such as source code, of the product.

Tailoring encompasses the "cosmetic only" and "add items only" parts of Table 11.3. Most COTS products require some amount of tailoring. Some tailoring is usually required just to install a product. Other tailoring options are designed by the vendor to help increase the utility of the product to the users, through mechanisms that can be used to enhance functionality or to ease integration. Products that involve database management systems also require tailoring of the schemas so that data fields and their names reflect the data needs of the users. Although some tailoring is generally necessary, don't underestimate the effort it will require to perform the initial tailoring or to redo it when product upgrades are released.

The appropriate integration techniques are used.   Integrate
Using an open, COTS-based systems approach is intended

---

2. *The COTS Book* provides guidance and criteria for the identification, selection, acquisition, logistics support, and testing of the various categories of commercial equipment, computer resources, and software.

TABLE 11.3 The Risks of Customization

Type of Customization*	Customized by Vendor	Customized by Contractor	Customized by You
Cosmetic only	OK	OK	OK
Change the software or firmware only	*Probably OK* if it is properly documented. Buy documentation from the vendor to show the change.	*Be careful!* This may build in problems, and the vendor may not support or warrant the resulting implementation.	*Avoid it!* Odds are, you'll degrade, not improve, the product. The vendor won't recognize the result, and a contractor probably can't help.
Add items only, no changes to existing implementation	*Probably OK.* The vendor should be responsible about inserting items from other sources. Get documentation for the resulting implementation.	*Be careful!* If there is no proprietary connection with the original or inserted item, the vendor may not be sensitive about latent glitches or induced failures.	*Be careful!* If problems arise, it's usually easier to plug in new functionality than to get help from either source.
Change the essentials of the implementation, including repackaging or ruggedizing	*Be careful!* This could mess up an otherwise reliable product. The vendor may abandon the resulting implementation when you need support.	*Avoid it!* The contractor has no understanding of the product's internal configuration and may do whatever works at the time. Usually, no reliable documentation is available, and it usually voids the supplier's warranty	*Avoid it!* Who will help when the trouble starts?

* Cosmetic changes include the addition of decals or color changes. Items added only include ones that you can plug in or bolt on without affecting the operation of the implementation. Essential changes refer to changes in function. Repackaging and ruggedizing refer to changes in form or fit.

in part to reduce the difficulties encountered when integrating COTS products from diverse sources. For example, if products use the same interface standard, they can be integrated directly, using those interfaces. But the use of open, COTS-based systems cannot completely eliminate all integration problems. It will probably still be necessary to alter how some products look to the rest of the system. Applicable techniques are

- Building filters that make one product's output usable as input to another
- "Wrapping" a product to alter its externally observable behavior

Filters and wrappers are examples of the use of glue code. Such "glue" provides the means to create a deployable system.

Integration can be done a little at a time or all at once. It should be more likely to go smoothly where standard interfaces are concerned; however, planning should anticipate possible problems.

The system is tested to be sure that it fulfills its func- **Test the system** *tional and other requirements.* For example, if a functional requirement for the system is that output must be in a particular format, you should test that function.

Besides testing individual functions and other requirements, such as expected user capacity, integration testing should also be performed. This ensures that all the system's component implementations interact properly to produce the desired results.

One common problem with the use of COTS products is management that clings to the myth that "I don't have to test any more." Even if the whole system has been acquired from a single vendor, it is necessary to ascertain whether the system meets its objectives and requirements. Just because the parts are "off-the-shelf" does not guarantee the behavior of the overall system. Not only is that a myth, but some forms of testing required for COTS products, especially those that are part of an open systems approach, are different from, and may be more extensive than, what is normal for custom-developed systems.

Many of the testing techniques for COTS-based systems are similar to those used for any system. However, if problems are discovered, determining exactly what has gone wrong may be a special challenge. In the case of custom-developed systems, the developers have full knowledge of the internals of the systems implementation, and this knowledge generally makes it easier to solve detected problems. However, with COTS-based systems, it might be necessary to use special tools and techniques to determine the source of a problem. The tools are those available on all systems for detecting component behavior from "outside" its implementation. The technique is a straightforward application of the scientific method, in which hypotheses are successively formed and tested until the product mismatch has been uncovered [Hissam 97; 98].

Test for open systems goals

Specific open systems goals are tested. Three common goals of open systems are interoperability, portability, and scalability. Because achieving these goals is often what motivates people to pursue an open systems approach, you may also want to test for these goals explicitly, using them as criteria to judge the openness of your system against scenarios that hypothesize changes the system may encounter in the future.

11.7 Deploy and Support

One key maintenance consideration is that the activities required to effectively support open, COTS-based systems resemble those used to initially create the system. In particular, it will be necessary to incorporate new versions of vendor products as time goes by. The tailoring and "glueware" that were created to integrate a product into the system initially will have to be reconsidered and potentially modified or even completely redone for each new product release.

Even more disturbing to our usual notions of maintenance is what occurs when a COTS product needs to be replaced. This may occur because the vendor has chosen to discontinue support of the product, because the vendor has gone out of business entirely, or because a new technology that will improve the system has arrived. In any of these cases, the support organization will have to repeat the "development" activities detailed earlier, such as criteria development, product evaluation, product tailoring, and integration. It's a never-ending cycle.

When deploying and supporting the system, ensure that the following are accomplished.

Maintain the system

The open, COTS-based system is maintained in a manner that preserves the openness and COTS product basis. Maintenance is of special concern for open, COTS-based systems. System lifetimes are measured in decades today, particularly for government systems. But product lifetimes are measured in months, and many technologies in fewer than five years.

Commercial sources are used for distribution, data configuration, and data management. The vendor or the integration contractor probably has the knowledge and experience to execute the support tasks with minimum disruption. They also will have the experience to recognize and to address problems as they occur.

Complexity resulting from multiple commercial support sources is anticipated. The more products the system contains, the more commercial support sources may be involved. All these sources of support must be coordinated, sometimes by a prime contractor.

Disputes sometimes arise among support providers about the responsibility for problems. For example, the software vendor may blame the hardware, and the hardware vendor may blame the software for the problem.

As more players and more products are integrated to constitute one system, it is necessary to have a clear plan for handling problems and disputes. One source of problems may be either unspecified or ambiguously specified parts of an interface specification, indicating a point at which the profile should be strengthened.

But even with well-specified interfaces, two or more products may conflict, even though they are each implementing the standards or other specifications correctly. Well before this happens, you need an effective plan for determining responsibilities and correcting the situation. Establish processes that explicitly define how to

- Identify where problems occur
- Determine who is responsible for a problem
- Handle disputes about problems
- Determine how and when changes and updates may be installed

Defining processes that address these issues *ahead of time* and getting agreement of key players will save time and confusion when the support is needed. This is something on which you should obtain vendor concurrence as part of negotiation of vendor agreements.

Use commercial sources

Plan for complexity of support

11.8 Summary

In this chapter, we covered engineering strategies. Engineering strategies address

- Determining concepts, requirements, and reference models
- Defining architectures, components, and interfaces
- Selecting standards
- Selecting implementations
- Acquiring implementations
- Integrating and testing the system
- Deploying and supporting the system

11.9 Food for Thought

1. What does the current baseline for your system look like, assuming there is one? If there isn't, use another system with which you are familiar. How open is it? How would you describe how well it exploits the marketplace?

2. Are there any existing reference models for the domain of your system or for any part of it? Develop the top-level decomposition of a reference model for the system you want to develop. Make sure that the reference model doesn't have any implementation decisions in it!

3. How much do you know about the marketplace your system will need to exploit? Take 30 minutes and see how much you can discover by surfing on the World Wide Web for products in a market segment in which you are interested. How will you decide what qualities you will use to decide which market segments and products might be of interest?

4. Stop to think how you would use each of the prioriti-
   zation considerations listed in Section 11.2 to make
   prioritizations for your system. Do they all apply to
   your system? Can you think of others not listed here?

5. Under what circumstances would you find it advantageous to participate full time on a standards body?
   Where would you get the resources to support this
   participation?

6. How will you handle conformance testing? What will
   you do if conformance test suites are not available for
   a standard you want to use?

7. Suppose that you wanted to evaluate a vendor. What
   are some of the criteria you would include, and why?
   Who would you get to do this?

8. A subordinate comes to you and says, "This product
   will *almost* do what we need. But it just doesn't use
   our preferred formula for this one calculation. Let's
   just get the source code from the vendor and make the
   fix ourselves." How do you answer him? Why? Then
   he goes on to say, "And, by the way, our old system
   displays money less than a dollar in cents, rather than
   $0.xx, so while we're in there, let's just change that,
   too." Now what do you say? Why?

9. What do you think the testing challenges will be for
   your new open, COTS-based system?

10. How will you handle the coordination of vendor's
    upgrades with new releases of your system? List key
    items that will need to be updated or redone every time
    you present your users with a new system release.

11. Your system integrators have everything working,
    using a number of COTS products, and you've fielded
    your first release of the system. But one of your help
    desk personnel comes to you, saying that she has had a
    flood of calls from users who complain that the system
    is not providing timely response. Describe a method
    you could use to figure out what is going wrong
    among those products.

12. You are in charge of a division that has several projects doing open, COTS-based system acquisition. Will this change how the individual projects are staffed? For example, do you take some staff from each project to put on a central COTS product IPT that is a resource for all the projects? What are the pros and cons of this approach? Has power changed in the organization?

13. Many people believe the total cost of an open, COTS-based acquisition is cheaper than custom development. Would you say that the cost of *managing* this type of acquisition—as opposed to a pure development model, for example—is also cheaper? What implications do you draw from this?

12

Procurement Practices

This chapter describes the procurement aspects of your approach to system acquisition. As we have defined it, acquisition covers all the activities performed to procure, develop, and maintain a system.

procurement ➡ The act of buying goods and services.

When it comes to procuring the services needed to create the system you want, you may have two choices. One might be to obtain the services from an internal organization. The other would be to contract for the services from outside your organization. Once you make that decision, you still must decide what services to acquire and how, when, and from whom to acquire them.

To do this, it is important that you understand the procurement approaches you can take. Here, we will provide information to help you assess your procurement practices for an open, COTS-based systems approach and to change them, if necessary.

12.1 Contracting Strategies

You can use a variety of contracting strategies when acquiring a system. They make up a spectrum of approaches, five of which—snapshots along the way—are depicted in Table 12.1. Each row in the table represents a selected step in the acquisition process. *You* in a cell means that you control the step, *Contractor* means that the integration

TABLE 12.1 Contracting Strategies

Steps	Strategy 1 Control	Strategy 2 Direct	Strategy 3 Guide	Strategy 4 Initiate	Strategy 5 Joint
Specify requirements	You	You	You	You	IPT
Select/recommend standards set	You	You	You	Contractor	IPT
Select/recommend standards	You	You	Contractor	Contractor	IPT
Profile standards	You	You	Contractor	Contractor	IPT
Conduct conform- ance qualification	You	Contractor	Contractor	Contractor	IPT
Select/recommend standards-based COTS products	You	Contractor	Contractor	Contractor	IPT
Integrate system	Contractor	Contractor	Contractor	Contractor	Contractor

contractor controls the step, and *IPT* (integrated product team) denotes joint responsibility.

We can recap these strategies as follows:

- Strategy 1 (Control): You specify the system requirements, standards, profile, and standards-based implementations and conduct conformance qualification. The contractor integrates the system.

- Strategy 2 (Direct): You collect and specify requirements, standards, and a profile. The contractor conducts conformance qualification, selects the standards-based implementations, and integrates the system.

- Strategy 3 (Guide): You specify system requirements and the set of standards you wish to use for the system. The contractor creates the standards profile, conducts conformance qualification, selects the standards-based implementations, and integrates the system.

- Strategy 4 (Initiate): You specify the system requirements. The contractor does the rest.

- Strategy 5 (Joint): You and the contractor share decision-making responsibility through one or more integrated product teams (IPTs).

The key difference among the five strategies is in how they spread the risks and responsibilities among various participants. For example, strategy 1 places a heavy burden on the acquirer with respect to both risk and responsibility, whereas strategy 4 shifts a large share of that burden to the contractor, and strategy 5 shares the risk and responsibility more equitably.

These are just some of the possible combinations. Strategy 5 is probably the preferred one. In fact, a major emphasis of govenment acquisition reform has been to shift acquisitions toward strategy 5.

Any system acquisition strategy must account for a broad range of requirements—for example, cost and usability requirements—beyond those for the use of COTS products and an open systems approach. Therefore, the contracting strategies discussed earlier must be part of your overall acquisition approach.

Depending on the contracting strategy you choose, each activity in the system acquisition process can be the responsibility of any combination of the following:

Your responsibilities

- Higher-level managers
- Project manager
- Project staff
- Contractors
- Vendors

You, as the project manager, must ensure that all the activities are properly addressed, regardless of who is responsible. Thus, you may need to ensure that sound criteria are used when selecting standards, standards profiles, and COTS products. You must be able to approve or to reject the contractor's or other technical team's choices with adequate knowledge and confidence. Remember, you are ultimately the one who has the greatest opportunity to make the acquisition a success.

Controlling the acquisition and managing risks can be more challenging than ever before because you must do more than just ensure that the implementations satisfy the requirements. You must also ensure that the implementations conform to the selected standards and represent sensible use of the marketplace.

12.2 Contracting Documentation

At the heart of any contract are the documents that embody the agreement. The following sections describe strategies and guidelines for the four key aspects of contract documentation: requests for proposals, statements of work, instructions to offerors, and evaluation factors. These documents and the processes used to create and manage them can be used by both industry and government contracting.

12.2.1 Contract Types

Procurement is accomplished through the use of a *contract*. Various types of contracts are used by both industry and government. For example, following are some of the more frequently used types of contracts in government [DSMC 98].

- A *fixed-price contract* provides a price that is not subject to any adjustment on the basis of the contractor's cost experience in performing the contract. One variation on this is a *fixed-price incentive firm contract,* which uses an incentive whereby the contractor's profit is increased or decreased by a predetermined share of an overrun or underrun. A firm target is established from which to later compute the overrun or underrun, and a ceiling price is set as the maximum amount the government will pay.

- A *cost-reimbursement contract* promises payment to the contractor of allowable costs incurred in the performance of the contract, to the extent prescribed in the contract. It establishes an estimate of the total cost for the purposes of obligation of funds and establishing a ceiling that the contractor may not exceed, except at its own risk, without prior approval or subsequent ratification of the contracting officers. Among variations on this are

  - *Cost-plus-fixed-fee*, which provides for the payment of a fixed fee to the contractor; once negotiated, the fee does not vary with actual cost but may be adjusted as a result of any subsequent changes in the scope of work or services

- *Cost-plus-incentive-fee*, which provides for a fee that is adjusted by formula in accordance with the relationship of total allowable costs to target costs; the provision for increase or decrease in the fee, depending on allowable costs of contract performance, is designed as an incentive for the contractor to increase the efficiency of performance

- A *time and materials contract* promises an hourly rate for labor and a fixed price for materials owed to the contractor for the entire transaction described in the contract.

12.2.2 Requests for Proposals

Part of using contractors or a technical development organization for system development is developing a request for proposal (RFP) or equivalent outline of what you want done.

Before developing an RFP, *the contracting strategy—* refer to Table 12.1—*you plan to follow is determined*. The strategy you choose determines the contractor's responsibilities and risks on the project and therefore influences how you write your RFP.

Determine your contracting strategy

One important element of your contract approach should be attention to incentives. How are you going to encourage your contractor to be faithful to the tenets of open systems and to truly work to optimize exploitation of the marketplace?

Incentives

No one is motivated by the prospect of making less money. A contractor who is simply squeezed will find reasons and ways to do more work. For example, if the contractor is used to earning his money from doing lots of programming, you will have to find a way to make use of COTS products equally lucrative for the contractor's enterprise. You might want to make use of award fees that recognize the contractor's technology refresh efforts. One program projected the opportunities for reducing the number of cards in a command and control system; for every dollar the contractor saved through technology refresh, by reducing the number of cards more than the projection, the contractor got $0.50. You need to find similar ways for rewarding contractors for making use of standards and COTS products rather than custom developing everything themselves.

Determine contractor qualifications

When developing your RFP, *contractors with appropriate open and COTS-based system qualifications are sought*. Look for contractors who

- Have relevant COTS and open system experience
- Share your vision of open and COTS-based systems
- Are likely to succeed in an open and COTS-based systems approach

When you develop an open or COTS-based systems RFP, focus on[1]

- The statement of work (SOW) and specifications
- Instructions to offerors
- Evaluation factors

These are the sections in which you can do the most to make clear your open and COTS-based system intentions.

Balance your needs

A balance is struck between system requirements and the need to create an open or COTS-based system. This need for balance can be described as follows:

> Achieving standardization is often in direct opposition to the use of performance specifications and COTS (commercial off-the-shelf) software. It is necessary to obtain a balance between these two ends of the spectrum by using good business and technical judgement in determining the best approach to reduce the total cost of ownership. [DON 96]

This "balancing" will require you to make trade-offs. For example, you may initially have a requirement for a multilevel secure system. However, no product may meet the multilevel security requirements, but other products may be available that will suffice if you are willing to make the trade-off.

12.2.3 Statements of Work

A statement of work (SOW), a necessary document in the contracting process, identifies the tasks to be completed under the contract. The SOW is traditionally part of the RFP.

---

1. In government, these three focus areas correspond to RFP sections C, L, and M, respectively.

More recently, the federal government and other organizations have been using a different approach to the development of SOWs, as a result of acquisition reform. This approach is based on the notion of a *statement of objectives* (SOO). A SOO is a very short—in some cases, less than a page—statement of general direction for the intended qualities of the resulting system. Using the SOO shifts the responsibility of preparing the SOW from the government to those responding to the solicitation. The rationale for this approach is to lower costs by encouraging innovative contract options and flexible design solutions. The SOO captures the top-level requirements and objectives for the solicitation and allows the bidders significant freedom in the structure and definition of SOW tasks.

The following topics should be covered when developing your statements of work or objectives and specifications. Who performs the work on each of these items depends on the contracting strategy you select.

The use of open system implementations is required in your statement of work or objectives. Information about the degree and the nature of openness for each implementation needs to be made available. Depending on the contracting strategy, require that the contractor specify which standard or standards will be used, how they will be used in the system, and why. Require that the products not only *implement* interface standards but also *use* the standard interfaces to interact; that is, the standards define the interactions among the components. The phrase "shall provide and use the functionality defined . . ." instead of "shall implement" may help when it is difficult to find implementations of a standard.

Specify openness and use of COTS products

A migration[2] plan is required for nonconformant implementations. This plan provides a chance that you can bring the implementations into conformance over time, even

Require migration planning

---

2. For the purposes of this book, we use the term migration to refer to the gradual evolution of a system from being predominantly custom built to being predominantly open systems and COTS-based. In contrast, the term transition is used to refer to the evolution of an organization from custom-development practices to COTS-based and open systems practices.

Specifying Openness Carefully

In 1992, the United States Coast Guard needed a new common workstation and wanted it to be an open system. The Coast Guard wrote the RFP accordingly, specifically requiring a POSIX-conformant operating system. The contract was awarded to a bidder whose implementation included Windows NT. However, the award was protested, based on the assertion that the winning bidder had not provided an open system. The General Services Administration (GSA) Board of Contract Appeals upheld the award, despite the fact that Windows NT's main claim to fame has nothing to do with its POSIX-conformant interface. (Yes, it does in fact have such an interface.) What happened?

In the words of the RFP, there was no requirement that the standards-conformant interfaces be the means by which the interactions of the (open) system took place. It was sufficient to meet the terms of the RFP for the components to support the specified interfaces: They didn't have to *use* them. As a consequence, the GSA Board of Contract Appeals determined that a system that had those interfaces present met the terms of the RFP and upheld the award [GSA 95].

if it is not possible now. Be sure to request cost-benefit analyses in migration planning.

Require market research

Market research is required and should include such topics as

- Availability of COTS products
- How closely COTS products correspond to requirements
- Vendor supportability plans
- Planning for replacement of obsolete COTS products
- Pin-for-pin interchangeability for hardware and software product interchangeability

Refer to Section 11.2, in particular the section Perform market research.

Frame your requirements

Requirements are framed in either a "thick" or a "thin" statement of work (SOW). A "thick" SOW includes all the requirements relevant to the RFP. A "thin" SOW generally includes only the *mandatory* requirements.

Using a "thin" SOW and specifications document allows contractors to propose solutions that may include the latest technology. Also, the evaluation of solutions can be based on the proposal with the "best value." The SOO represents the extreme version of a "thin" approach.

State the material requirements in terms of performance, form, fit, and function rather than design. Tell the integration contractor what you need, not how to build it.

Material requirements

A technology refreshment/enhancement clause is included in your statement of work because all standards specifications and COTS products, mature or not, are likely to evolve over the life of your system. Often, when you use immature or nonstandard specifications, you may include those specifications in the RFP, thereby preventing the developers from taking advantage of ongoing improvements to the specification. Including text about technology refreshment or technology enhancement allows you to include the specification in the RFP *and* account for growth and advancement of the system. Doing so will also support your ability to upgrade underlying technologies and COTS products even if the standards do not change.

Plan for technology refreshment

Integrated product teams (IPTs) are used where appropriate. They are designed to combine the skills and strengths of your team members, whether acquirers or developers, or contracting or engineering professionals.

Use IPTs

> **integrated product team** ➟ An interdisciplinary team composed of representatives from appropriate functional disciplines working together to build successful programs, identify and resolve issues, and make sound and timely recommendations to facilitate decision making [DSMC 98].

IPTs are broad-based teams that include your organization and contractors and perhaps other stakeholders as well. These interdisciplinary teams develop products—specifications, designs, software, integrated subsystems—by drawing on the strengths and knowledge of each team member.

Training in open systems and COTS products is required for the contractor team, including specifications to measure the effectiveness of training, as part of the statement of work. There may come a point in time when this will no longer be necessary, but until an open, COTS-based systems approach is part of everyone's training and experience, training will still be essential.

Require training

Integrated Product Teams

We hear a lot about the use of IPTs and the assumption that their use will almost guarantee success. The following is based on a true story. A very senior manager was faced with a serious problem, and an underling in his organization suggested forming an IPT to address it. "No!" the manager said, almost yelling. "I don't want some damn IPT. Get a couple of smart people, put 'em in a room, and tell them to solve this thing!"

12.2.4 Instructions to Prospective Responders

In addition to the request for proposal and SOW or SOO, you may want to provide additional instructions to bidders, depending on their responsibilities on the project. The following paragraphs are examples of other information you may want them to provide.

Solicit definition of "open system"

Bidders are required to define what "open systems" are as part of their response. This not only ensures that you share the same understanding of open systems but also reinforces your commitment to open systems. Without this reinforcement—and attendant insight into the bidder's point of view—the bidder might otherwise see the solicitation for opinions and alternatives as a way out of pursuing an open systems approach.

Solicit experience with open and COTS-based systems

Evidence of the bidder's past experience is required. Special emphasis is put on the experience with and understanding of open systems and the use of COTS products. Evidence of experience might include past performance and lessons learned, especially when using standards and standards-based COTS hardware and software.

Evidence of understanding might include describing how system features provide portability, interoperability, maintainability, vendor independence, technology insertion, compatibility with other products, reusability, scalability, and improved user productivity. How they prove conformance of their implementations to the profiles and standards cited in your specifications could be used to indicate how well bidders understand the nuances of open systems. Bidders' demonstration of familiarity with the marketplace will indicate some of their other qualifications for your job.

An outline of the open systems migration plan and the project's major tasks is required when there is an existing system. A migration plan includes the bidders' definitions and analyses of the current system, the target system, and the migration strategy.

Plan the migration

The bidders' opinions of the specifications, standards, SOW, cost, and schedule are invited. The bidders are also asked to offer alternatives with rationale. Ask bidders for a cost-benefit analysis as part of their proposals. When asking for such input, reiterate your commitment to openness and the marketplace.

Solicit their opinions

Search for Insight

One very experienced project manager said that his real concern was finding out how smart the contractor was. "You can put out lots of requirements, lots of specifications, and tell the contractor exactly what you would like them to do. But that's the easy thing for them to respond to. I always ask them a sprinkling of very hard questions; I want to see how they respond to see if they know enough to pull this thing off."

12.2.5 Evaluation Factors

To be sure that the factors you use to evaluate prospective contractors are clear and well understood, do the following.

Your open system philosophy is clearly stated, as well as your commitment to open, COTS-based systems.

State your philosophy

The evaluation factors that are specific to open, COTS-based systems are defined and, if possible, numerical weights, or priorities, are assigned to them. These new evaluation factors may include

Define factors

- Open systems architecture
- Life-cycle support proposal
- Strategy for using COTS products
- Technology refreshment program
- Strength of experience and understanding of open, COTS-based systems

- Understanding of open, COTS-based systems and their role as an objective in this acquisition
- Adherence to an open systems approach
- Inclusion of optional requirements
- Quality of alternative proposals put forward by the bidder
- Strength of market knowledge
- Validity of business case analysis

Warn prospective contractors that you may award the contract to someone other than the low bidder and that you will use your prior knowledge and experience with them as well as their past performance references to validate claims in the proposals. Although these provisions are normal in dealings between commercial enterprises, they may be relatively new behavior for some government project staffs.

12.3 The Role of the Players

In this book, our goal is to address acquisition for both industry and government. There are several differences in the way that government and industry conduct business. To help you understand these differences, we compare the way government and industry usually buy things.

12.3.1 Government Procurement

The rules

Because of multiple constraints, government procurement is more complex and difficult than industry procurement. The effort to streamline government acquisition regulations is meant to harmonize government practices with those of industry and thus save money. Many of the rules that the government must follow are meant to protect taxpayer money, promote social change, and ensure fairness in the process.

Factors

When it contracts for something, the government is driven by factors that go beyond system requirements. The government must

- Comply with regulations that dictate the contracting process and other aspects of acquisition
- Meet government needs that are beyond the requirements documented for the system
- Maximize the opportunity for offerors to sell to the government, by ensuring open competition and providing a protest mechanism
- Protect taxpayer dollars by ensuring that money is spent wisely
- Consider socioeconomic factors, such as promoting opportunities for minority-owned businesses

Why Is the Government Different?

When discussing acquisition, especially procurement, it is important to understand why government is different from industry. The article "Acquisition Reform: It's Not As Easy As It Seems" [Cancian 95] contains the following list of eight reasons that the defense industry is different. Although the government has been working to decrease such differences, most will continue to exist and play a role in government acquisition.

1. There is one buyer—a monopsony—and hence no true market.
2. For any particular item, there is often only one or at most a very few sellers.
3. The user's "bottom line" is not financial but performance. Competition therefore strongly emphasizes performance over price.
4. Major contracts are signed years before actual results are available and therefore must be based on estimates of cost, schedule, and performance.
5. Performance is difficult to judge, and is often judged subjectively, except for the rare occasions when the nation actually uses military force on a large scale.
6. The enterprise operates with public funds, the use of which is held to a different standard than private funds.
7. Decision making power is diffuse, being shared between the executive branch and the legislative branch (with its many committees and subcommittees).
8. Decisions and operations are conducted in the open, under great public scrutiny.

Recent changes

The government has experienced major changes in its procurement practices, such as

- A decline in the use of MIL-SPECs and MIL-STDs
- An increase in the use of commercial products
- A decline in the number of standards and specifications imposed on a contractor
- A change in the emphasis of economic considerations

Note that these changes apply to buying solutions and represent a movement toward participation in the open marketplace for products and standards. However, these changes can also affect building solutions as well as buying them. For example, VME (Versa-Module European) bus cards are not being developed to full military specifications, because the rest of the VME device consists of products that conform to industry standards.

Reducing Military Specifications and Standards

The Cooperative Engagement Capability (CEC) program office, a Department of Defense program, changed its acquisition practices in keeping with acquisition reform, revising its system specification and statement of work so that the contractor had no design restrictions. It was the responsibility of the contractor to develop a program plan that explained how it would meet the requirements of the system specification. Because the CEC did not force military specifications and standards on the contractor, the number of military specifications and standards in the CEC contract dropped from 125 to 17 [Strickland 95].

These changes also generate changes in the government's approach to support, prompting the government to

- Use existing commercial support and data
- Develop new, in-house support only if there is a critical-mission need or substantial cost savings
- Modify existing support to allow maximum COTS product use, if necessary

- Use manufacturers' or suppliers' distribution channels
  when cost and effect on readiness and supportability
  are acceptable.

Focus on continual investment when you consider
support for COTS products. For example, if you are contracting for support, you may need to use procurement
techniques, such as warranties and data rights escrow.
These techniques are alternatives to new development.

The trend in government acquisition is clear. The fed- **Future**
eral acquisition laws are becoming increasingly oriented
toward nondevelopmental items and commercial practices.
It is possible that the government may become more like
a commercial entity; some call it commercial-military
integration.

The streamlining of acquisition laws[3] has

- Created stronger language about the use of nondevel-
  opmental items
- Extended the definition of commercial products to
  include services
- Changed regulations about data rights
- Changed regulations about technology transfer

The DoD, the Department of Justice, and the Federal
Trade Commission (Bureau of Competition) have jointly
worked to examine antitrust regulations in anticipation of
DoD downsizing. These agencies have recommended that
no antitrust exemption be given for the defense industry
and are examining mergers to make sure that there is still
competition.

Systems development in the DoD is very volatile. Laws
are changing, the regulations are changing, and the way to
conduct business is changing too. To be successful in the
midst of all of this change is to learn to make these changes
meet your needs or learn to meet your needs despite these
changes.

---

3. For a thorough, interesting discussion behind acquisition reform, see
[DoD 93]. Despite being about 6 inches thick and weighing more than
10 pounds, this document is extremely complete, including some of the
history behind particular acquisition laws.

12.3.2 Industry Procurement

The rules

When acquiring systems, industry has few rules to follow beyond those that govern all business in the country or state. If a company wants to buy products or services from another organization, few rules limit those purchases.

State governments, not the federal government, are the primary source for laws dealing with commercial transactions in the United States. In general, these laws are described in the *Uniform Commercial Code*. This code deals with laws that govern such aspects of commercial transactions as sales, letters of credit, investment securities, and contract rights. Thus, each state may tailor the code to suit its own needs—similar to a standards profile.

Factors

When companies in industry contract for something, they are driven primarily by economic factors. These factors include

- Maximizing profit and efficiency by getting the best value for the company
- Meeting company needs, such as maintaining excellent customer service and increasing market share

Contract types

The contracts that industry uses can be tailored to every transaction. Most vendors have standard contracts they like to use; however, the company buying products and services can sometimes negotiate the contract to include provisions that protect the rights of the buyer. A vendor that has many buyers may dictate the terms and conditions of the contract, in spite of the buyers' wants and needs.

Changes

Industry has experienced some change in its *acquisition* practices as well but few changes in its *procurement* practices. These changes include

- An increase in the use of and attention to standards
- Increased membership and participation in standards development groups, particularly consortia
- Increased cooperation between companies to increase their influence on the overall market in terms of de facto standards, such as Java

Note that these changes apply mainly to cooperation with, and attention to, entities that influence system development decisions outside of the corporation.

Procurement by industry is less likely to change sig- **Future**
nificantly, although e-commerce is a distinct exception.
However, companies must take a broader view of the marketplace, technology, and standards. Being aware of the
business climate and trends for these three areas can mitigate the risk of becoming permanently tied to suppliers
and products that do not change with the requirements of
your system.

12.4 Government Contracting Concerns

Differences among contracting officers and their interpretations of regulations may affect your ability to do all you
need to for a successful open, COTS-based acquisition. A
contracting officer's flexible interpretation can be very
useful and important to your success, but a conservative or
narrow viewpoint may create roadblocks. Laws define the
government's relationship with its contractors; therefore,
you might not always be able to do all the things that are
considered best commercial practice. Best commercial
practice is not necessarily legal government practice, even
if it should be.

Greater benefits of open, COTS-based systems may
occur *across* programs and *across* departments or sub-
units. (One risk of this, of course, is that new dependencies
may emerge.) For example, the Office of the Secretary of
Defense (OSD) has policies for commonality and for sharing of widely used products across systems, such as the
Defense Information Infrastructure Common Operating
Environment (DII COE). This can be a double-edged
sword. Commitment and support at high levels may help
and may lead to enforcement of standards, but it may also
lead to restrictions and demands that managers conform to
greater levels of commonality than necessary or desirable
from the isolated viewpoint of a single system.

Elements of the open systems movement include
Department of Defense Directive (DODD) 5000.1 and
Department of Defense Instruction (DODI) 5000.2 [DoD
00d; 00e]. Other important references are the Federal

Acquisition Regulations (FAR) and the Defense Federal Acquisition Regulation Supplement (DFARS), the *Buying Commercial and Nondevelopmental Items (CANDI): A Handbook* [SD-2], and documentation about market research [SD-5]. Other useful information can also be found on the Defense Acquisition Deskbook [DAD].

12.5 Summary

This chapter has addressed procurement in the context of open, COTS-based acquisitions.

Contracting strategies

We described a number of alternative contracting strategies, which are distinguished by division of responsibility among the relevant parties. The contract strategies include

- Control
- Direct
- Guide
- Initiate
- Joint

Contracting documents

We described various contract types and key contracting documents:

- RFPs
- SOWs or SOOs
- Additional instructions to responders
- Proposal evaluation factors

We closed with some discussion about how industry and government approach procurement.

12.6 Food for Thought

1. Are your acquisition people ready to make the transition to open and COTS-based systems? Think about each of your people individually. Which ones are

likely to be enthusiastic about the changes? Which ones are likely to present barriers and challenges? Remember to consider the technical personnel who are key to acquisition, as well as your contracting officers and buyers.

2. How do you expect to differentiate between contractor proposals for an open, COTS-based systems project? What contractor qualifications or attributes will be most critical for your success? How will you ask for the things you need to know to make this choice among competitors?

3. Contractors need to have incentives for changing their old habits. What ways can you use award fees or incentive fees to encourage good open, COTS-based system engineering?

4. It is generally accepted that 50 percent or more of the life-cycle cost is in maintenance. Given this, how would you put a weight on an evaluation factor for maintenance to reflect that?

5. A government proposal is issued for what looks like a large, complex system. The proposal calls out an open system approach and heavy use of COTS products. Then, you notice that it will be a firm, fixed-price contract. Does this type of contract change your approach to responding and, if so, how?

6. You are contracting for a system that has many component implementations, and you expect multiple suppliers. Develop a process and a draft agreement, to which you want vendors to agree, to handle the situation when there are integration problems.

7. How does your choice of a contract type, such as cost-plus versus fixed-price, depend on your overall acquisition model? For example, if you use a waterfall model versus an evolutionary model, what are the implications for the contract types you may consider using?

PART FOUR

Considering Acquisition

By now you know that acquisition of systems based on open standards and COTS products represents a different way of doing business. All acquisition is done in some *framework,* and we want to describe the properties of a general framework. We can then create various acquisition *models* based on that framework. We want to show you how that approach can provide you the information you need for your own acquisition. But we also need to indicate some of the details of the activities that you will no doubt perform for the acquisition of your open, COTS-based system, and that is addressed here. It is the richness of living in this new world that brings you challenges— and opportunities.

Chapters in Part Four

13

An Acquisition Framework

One of our concerns in this book is the role of open systems and COTS products in the context of acquisition management. Recall that by *acquisition,* we mean the activities associated with the procurement, development, and maintenance of a system.

Our previous focus has been on the principles and details associated with the use of open systems and COTS products. In this chapter, we will develop a general acquisition framework. This will give us a common background on which to later address specific acquisition models and how open systems and COTS products affect acquisition.

13.1 Defining a Framework

All acquisition is performed in the context of an overall framework. But, as we will see, various acquisition models can be constructed from a common framework.

> **acquisition framework** ➡ A description of a general set of acquisition activities, acquisition events, and the relations among them, including timing properties.

Acquisition frameworks are important because they provide a common language and concepts that can be used to discuss an acquisition model. Then, a particular acquisition model can be thought of as an instance of the framework. Understanding the framework allows us to gain insight into the models that are derived from that framework. Stated differently, we can reuse our knowledge about the framework in the context of models based on that framework. This should remind you of an architecture; recall that some key properties of an architecture are components and their functionality, as well as connectivity (see Section 5.3).

13.2 Acquisition Activities

Successful acquisition of a system, including hardware and software, is a result of performing a number of acquisition *activities*. These activities are the building blocks that describe the work to be performed. We separate these activities into two groups so that we can manage the overall complexity of the acquisition in a simpler way—an example of the *divide-and-conquer* approach. The delineation of management and technical activities also suggests characteristics of the people responsible for each activity.

Technical
activities

Many different acquisition activities are possible. We have spent a good part of this book on technical activities for open systems and the use of COTS products. An example of a set of traditional technical acquisition activities includes

- *Feasibility analysis:* concept models and life-cycle feasibility
- *Requirements definition:* requirements specification and management
- *System design:* architecture specification, top-level and detailed design, interface specifications, and draft user manuals
- *Implementation:* development of code and unit testing
- *Integration:* integration of implementations and verification of function and performance at a system level
- *Operation and maintenance:* system deployment, defect correction and addition of minor changes, as well as major upgrades

We will treat these activities as a basic set of technical acquisition activities.

In addition to technical activities, some activities focus more on the management aspects of the acquisition. A minimal set of such activities includes:

Management activities

- *Project management:* planning and tracking of budgets, costs, and schedules
- *Risk management:* identification, tracking, and mitigation planning for project risks
- *Contract management:* contract specification, proposal evaluation, contract award, tracking, and oversight

We will treat these activities as a basic set of management acquisition activities.

13.3 Acquisition Events

An acquisition event is a condition whose existence requires a response by an activity in the framework. Acquisition events are important because they provide the basis for linking acquisition activities together to model an acquisition process.

Acquisition events can be *internally* or *externally* initiated with respect to the scope of the acquisition project. An internal event is one that is initiated within the scope of the project. An example of this might be initiation of a risk management review. In contrast, an externally generated event is one that is initiated outside the project. For example, if a project is using a particular hardware platform and the manufacturer upgrades the platform, this represents an external event. It is important because the project must respond to the event, deciding whether to upgrade future purchases of the hardware platform.

Internal and external events

Just as acquisition activities can be grouped into management and technical categories, so too can acquisition events. For example, a decision to allocate or reallocate budget to a project is essentially a management choice and could be represented as a management event. On the other hand, initiation of a critical design review associated with a development is primarily technical in nature.[1]

Acquisition decision points

Some acquisition events are termed *acquisition decision points*. These events signify "go-or-no-go" decisions. The statement that "the project can proceed to system integration testing when a certain defect density has been achieved in all its subsystems" is an example of an acquisition decision point. Acquisition decision points can be either technical or management in nature.

13.4 Relations among Activities and Events

The two main relations that are important to an acquisition framework are relations among acquisition activities and among events and activities.

Relations among activities

Relations among acquisition activities typically indicate some form of dependency. For example, the activity of requirements specification might be followed by the activity of high-level system design. This indicates that the system design is dependent on the requirements specification. Note that *chains* of activities are possible, which means that several activities are related to one another, in a serial fashion.

Relations among events and activities

Also possible are relations among events and activities and vice versa. Two examples of this follow.

- An acquisition event representing release of project funding may initiate an activity representing acquisition budget planning.
- Completion of unit testing—an activity—may initiate a decision—an event—to place the tested code under configuration management.

Examples such as these also indicate some form of dependency between the activity and an associated event.

---

1. Sometimes, the question arises of how to characterize an event, either technical or management. In many cases, the type of event—technical or management—is determined by the type of the activity responsible for dealing with the event.

13.5 Timing Considerations

Timing is everything, they say. This remark also applies to
the acquisition framework. Until now, the discussion has
been focused principally on the *structural properties* of the
framework and relations among its elements. For example,
activities provide a structure, and relations and events help
express the connectivity among the structural components.

But this structural aspect is not the whole story. To the **Timing**
contrary, it lacks an especially important ingredient. That is, **properties**
a basic question relates to *when* activities are performed and
when an event occurs. Thus, a framework has a temporal
aspect to it because we need to know when things happen.

In fact, the temporal aspects permitted in the framework are a key point that allows us to differentiate acquisition models that are based on that framework. For example,
suppose that we have three activities, denoted A, B, and C.
There are a number of different ways these activities can
be performed.

Figure 13.1 shows two cases illustrating different ways
the acquisition activities can be ordered. In the first case,
the three activities are performed one after another, in a
serial manner. However, in the second case, the same
activities are performed in parallel, at the same time.

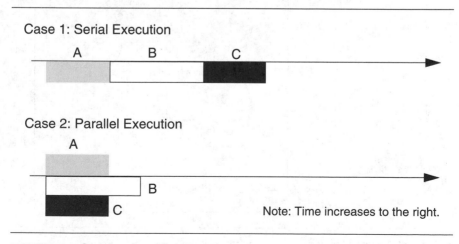

Case 1: Serial Execution

A B C

Case 2: Parallel Execution

A

B

C

Note: Time increases to the right.

FIGURE 13.1 Serial and parallel execution.

Importance of timing properties

The alternatives shown in Figure 13.1 represent two extremes; in reality, some activities may be performed in parallel and some serially. The point to note, however, is that the amount of potential parallelism can have major implications for the execution structure associated with the framework. The timing properties of how an acquisition is conducted is fundamental to both the acquisition and the management of that acquisition!

13.6 Framework Summary

Figure 13.2 summarizes the discussion of the framework, illustrating the relations between acquisition activities and internal and external acquisition events. For example, the

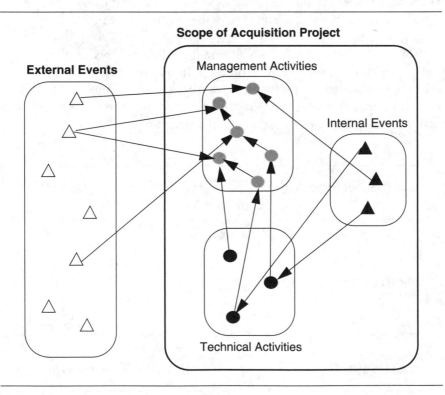

FIGURE 13.2 Illustrating the acquisition framework.

relations between both internal and external events and acquisition activities can be management or technical in nature. Note also the relations among various acquisition activities. However, Figure 13.2 illustrates only the static aspects of the framework elements; we do not show the timing characteristics of the framework.

This presentation is primarily intuitive in nature. But some work has formalized the nature of the acquisition framework [Meyers 2001]. Rather than pursue a formalization of the model, however, we will illustrate applications of the framework in the next chapter.

13.7 Acquisition Strategies

Understanding acquisition activities, especially in the context of an overall acquisition framework, is an important consideration for a project manager. But another element must be accounted for: the acquisition strategy.

> **acquisition strategy** ➡ A pattern of acquisition actions designed to accomplish the goals of a project.

A strategy is a high-level concept. Some of the questions that a project manager must consider when developing an acquisition strategy follow.

- What are our overriding goals and constraints? For example is the schedule rigid but the cost somewhat flexible?

- What acquisition approach and model are most relevant?

- What are the key assumptions on which we base our strategy? For example, what do we believe about future technologies or the likelihood of changes to the system?

- How much of a given activity will be performed by our staff rather than others, such as contractors?

- What alternative plans do we need, and when do we change our current plan?

An acquisition strategy provides guidance to the overall project. The acquisition strategy helps you translate an acquisition framework into an acquisition model that meets your needs. Success of an acquisition project depends on a sound acquisition strategy and an acquisition model that conforms to that strategy.

13.8 Summary

We defined an *acquisition framework* as a set of acquisition activities, acquisition events, the relations among them, and their associated timing properties. We also specified a set of basic *acquisition activities*, both management and technical in nature. A minimal set includes those shown in Table 13.1. We also discussed some aspects of acquisition strategies.

13.9 Food for Thought

1. How do the acquisition activities listed in Section 13.2 compare to those you are currently using? What are the differences?

2. It is sometimes helpful to discuss acquisition phases. An *acquisition phase* is simply a group of related acquisition activities having an overall timing charac-

TABLE 13.1 Basic Acquisition Activities

Management Activities	Technical Activities
Project management	Feasibility analysis
Contract management	Requirements definition
Risk management	Product design
	Implementation
	Integration
	Operation and maintenance

teristic, such as beginning and ending dates. How could you include phases in an acquisition framework?

3. Consider a table whose rows and columns denote acquisition activities. Pick at least five such activities and put a checkmark in the cell of the table where the activities can be performed in parallel. What are the advantages of possible parallelism? What other activities require synchronization? Does it look as though a parallel model is in some sense *better* than a serial model? Why or why not?

4. Knowing that we discussed acquisition decision points, your boss thinks they're a neat idea. She also heard about *exit criteria* that must be satisfied in order to proceed with an acquisition. That is, if the exit criteria are not satisfied for a given decision point, some action must be taken. What exit criteria do you choose, and why? Finally, whom in your office do you ask to review this work you've done, and what made you pick that person?

5. Describe the relative strengths and weaknesses of executing acquisition activities in a serial versus a parallel manner.

6. How would you describe your organization's current acquisition strategy?

7. You would probably agree that versatility in acquisition is important for your project. How much of your management resources do you apply to developing and modifying alternative acquisition strategies?

14

Acquisition Models

In this chapter, we apply the acquisition framework to describe a number of well-known acquisition models. This information will help us when we consider open systems and COTS products in the overall acquisition context. That subject will be discussed in Chapter 15.

14.1 Characterizing Acquisition Models

The acquisition framework we discussed in the previous chapter provides a general approach. We now define acquisition model.

> **acquisition model** ⟼ A particular description of acquisition activities, acquisition events, and the relations among them, including timing properties, based on an acquisition framework.

You may hear people talk about a *waterfall model* or an *evolutionary model*. Each of these models can be cast in the context of an acquisition framework. Some characteristics that differentiate one model from another are

- Acquisition *activities*. The set of activities included in the model is a key differentiator. For example, a pure development model may have an activity for software coding, but that same activity may not be present in a pure COTS-based acquisition model.
- Acquisition *events*. The main importance of including acquisition events is that they indicate that some

acquisition activity must be performed. For example, vendor upgrade of a COTS product is an acquisition event that may warrant evaluation of the new product release.

- The *relations* among activities and/or events. Given a set of activities and events, the manner in which they are related is another static characteristic of the model. For example, performing unit test after code development illustrates a relation between the activities unit test and code development.

- *Timing considerations.* The last differentiator deals with the timing properties associated with the elements of an acquisition model. As we noted in Section 13.5, activities can be performed in either a serial manner or a parallel manner. The same activities can be performed in different order, yielding different model behavior.

Many different acquisition models are possible. A few models are well known, and we will describe them in this chapter. One of the key jobs of a project manager is to clearly define the model that is relevant to a particular project. Sometimes, project managers need to step back and look at the big picture. Ask yourself what acquisition model you use. How does it work? How can you make it work better?

14.2 Waterfall Model

One basic acquisition model is based on the technical activities defined in Section 13.2. In addition, we assume that each activity is performed in sequence. The simplicity of this basic model stems from the fact that there is little synchronization among various activities performed. In fact, this simple model is related to the well-known *waterfall model* [Royce 1970]. Among other things, this model places emphasis on the development of documentation.

You may already be familiar with the waterfall model. We use it here to illustrate how the framework is applied to create an acquisition model. Figure 14.1 shows the traditional view of the waterfall model. An alternative way to show

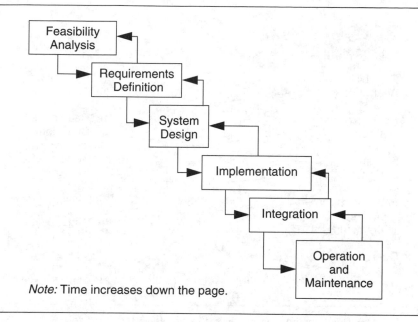

Note: Time increases down the page.

FIGURE 14.1 Simple waterfall acquisition model.

the relations between the activities, which we introduce here and will use for the more complex case of open, COTS-based systems, is shown in Figure 14.2.

We can relate our specification of the basic waterfall model to the general framework as shown in Table 14.1. Some of the principal characteristics of this model are

- *Highly serialized* between different activities: a timing property
- *Minimal iteration* between different activities:[1] a property of relations among activities

The emphasis of the waterfall model is on a development perspective. However, development is only one aspect of the acquisition process. Next, we show how to refine the waterfall model by considering additional acquisition characteristics.

---

1. The original work on the waterfall model emphasized close coupling between neighboring activities but recognized that the coupling could also extend to other neighbors.

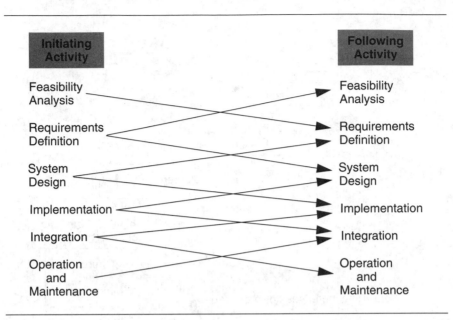

FIGURE 14.2 Relations between activities in simple waterfall model.

TABLE 14.1 Aspects of Simple Waterfall Acquisition Model

Acquisition Aspect	Descriptions
Technical activities	Feasibility analysis, requirements definition, system design, implementation, integration, and operation and maintenance
Events	Initiation event: Start of an activity Completion event: End of an activity
Relations	▪ Completion of one activity initiates another activity. ▪ Iteration between neighboring activities is permitted
Timing Properties	Only one activity is performed at a time

14.3 Refined Waterfall Model

The basic waterfall model shown in Figure 14.1 can be refined in a number of ways. The basic model was developed only in terms of a number of technical activities. Now we will embellish that model by adding management aspects.

For the technical activities in the refined waterfall model, we will use the same activities as for the basic waterfall model. We now add a set of management activities to the model. For example, we will include a management activity associated with the budget process.

Acquisition activities

The next aspect of the refined model is to introduce explicit acquisition events. Because we are considering management and technical activities, we will also separate the associated acquisition events.

Acquisition events

Furthermore, we will permit synchronization between activities. Thus, for example, we will allow synchronization between a technical acquisition activity and a management acquisition activity.

Relations among activities

As we did for the basic model, Table 14.2 summarizes the refined waterfall model.

Model summary

An alternative to the textual description of the refined waterfall model is a graphical representation. Figure 14.3 illustrates the graphic representation, highlighting the main activities, events, and relations.

TABLE 14.2 Elements of Refined Waterfall Model

Acquisition Aspect	Descriptions
Activities	■ Technical: Feasibility analysis, requirements definition, system design, implementation, integration, and operation and maintenance ■ Management: project management (including planning and budgeting), contract management, and risk management
Events	■ Technical – Initiation event: Start of an activity – Completion event: End of an activity ■ Management – Activity-specific events: quarterly project management review notifications, periodic budget availability notifications, and risk management review announcements
Relations	■ Technical – Completion of one activity initiates another activity – Iteration between neighboring activities permitted ■ Management – Relations among management activities permitted: project planning depends on budget allocation ■ Coupling between management and technical activities permitted: requirements definition activity may have associated risk management activity
Timing Properties	■ Only one technical activity performed at a time ■ Management activities performed in parallel

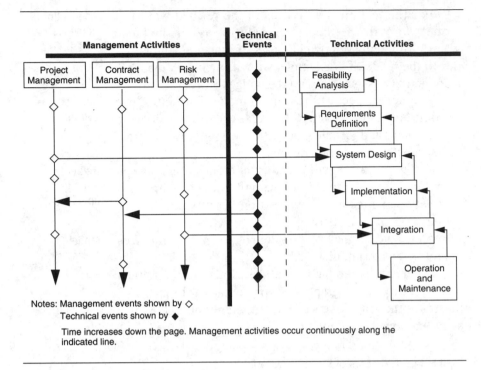

FIGURE 14.3 Refined waterfall model.

In Figure 14.3, we have separated the technical and management activities in the refined model. Some of the characteristics of the model are

- *Highly serialized* technical activities
- *Continuous* management activities
- *Parallelism* in management activities

The relations shown in Figure 14.3 illustrate

- Project management (management event) and system design (technical activity)
- Contract management (management event) and project management (management activity)
- A technical event and contract management (management activity)
- A risk management event and integration (technical activity)

Among other things, the inclusion of management activities has increased the complexity of the model. Note also the parallelism of management activities that is not present in the technical activities. Furthermore, relations among various activities, such as between a management activity and a technical activity, illustrate the further complexity of the overall acquisition model.

It is one thing to have complex activities, whether they be technical or management in nature. It is another thing to successfully deal with the *relations* of these various activities. The complexity of individual elements— activities, events, and their relations—is greatly compounded when they must be treated collectively. This illustrates the challenge of dealing with the total acquisition.

This basic waterfall model served well for a long time and is still used today in some acquisitions. It is generally no longer in vogue, however, and is sometimes disparagingly referred to as "requirements, delay, surprise." However, many characteristics of the waterfall model are still present in other, currently popular acquisition models. In that sense, the waterfall model has been subsumed by other models.

Some major criticisms of the model were its

- Assumption that requirements were completely known at the beginning of a project
- Serialization of technical activities
- Overreliance on documentation

The fallacy in the waterfall approach was to assume that we really knew what we wanted when we started to acquire a system! Realizing that we did not fully know the requirements at the start of the acquisition led to the development of more evolutionary models.

14.4 Spiral Acquisition Models

Other acquisition models are possible with an emphasis on acquisition activities performed in an evolutionary manner. One well-known model is the spiral model, originally based on the work of Boehm [Boehm 88]. This model is partitioned into four major stages:

- *Planning:* identification of objectives, alternatives, and constraints
- *Risk analysis and mitigation:* identification of potential risks and mitigation approaches, such as prototypes, benchmarks, and modeling
- *Engineering:* the process of developing and verifying part of the overall system
- *Customer evaluation:* assessment of the system by the customer with respect to characteristic features and usability

Figure 14.4 shows a spiral model as it is typically represented.

The heavy line in the figure is like the hand of a watch. As it sweeps around (clockwise, of course!), it goes through major activities of the model, namely, planning,

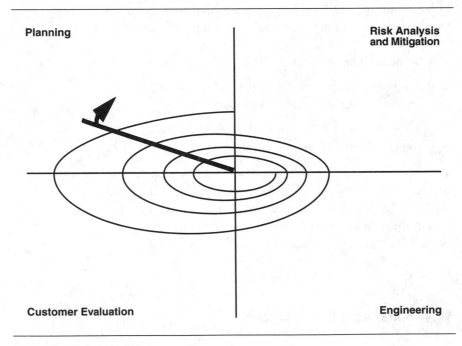

Planning

Risk Analysis and Mitigation

Customer Evaluation

Engineering

FIGURE 14.4 Spiral model.

risk analysis and mitigation, engineering, and customer evaluation. After we complete one cycle of the model, we return to the starting point and begin the process again.

Figure 14.5, in the style of Figure 14.3, shows how we "unwind" the spiral model. Of the activities shown, only one is considered technical in nature: the engineering activity. Assignment of the other activities to the management category simply indicates that primary responsibility lies with

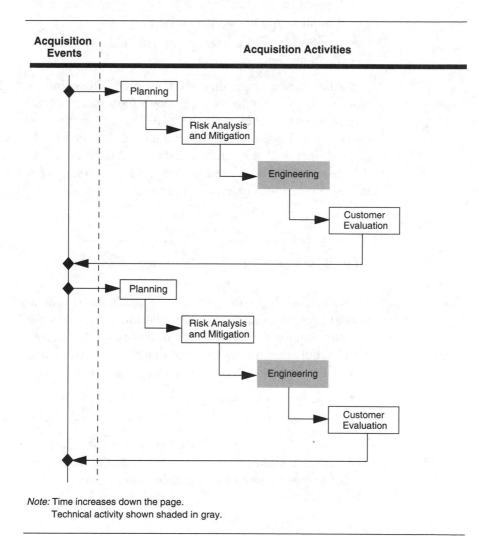

Acquisition Events   **Acquisition Activities**

Planning

Risk Analysis and Mitigation

Engineering

Customer Evaluation

Planning

Risk Analysis and Mitigation

Engineering

Customer Evaluation

Note: Time increases down the page.
Technical activity shown shaded in gray.

FIGURE 14.5 Alternative representation of spiral model.

management. This is not to say that technical staff do not support the activity. Note further that two primary acquisition events are shown, representing the beginning and the end of an acquisition spiral.

The timing properties of the spiral model as we have discussed it here are based on stages that are performed serially. On completion of one cycle, a new cycle begins.

The primary advantages of a spiral approach include its

- Evolutionary nature, which provides alternatives to minimize overall acquisition risk
- Emphasis on risk management principles, such as risk identification and mitigation

Another advantage, implicit in the preceding points, is that the use of a spiral approach allows for greater interaction between the developing agent and the customer and/or users. By and large, the more interaction, the more likely the customer and user will be satisfied, and the more likely the acquisition will succeed. As project managers know, it is the customer who determines success!

14.5 Summary

We defined an *acquisition model* as a particular specification of acquisition activities, acquisition events, and the relations among them, including timing properties, based on an acquisition framework. To illustrate our acquisition model approach, we described two well-known models:

- Waterfall model, including a refined version
- Spiral model

Table 14.3 compares these two acquisition models. The table is simplified in order to illustrate the fundamental differences between the two acquisition models.

TABLE 14.3 Comparison of Waterfall and Spiral Models

Aquisition Aspect	Waterfall Model	Spiral Model
Activities	Emphasis on technical activities	Emphasis on management activities
Events	Start and stop of activity	Start and stop of a cycle of activities
Relations	Closely coupled technical activities	Closely coupled technical and management activities in a stage
Timing	▪ Only one technical activity performed at a time ▪ Management activities performed in parallel	Repeated cycles of technical and management activities

14.6 Food for Thought

1. If you were given two different acquisition models, what criteria would you use to determine which model is better?

2. What is the acquisition model you use when you go shopping to buy someone a present? Is the model the same as when you go out to buy something for yourself? Do the models vary by cost or significance of the selected item?

3. Consider the waterfall model shown in Figure 14.1. Although it was intended originally for software development, to what degree does it apply to a hardware acquisition?

4. Suppose that a system is being developed as a series of incremental builds. What do you understand this term to mean? Does this imply that a spiral approach is being followed? Why or why not?

5. Compare the challenges in managing a waterfall acquisition model and a spiral acquisition model. Which model do you think is more difficult to manage, and why?

6. Suppose that a system is developed by two independent, equally talented teams. One team uses a waterfall

model, and the other team uses a spiral model. Which team do you think will get done first? Which will have greater cost? For which team can you, as project manager, have greater impact? Why?

7. You're in charge of acquisition for a system. One subsystem is being done using a waterfall model, and another subsystem is being done using a spiral model. How do you, as the project manager, integrate the two approaches? What problems do you foresee, and what risk mitigation strategies can you apply?

15

Acquisition Models for Open, COTS-Based Systems

In this chapter, we develop acquisition models that focus specifically on open systems and COTS products. The models are based on the framework developed earlier (see Chapter 13). Here, we consider

- Acquisition activities
- Acquisition events
- Relation between acquisition activities and events
- Timing considerations

These topics are considered for both standards and COTS products. We then integrate the discussion of standards and COTS-based acquisition considerations to show how various acquisition models can be developed. We conclude the chapter with some remarks about organizational considerations that can affect multiproject acquisition.

We focus on the role of standards and COTS products in an open system context because they are fundamental to the overall approach. We do not address other system engineering activities that are outside the standards and COTS envelope; for example, we do not discuss details of architecture specification or custom development.

The value of this chapter is that it provides an approach to acquisition modeling that you can use to reason about the acquisition of open, COTS-based systems. In particular, this chapter gives you information for taking the activities discussed throughout the book and putting them together in a process that you can use in your acquisition.

15.1 The Overall Context

Although this chapter focuses on an acquisition model with emphasis on standards and COTS products, it is important to set an overall context. Certainly, acquisition of a system involves more than just standards and COTS products. The overall context is illustrated in Figure 15.1.

Figure 15.1 illustrates our division of the acquisition aspects related to open, COTS-based systems. At the same time, we must be able to address other acquisition elements, such as

- Requirements management
- Architecture specification and evaluation
- System design
- System testing
- Deployment
- Maintenance

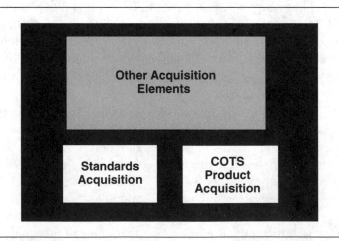

FIGURE 15.1 Overall context for open, COTS-based acquisition.

Our purpose here is not to develop a particular acquisition model that includes the details associated with the elements listed. There are several reasons for this. First, there are a number of variations in what elements one seeks to include in the overall context; to pursue that path would take us too far afield. Second, the amount of material necessary to fully cover all the acquisition aspects for the listed elements is very large, and much of that material is independent of open systems and the use of COTS products. Finally, you are already familiar with many of the acquisition aspects, such as requirements management and system integration. In this chapter, we focus on acquisition model considerations for open, COTS-based systems.

15.2 Standards

Table 15.1 presents a sample list of acquisition activities associated with standards. In order to give an integrated view, we do not separate activities into management and technical activities; that will be done later.

Acquisition activities

The activities listed in Table 15.1 are at various levels of detail, and each activity may include several further levels of detail. For example, standards evaluation may range from simple questions to obtaining one or more conforming implementations and testing them for suitability in an operational environment. Note also that some of the activities may or may not be part of a project's scope. For example, if a project team feels that it is not necessary to liase with a standards organization, as determined by the survey of standards organizations, the associated acquisition activity would not be present in the project acquisition model.

Consideration of acquisition events is important for a number of reasons. The primary reason is that an acquisition event initiates an acquisition activity. This is most likely to occur for external acquisition events that are initiated by an agent outside the scope of the acquisition organization. In fact, it is the necessity to deal with external events for standards and COTS products that is a fundamental,

Acquisition events

TABLE 15.1 Acquisition Activities for Standards

Activity	Description
Standards business strategy management	Develop and manage the project business strategy for the use of standards.
Standards risk management	Perform risk management activities—identification, development of mitigation strategies, and so on—for standards use.
Standards requirements management	Assess and iterate system requirements and their ability to be satisfied through the use of standards.
Standards solicitation language development	Develop standards-related language for statements of work, requests for proposals, and proposal evaluation criteria.
Standards organization surveys	Determine the various standards bodies that may be relevant to the domain, including knowledge of their processes and the degree to which you can participate.
Standards organization liaison	Perform activities to gain deeper understanding of, and possible collaboration with, selected standards organizations. You may also include activities to establish a formal association, such as membership or a memorandum of understanding.
Standards development	Participate in the development of a standard.
Standards balloting	Participate in a ballot to exert influence over a standard.
Standards suitability assessment	Perform high-level assessment of suitability of a set of standards for inclusion in the system; develop and maintain assessment criteria, which might include, for example, breadth of acceptance, extensibility of the standard, maturity, quality of documentation, and availability of conformance tests.
Standards evaluation	Perform lower-level assessment of the candidate standards; develop and maintain evaluation criteria, which might include, for example, the ability of features in the standard to meet system requirements and the degree of implementation dependence permitted.
Standards selection	Select a particular standard from a set of candidate standards, based on previous evaluation results.
Standards procurement	Procure a selected or candidate standard.
Standards conformance test management	Obtain conformance tests for a standard; develop them if none exist. This may include collaboration with others, including the relevant standards organization.
Standards profile management	Develop and maintain the standards profile for your project, including any necessary "glue" specifications.

distinguishing factor of open, COTS-based acquisition. The fact that such events may occur continuously means that the project must be prepared to deal with such events continuously. Some examples of these events and possible acquisition responses are shown in Table 15.2.

TABLE 15.2 Standards Acquisition External Events

External Event	Description
Announcement of new standard	Announcement of intent to develop a new standard
New standards organization	Announcement of formation of a new standards organization
Selected standard approval	Formal approval of a previously selected standard by its governing body
Selected standard revision	Revision of a previously selected standard by its governing body
Selected standard withdrawal	Withdrawal of a previously selected standard by its governing body

Internal events also are associated with standards acquisition. These events are initiated within the scope of the project and signal activities that need to be performed. Some examples of internal acquisition events related to standards are shown in Table 15.3.

One of the characteristics of the general acquisition framework we discussed in Section 13.1 is the relations among various acquisition activities. Figure 15.2 shows an example of this for the sample activities listed in Table 15.1. **Relations among activities**

To illustrate the relations in Figure 15.2, consider the standards development activity located on the left-hand

TABLE 15.3 Standards Acquisition Internal Events

Internal Event	Description
Standard selection recommendation	A recommendation for selection of one or more standards
Standard procurement	A request to procure a particular standard(s)
Standards review	A review, perhaps periodic in nature, of currently selected standards
Selected standard unsuitable	Determination that a previously selected standard is unsuitable, perhaps because of new system requirements or failure of existing COTS products to meet new requirements, such as for performance or security

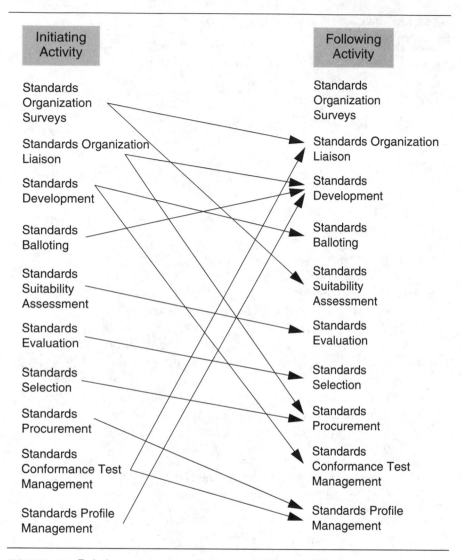

FIGURE 15.2 Relations among standards acquisition activities.

side of the figure. This activity is related to the following activities on the right-hand side of the figure:

- *Standards balloting:* It may be that an organization wishes to influence a standard through its balloting process, and this may be related to the standard development.

- *Standards conformance test management:* An organization may feel that it is important to have conformance tests for a standard. This activity can thus be related to the standard development effort.

You might be inclined to think that standards balloting and conformance test development are a subset of standards development, but this is not necessarily the case. For example, in many cases, you can ballot on a standard without being part of its development effort. You can also develop conformance tests without being part of the development effort for that standard. The fact that these activities are listed separately simply means that they can be performed independently of another activity. The independence of the activity is what causes it to be treated as one of the basic acquisition activities.

Another characteristic of the acquisition framework is the relations among events and acquisition activities. We show an example of this for standards in Figure 15.3. Suppose that a standard is revised, an example of an external event. An announcement of a revision to a previously selected standard causes the activity *standards suitability assessment* to be initiated.

Relations among events and activities

Note that not all standards activities are listed on the right-hand side of Figure 15.3. The reason is that some activities may not be directly initiated by an event but may instead be initiated by other activities. For example, consider *standard evaluation,* an activity not present in Figure 15.3. If a standard is revised—external event—it will initiate an activity—*standard suitability assessment*—which in turn may cause the activity *standard evaluation* to be performed. We see, then, that *chains of activities* may be present in the overall project acquisition.

In accordance with the general framework, it is necessary to describe the timing properties associated with events and activities. In this regard, we note the following:

Timing properties

- When an external or internal event occurs, its associated activity is initiated at some later time. For example, a *new standard announcement*—external event— will be followed in time by the *standards organization liaison* and the *standards suitability assessment* activities.

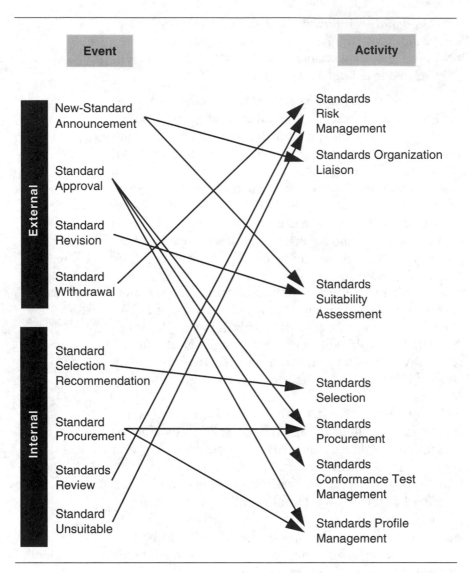

FIGURE 15.3 Relations among standards events and activities.

- When an activity completes, at some time, if there is a relation between that activity and another activity, the other activity is initiated at a later time. For example, the activity *standards evaluation* is related to the activity *standards selection* and indicates that *standards selection* is performed after *standards evaluation*.

Thus, the timing properties are a manifestation of the *dependencies*, expressed as relations among activities and events. Recognizing the temporal dependencies is more important here than specifying a particular value of time when an activity is initiated, which depends more on how your project organizes your acquisition model.

15.3 COTS Products

Table 15.4 presents a candidate list of acquisition activities associated with COTS products. At this point, we do not separate them into management and technical activities.

Acquisition activities

TABLE 15.4 Acquisition Activities for COTS Products

Activity	Description
COTS product business strategy management	Develop and manage the overall COTS business strategy.
COTS product risk management	Perform risk management activities—identification, development of mitigation strategy, and so on—for COTS products.
COTS product requirements management	Assess and iterate system requirements and knowledge of the COTS product capabilities.
COTS product cost estimation	Develop, apply, and monitor cost estimation models for COTS products.
COTS product solicitation language development	Develop COTS-related language for statements of work, requests for proposals, and proposal evaluation criteria.
COTS product market research	Perform top-level assessment of market for COTS vendors and products to meet a need for the system in question.
COTS product vendor qualification	Develop vendor qualification criteria and apply to one or more vendors.
COTS product vendor liaison	Perform activities associated with a particular vendor of a COTS product.
COTS product suitability assessment	Perform high-level assessment of suitability of a given COTS product for inclusion in the system; develop and maintain high-level criteria, which might include, for example, breadth of acceptance, extensibility of the product, maturity, quality of documentation, and availability of conformance test results for associated standards.
COTS product evaluation	Perform lower-level assessment of candidate COTS products; develop and maintain evaluation criteria, which might include, for example, the ability of features in the product to meet system requirements and degree of implementation dependency.

continued

TABLE 15.4 Acquisition Activities for COTS Products *(continued)*

Activity	Description
COTS product selection	Select a particular product(s) for the component, based on vendor qualification and product evaluation results.
COTS product procurement	Procure a selected or candidate COTS product. This also includes license negotiation and license management, as well as dealing with possible escrow issues.
COTS product conformance test management	Apply existing—either by others or project-developed—conformance tests to COTS product.
COTS product training	Train users in the use of the selected COTS product.
COTS product configuration management	Develop, maintain, and manage COTS product configuration information.

One striking point that results from considering Table 15.4 is this: There is considerable *symmetry* in the activities associated with COTS products and the standards they implement. This commonality should be expected. For example, the acquisition of a standard or a COTS product may be performed, or an assessment of a standard or a COTS product may be performed. The details of *how* the assessments are performed are different, but the essence of the activity is the same.

Acquisition events

Acquisition events for COTS products are both internal and external in nature. The symmetry between standards-based events and COTS-related events may be exploited to develop the relevant set of events for COTS products. Examples of events that we would expect are

- Announcement of new COTS product
- Upgrade of existing COTS product
- Withdrawal of COTS product
- Procurement of COTS product
- Advent of a new technology

Note that all of these are external events. This illustrates the marketplace dynamics that must be considered when doing an open, COTS-based acquisition.

Relations among activities

Just as there are relations among standards activities, there are relations among the COTS activities. We will not explicitly list these relations; the symmetry we described previously suggests that simple changes to Figure 15.3 can be made to develop the required information.

The timing properties for COTS events and activities are similar to those discussed in connection with standards (see page 279).

Timing properties

15.4 Integration of Standards and COTS Product Acquisition Elements

15.4.1 Relations among Acquisition Activities

Now we can integrate the acquisition activities associated with standards and COTS products to identify relations among the main activities. We illustrate this in Figure 15.4. This model is intended to be more suggestive than complete. This is to avoid clutter in the figure, in the interest of presenting the basic character of the model. For example, we have not included all acquisition activities that are listed in Tables 15.1 and 15.4.

We have indicated a few key relations between standards activities and COTS product activities in Figure 15.4. These relations are related to standards assessment and evaluation and COTS product considerations, namely, market research and product evaluation. The relation between the standards acquisition activities and COTS product acquisition activities is fundamental to the overall model.

Some of the items we have *not* explicitly shown are

- Relations among standards acquisition activities and relations among COTS acquisition activities: Some of the relations between standards-based acquisition activities appear in Figure 15.2.

- Relations between events and activities: Some of these are shown in Figure 15.4, such as an external event indicating a change to a selected COTS product, which then initiates the activity to assess the suitability of the changed COTS product.

We also show relations between standards activities and COTS activities. Some examples of this are indicated in Figure 15.4. For example, the arrow connecting *standards*

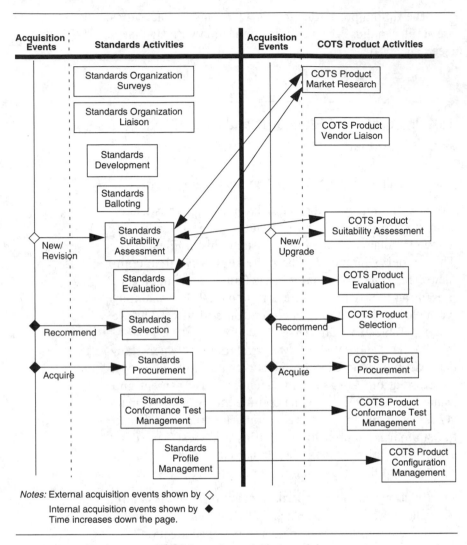

FIGURE 15.4 Basic open, COTS-based acquisition model.

evaluation and *COTS product evaluation* indicates a relation between these activities.

15.4.2 Iterative Nature of the Acquisition

Previously, we described relations among acquisition activities, such as standards and COTS product activities. But the acquisition model presented in Figure 15.4 does not highlight

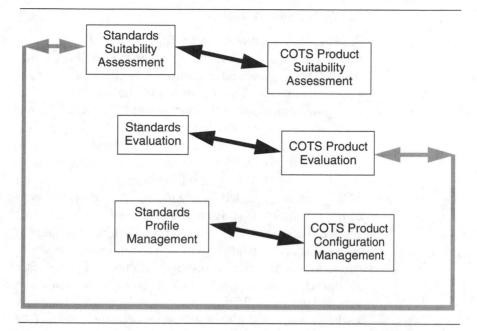

FIGURE 15.5 Iterative nature of acquisition process.

the iterative nature and possible feedback among the activities. These aspects are shown in Figure 15.5 for a few of the standards and COTS product activities.

Some of the key aspects of Figure 15.5 are summarized as follows:

- *Similarity in the activities.* These include, for example, assessment and evaluation. These activities can be performed for both standards and COTS products.

- *Interaction between analogous acquisition activities where there is significant iteration,* as indicated by the arrows in the center of the figure. For example, if a standard is evaluated, evaluation of a corresponding COTS product may be warranted.

- *The need for reassessment,* a form of iteration, as shown by the gray lines. For example, as a result of performing a *COTS product evaluation,* it may be necessary to return to performing *standards suitability assessment.*

15.4.3 Acquisition Threads

Another way to show the relations between standards and COTS product acquisition activities is to show some detail. This is presented in terms of a thread, or a sequence of acquisition activities. For example, the occurrence of an event may initiate a thread. A thread can terminate as a result of an acquisition activity in the sequence.

Consider the case of a revision to an existing standard, illustrated in Figure 15.6. The revision to a standard is an external event. Based on the information in Figure 15.3, one of the activities initiated for a standards revision is the *standards suitability assessment*. Then, we see from Figure 15.2 that a *standards suitability assessment* activity is related to the standards evaluation activity. We can follow the sequence of standards acquisition activities shown in Figure 15.2, recognizing that the result of each activity is the choice to proceed or to stop. Figure 15.6 shows a sequence of binary choices; the filled circles denote where the standard or COTS product does not satisfy the criteria and warrants no further consideration, thus terminating the thread.

Acquisition threads, such as we have shown here, are important for several reasons. First, they are useful in presenting the overall sequence of activities performed in the acquisition. Second, they illustrate the points where there is coupling to other threads. For example, as indicated by the shaded arrow in Figure 15.6, there is a relation between the activity *standards assessment* and the activity *COTS product suitability assessment.*

Note that when different threads are coupled, as in Figure 15.6, the point at which coupling occurs is very important. In the case shown in Figure 15.6, the thread for assessing the suitability of a COTS product is initiated early. Instead, one could have postponed the suitability thread for COTS products until it had been decided to retain the standard that was revised.

Initiating threads in parallel like this is both good and bad. Doing so will be good if there is a reasonable belief that the COTS products will remain fairly stable with respect to the changes in the standard. On the other hand, if the standard has undergone a major revision, it may be

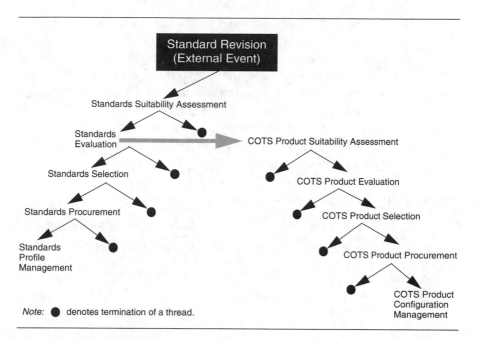

FIGURE 15.6 Acquisition thread for standard revision.

worth waiting until the nature of the revision is understood before initiating any acquisition thread for the evaluation of the COTS products. We are illustrating possible choices in considering the preceding example. This is where you need to exercise judgment in the performance of acquisition activities.

15.5 Acquisition Model Considerations

In Chapter 14, we provided an overview of a waterfall model and a spiral model in terms of our acquisition framework. What happens when we try to incorporate open systems and the use of COTS products in a particular acquisition model? We turn to that question in this section.

To begin, recall that acquisition consists of procurement, development, and maintenance activities. Furthermore, these activities may be management or technical in nature. Let us take the acquisition activities for standards

Partition of acquisition activities

and COTS products and place them in the overall acquisition context (Table 15.5).

Note that we have grouped development and maintenance activities together for simplicity. In addition, we see that a number of standards and COTS product management activities are a part of procurement, as well as development and maintenance. An example of this is a risk management activity, which may be staffed by people from various disciplines.

TABLE 15.5 Partitioning Standards and COTS Product Acquisition Activities

	Procurement	Development and Maintenance
Management	Standards business strategy management Standards risk management Standards requirements management	
	▪ Standards solicitation language development ▪ Standards procurement	
	COTS product business strategy management COTS product risk management COTS product requirements management	
	▪ COTS product vendor qualification ▪ COTS product cost estimation ▪ COTS product solicitation language development ▪ COTS product procurement	
Technical	▪ Standards organization surveys ▪ Standards organization liaison	▪ Standards development ▪ Standards balloting ▪ Standards suitability assessment ▪ Standards evaluation ▪ Standards selection ▪ Standards conformance test management ▪ Standards profile management
	▪ COTS product vendor liaison ▪ COTS product market research	▪ COTS product suitability assessment ▪ COTS product evaluation ▪ COTS product selection ▪ COTS product training ▪ COTS product conformance testing ▪ COTS product configuration management

Before dealing with the specifics of a particular acqui- **Overall model**
sition model, it is very important to specify certain **context**
assumptions. The following assumptions are fundamental
to the overall acquisition model. We require that the model

- Recognize that standards-based activities occur over
  the life cycle of the system acquisition
- Recognize that COTS products activities occur over
  the life cycle of the system acquisition

We now realize that although multiple acquisition
models are possible, the preceding assumptions have significant impact on any acquisition model that purports to
address open systems and COTS products. Remember the
fundamental point about the nature of open, COTS-based
acquisition: the need to deal with external events on a continuous basis. This requires that your acquisition model—
or "acquisition architecture," if you will—must deal with
the real world!

In Figure 15.7, the box represents the boundary of the
project scope. Standards and COTS-based activities must deal
with the events initiated in the external project environment.

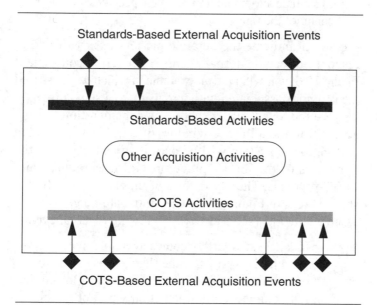

FIGURE 15.7 Acquisition context of open, COTS-based acquisition.

This constraint limits how various acquisition models can deal with the open, COTS-based systems environment.

Waterfall model

A well-known development approach is the waterfall model, which we discussed earlier; see Section 14.2. The striking characteristic of this model is that it is predominantly serial in nature and based on custom development. How can this approach be extended to account for standards and COTS products?

We accept the premise that external events, for standards as well as for COTS products, can occur at any time. *The important question is when these events are allowed to affect the system development.* You can think of a window associated with an event; is the window open at the time of the event? And how long is the window open?

It is not possible to give the details of a full model in a simple picture, just as it is not possible to give the details of an architecture in a simple picture. However, we illustrate the considerations for a waterfall acquisition model in Figure 15.8, showing three major aspects of the acquisition:

- Standards-related activities, at the top of the figure
- COTS-related activities, at the bottom of the figure
- System development and maintenance activities, at the center of the figure

We do not indicate the detailed processing performed in response to each external event. However, if you look at Figure 15.6, you will note an example in which we illustrated the activities associated with a revision to a standard.

We indicated earlier that a key consideration for any acquisition model is the window of time during which a change to the system will be permitted as a result of the dynamics of the marketplace providing standards and COTS products. These windows of time are shown by the shaded areas in Figure 15.8. They illustrate ranges of time associated with responses to the following external events.

- When a new standard becomes available, it can be accepted in the system in the shaded area at the top left of Figure 15.8. In this case, it will be allowed during requirements definition but only part of system design. The decision to consider a new standard during

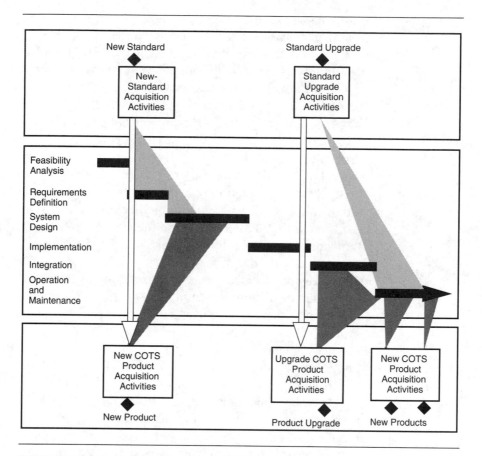

FIGURE 15.8 Acquisition context for waterfall model.

only part of system design minimizes perturbation of the system that is under development.

- When a new COTS product is available during development, it is permitted to be incorporated in the system only during system design. Late in system design, we assume that the design has been frozen, and no new product upgrades are allowed.

- During operation and maintenance, a new COTS product or an upgrade to an existing product can be incorporated in the system at appropriate times.

The ranges of time can be thought of as windows of opportunity for insertion of standards or COTS products into the system. Inserting new or upgraded products into a system introduces volatility. Hence, as indicated in Figure 15.8, there are times when such volatility is not permitted; real developments are volatile enough! We assume, of course, that in certain circumstances, a COTS product upgrade can be permitted just about any time. For example, if a major bug that adversely affects the project is fixed and a new release of the product becomes available, it is likely that the project will make every effort to insert that fix into the system. (Of course, the ideal project should not get a surprise like a major bug fix in a critical element!) Note that although the windows of opportunity for insertion of standards and/or COTS products into the system are limited, the acquisition activities for these items are performed continuously and concurrently.

A key point in the preceding discussion of the waterfall model deals with the choice of windows of opportunity for insertion of either new standards or products in the system. The decision about when a new product can be inserted can vary from project to project and also depends on the acquisition model. We will show another example of this later, when we discuss a spiral acquisition model.

In reality, the acquisition of a system typically includes maintenance. When we look at the maintenance activities, they will often appear to be a repeat of the development activities: requirements changes, design, code, and integration testing. In this sense, a waterfall model begins to look like a series of increments, which is what it becomes in practice. Note, however, that none of the above discussion would change the view of how open, COTS products are incorporated into the system.

The preceding discussion of how one may incorporate open, COTS products in a waterfall model has some difficulties. In particular, the assumption behind the waterfall model is that when the development is initiated, the set of all requirements is known. This cannot be assumed when one considers an open, COTS-based modification to the model. That is, assuming that the system requirements are fixed, without consideration of the impact of COTS products on those requirements—requirements negotiation—

directly conflicts with the assumed role of COTS products in an acquisition approach.

The implication of the preceding is that including open, COTS-based acquisition activities in a waterfall model leads to a contradiction. What we need is a more flexible approach that allows us to gain benefits of an open, COTS-based approach.

One of the basic tenets of the spiral model is its funda-   **Spiral model**
mental iterative nature; see Section 14.4. Recall that the major cycle of the spiral model can be characterized by activities related to planning, risk management, engineering, and customer evaluation. We can linearize the various spiral cycles of the model, as we illustrated in Figure 14.5. If we incorporate open, COTS products in the spiral model, the result is as shown in Figure 15.9.

The shaded areas in Figure 15.9 illustrate the windows of opportunity during which a standard or a COTS product might be incorporated into the system. For example, although not all possible shaded areas are shown in Figure 15.9, those that are have the following character.

- When a new standard becomes available, it might be accepted in the system in the indicated shaded areas. In particular, the new standard might be accepted throughout the planning and risk management stages. However, it might be accepted during only *part* of the engineering stage. The reason for this is the same as in the waterfall model: We seek to minimize volatility during the system development.

- When a new COTS product has been selected, it might be permitted to be incorporated in the system only during the risk management and engineering stages. For example, during the risk management stage, the upgraded COTS product could be undergoing evaluation to determine whether it is acceptable for inclusion in the system.

Both the waterfall model and the spiral model share a number of characteristics. A major concern is how they deal with external events in the sense that an external event can affect the system being acquired. A greater window of opportunity allows for more frequent upgrades to the system. But

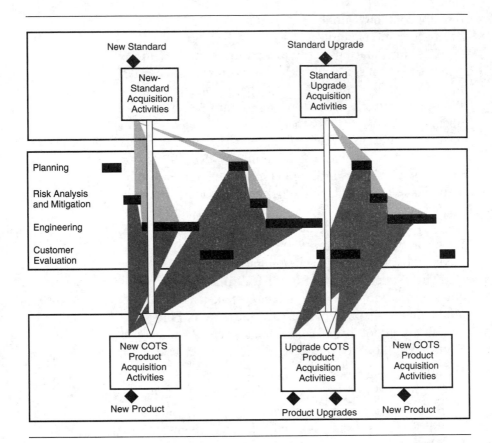

FIGURE 15.9 Acquisition context for spiral model.

this comes at a cost. To balance stability in the development stages of the acquisition with the demands of the marketplace is a key to overall project success.

The preceding discussion of Figure 15.9 also shows why spiral development fits better with an open, COTS-based systems approach. Spiral development is better able to deal with external events.

Other choices   Subject to the acquisition constraint of dealing with external events from multiple sources, namely, standards and COTS products, it is natural to ask whether other choices for an acquisition model are possible. This question gets to the heart of what many current—and future— acquisition projects must face. However, the current state of the acquisition practice lacks a well-specified acquisition model that includes standards and COTS product activities in an integrated manner. Present approaches graft some acquisition activities onto an existing acquisition context. Thus, there is a lack of an integrated process (sound familiar?) based on well-defined acquisition activities, events, and the relations among events and activities.

On one hand, the preceding discussion is a bit disconcerting. The lack of well-defined acquisition models that incorporate standards and COTS products illustrates some of the turmoil in the current acquisition climate. On the other hand, it is our hope that you can take the material developed in this book—with its intended emphasis on open, COTS-based acquisition—and apply those ideas and principles to *your* acquisition project. The time spent in developing a sound and rigorous acquisition process can pay significant dividends in the end. There may be wrong turns along the acquisition road, but a well-defined model can keep you pointed in the right direction.

15.6 Management Implications

The preceding discussion of acquisition model considerations leads to some implications that are particularly relevant to project managers.

- Both the standards and the COTS acquisition activities must be treated as equals. Managing only COTS products without an understanding of the standards they implement is not enough.

- Managing the interaction between standards and COTS products is crucial. Failure to recognize the coupling between standards and COTS products is a sure path to pain and agony.

- Minimizing the amount of reassessment of standards and COTS products is a key to successful acquisition. Both the amount of reassessment and the timing of the activities in relation to the system lifecycle are very important.

- The dynamics of this acquisition approach require versatility and the ability of the staff to deal with more complex environments than in the past. This observation also applies to the project manager!

Gene matching   The external environment represents a source of both standards and COTS products. The ability to identify the individual standards and products and to determine their relation is extremely important. We can illustrate the relation between standards and COTS product acquisition by an analogy from genetics.

For both standards and COTS products, analogous activities are performed. Suppose that we represent these common activities as I (Identify), E (Evaluate), S (Select), P (Procure), and U (Use). Associated with each of these activities are criteria that can be used to determine the acceptability of the item under consideration. Figure 15.10 shows the common activities as they relate to standards and COTS "genes." The problem for a project is to be able to determine when a proper gene match has been found. By match, we mean that both a standard and its associated COTS product satisfy corresponding criteria.

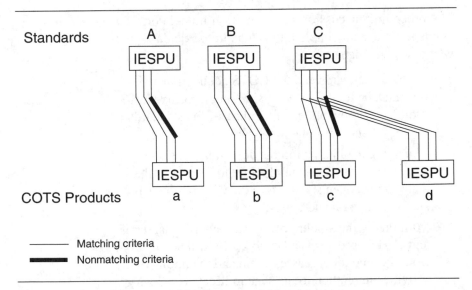

FIGURE 15.10 Standards and COTS gene-matching sequence.

Figure 15.10 highlights the following points.

- Standard A has a corresponding COTS product, labeled "a." In this case, the identification and evaluation activities match, but the activity for selection does not.

- Standard B has a corresponding COTS product, labeled "b." All the acquisition activity–related criteria match except the one for usability, and this mismatch is shown by the heavy line. Hence, product "b" is deemed unsuitable.[1]

- Standard C has two corresponding COTS products, labeled "c" and "d." Product "c" does not match on all the criteria, but product "d" does. Hence, product "d" would be suitable for inclusion in the system.

Figure 15.10 illustrates the interaction of standards and COTS activities in an acquisition. In some cases, there will be a match, but in others, there will not be. The gene pool is large, and much work must be applied before a gene is added to the gene pool for *your* system!

15.7 Multiproject Acquisition

For a single project to successfully apply any acquisition model, such as described in Section 15.4, is difficult. Part of the reason for the difficulty is the inherent complexity of the model, in its attempt to reflect the reality of COTS products and open systems. But note that the complexity of the use of COTS products and open systems stems from the need for greater interaction with the external environment.

---

1. You might be inclined to think that if you get all the way to usability testing of a COTS product and then determine that something is wrong, you should have known that fact sooner. We understand your concern. But it illustrates another item of reality: Sometimes, the evaluation and selection criteria we develop and apply aren't perfect. Hence, you may not find out until much later than you'd like that your assessment approach has a flaw. All the more reason to put the emphasis up front, minimizing later surprises.

The result is that an open, COTS-based acquisition is both more complex and of greater scale than traditional, development-centric acquisition approaches.

How, then, does a project deal with an increase in the complexity and scale of its management activities? One approach is through collaboration in the performance of those acquisition activities that are common across projects. We recognize—and emphasize—that collaboration with other, related organizations may provide significant benefit, limit risks, and allow greater flexibility for a project manager. If several organizations are each performing the same activities and dealing with similar external events, multiple projects may be able to share the load. For example, assessing standards may be either haphazard or unspecified in any formal way in an isolated project with limited resources. However, if multiple projects cooperate, there is an opportunity to bring critical mass to bear on an activity.

To illustrate the ability of multiple projects to share responsibility for acquisition activities, consider Figure 15.11. This figure shows three separate acquisition projects, A, B, and C, which share a *common acquisition infrastructure*. There are a number of candidate activities to place in the common acquisition infrastructure:

- Standards organization surveys
- COTS product market research
- Standards conformance test management
- COTS product conformance testing

The particular choice of which activities should be part of the common acquisition infrastructure depends on how similar the individual projects are. The point is, however, that each of these common activities provides input to all the cooperating acquisition projects.

Adage

"In the multitude of counsellors there is safety."
—Proverbs

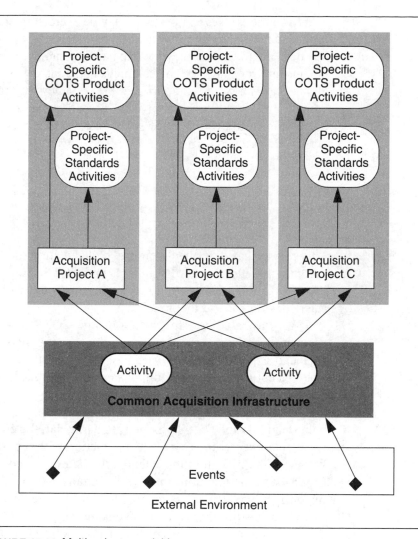

FIGURE 15.11 Multiproject acquisition.

The individual projects gain leverage not only from sharing common acquisition activities but also in another way. Note that in Figure 15.11, the common acquisition infrastructure deals with external events. For example, if there were a new standard announcement or an upgrade to a COTS product, the events are handled by the common infrastructure.

Even though several projects may be exercising similar acquisition activities and dealing with external events, this does *not* mean that they have to have the same acquisition model. One may take an evolutionary approach, whereas another takes a waterfall approach. Still another may take some hybrid acquisition approach. But all projects will need to perform evaluation of standards and COTS products. The word is *leverage*.

15.8 Summary

This chapter has described elements of acquisition models that incorporate the use of standards and COTS products. We described activities, events, relations, and timing characteristics for each of them.

We illustrated how the standards and COTS product acquisition activities, events, and relations can be incorporated into acquisition models. Then, we considered the important concept of windows of opportunity for standards and COTS product insertion into an acquisition.

There are strong implications for management for both standards and COTS products. In particular, the external events—representative of the interaction with the marketplace—signify the fundamental character of an open, COTS-based acquisition. In fact, the requirement to continuously and concurrently deal with many external events is what makes life in this world so challenging!

We also discussed multiproject acquisition. It is in this context that one may be able to gain leverage from joint efforts.

15.9 Food for Thought

1. One reason for paying attention to acquisition models is that they help a manager gain deeper understanding of a project. In what other ways can you gain this type

of insight? How often do you and your staff spend time trying to really understand your acquisition strategy rather than fighting the fire du jour?

2. What other acquisition activities, in addition to those listed in Table 15.1, do you feel are relevant for standards? What additional acquisition events should be included? Distinguish between internal and external events.

3. In Figure 15.2, which of the activities do you consider to be more important? Suppose that you had to denote important relations by using a heavy line. Which lines in the figure would you change? Would you add or delete any line(s)?

4. Develop a figure similar to Figure 15.3 for COTS products.

5. What other acquisition activities, in addition to those listed in Table 15.4, do you feel are relevant for COTS products? What additional acquisition events should be included? Distinguish between internal and external events.

6. Does every acquisition event for a standard mean that there should be an acquisition event for a COTS product? Why or why not? Discuss the couplings between these two classes of acquisition events.

7. Develop the details of the acquisition activities and events for standards and COTS products for your organization. Start with something like Figure 15.4.

8. As a new project manager, how would you allocate resources between acquisition activities associated with standards as opposed to COTS products? Next, how would you allocate resources for each acquisition activity?

9. What are the windows of opportunity for insertion of standards and COTS products for the system you are currently working on? Who determines the windows of opportunity, and how? Is anything in writing?

10. Suppose that you enter into a joint agreement with a COTS vendor to cooperatively develop a product. How would this change the acquisition model for COTS products?

11. In reality, most projects must deal with both open, COTS-based acquisition activities and custom development. How do you account for the activities of custom development in your acquisition model?

12. How would you modify the acquisition model to account for a portion of the work being contracted out while some of it is performed in-house?

13. You get that long-awaited promotion to a higher level of management. Your new boss, whom you thought a pretty good person to work for, knows that you took a course in managing open systems and COTS products. On your first day on your new job, the boss asks you to develop two work-breakdown structures: one for open systems activities and one for COTS-based activities. Do you agree with doing two WBSs? If you do, what will your first drafts look like? Would you want to own the acquisition process for open, COTS-based systems for your organization? If so, what is your strategy to get others to agree with you? If not, what else would you rather do?

14. Metrics are very popular these days to help manage a project, and for very good reasons. In keeping with that spirit, suppose that a friend defines an *acquisition efficiency metric* to be the ratio of time when a product may be inserted into a system, divided by the system development time (initiation to delivery). What's your opinion of this new metric? Clearly, if the efficiency is 100 percent, meaning that a product can be inserted any time, the system acquisition is completely flexible. What would you consider to be desirable values for this metric? How might it differ for standards versus COTS products?

15. You are the manager of a group of acquisition projects. Sketch out a policy for multiproject acquisition. Develop a set of criteria you can apply to determine

whether a collaborative, multiproject acquisition approach is warranted. Apply these criteria to your projects. What are your results?

16. Your friend, who likes to draw diagrams to help understand things, is wondering about multiproject acquisition. Your friend completely agrees in principle and then draws the diagram shown in Figure 15.12.

    Now your friend says, "I understand the benefits of having a contractor provide the common things to your project and my project. But what puzzles me is how to get contractor X to work with the two primes. Should I provide incentives to *both* the primes and contractor X so that they work together? And what happens if prime contractor A wins the job for the common acquisition infrastructure? This looks like another paradigm shift coming! Neat!" What do you say to your friend?

17. A person being honored at a retirement party, when asked to quickly review his career, says, "Things are so much harder today. We used to control a lot of things. But now we, sorry, I mean *you*, have to worry about lots of *external* things—things that are outside your control. Half the time, you're playing russian roulette. Frankly, I liked the good old days, and I really hope *these* days will become good old days for *you*. Thanks!" Do you agree with what he said?

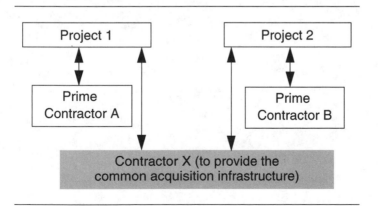

FIGURE 15.12 Diagram for proposed multiproject acquisition.

PART FIVE

Closing Thoughts

The one chapter in this part looks at the future of open, COTS-based acquisition. We describe what we anticipate for software acquisition and make some comments pertinent to government acquisition. We also identify some topics for additional study and development.

16

Looking Ahead

We have written a lot about the role of open systems and COTS products in a system acquisition. We've also spent a lot of time teaching it and discussing it with many people. We wanted to take a little time to look ahead at what we think the future holds for open systems and the use of COTS products. The following is directed especially toward project managers, but it has implications for those who must collectively work together to make an acquisition successful.

16.1 General Thoughts

This topic centers on the ability to establish relationships with "others." And let's be careful here: Others is meant to include not only people but also machines.

The world will continue to get smaller and smaller

This smaller world is attributable to interoperability among systems, which, in turn, is due largely to standards and implementations that conform to those standards. We should give a large cheer for the work of the IETF and the Internet standards that provide the communication backbone that allows applications to communicate meaningfully. Without those standards, there wouldn't be a World Wide Web.

A related aspect of this tendency for the world to get smaller is that pervasiveness of computing will increase. Despite the fact that the current infrastructure, namely, the

Web, is really based on a rather simple model, it is a powerful model. And, as we see daily, it allows for widespread collaboration.

Candy?

Schools are now teaching subjects in an integrated manner. One school couples reading and mathematics by offering the following problem: "Suppose the letter 'A' is worth one point, the letter 'B' is worth two points, and so on. Can you," the teacher asks her students, "find me a word that adds up to 100 points? If you do, you can have a piece of candy!" A friend got interested in this question and wrote a small program to generate the score for a given word. Then, off to the Web, hunting for word lists for various languages. In about 30 minutes, the problem was solved.

The point is that when searching on the Web, the person was not aware of what machines were involved, what applications were running on remote machines, or even what country they resided in. It was all plug-and-play, and that made life easy for the user. One result of this was that it appears that Italian has the greatest density of 100-point words. Another result is that the kid who brought in this list of 600 words became very popular with his classmates. Not so sure how the teacher felt! And one more thing: All this was brought to you by standards and conforming implementations!

Fads come and go, but open systems and COTS products are here to stay

Many new approaches and technologies have been heralded as the next *silver bullet,* only to subsequently fall out of favor. But open systems and COTS products do not appear to be simply fads. Their use is being driven by economic imperatives, and they will remain important, almost to the point of being taken for granted.

Even now, open systems are considered a bit passé in some circles. There is the perception that "of course my system will be open"; it's taken for granted. The same is even more true of exploiting the marketplace and making optimal use of COTS products. We see no reason that will not continue. In spite of how anyone seeks to define the terms, open systems and the use of COTS products have gained the acceptance of the community.

That does not mean, however, that acquisition is any easier. There will still be various definitions for the key terms, such as open system, not only from a conceptual standpoint but from a practical standpoint as well. In addition, as the marketplace grows, market research is likely to become more time consuming, ensuring conformance to standards may be more demanding, and integration of so many different products—even in the presence of interface standards—may be more difficult. The existence of more standards and products will require more time to evaluate them, and the increased variety of both products and standards means greater potential for difficulties in system definition and integration.

Standardization seems historically to start at the lowest level and to work its way up. This is exemplified by what has made the World Wide Web possible: Without the basic Internet standards from the IETF, the kinds of protocols and standard formats that make the Web work would not have been possible. In fact, it is only because the issues at the lower levels had basically been solved that it was possible to develop the higher-level protocols, such as HyperText Transfer Protocol (HTTP).

The level of abstraction of commonly accepted standards will continue to rise

The same is likely to keep happening throughout the standards community. Whereas most standardization activity in the past concentrated on things at the platform level, such as operating systems and networking protocols, today more attention is focused on application-level interactions and the standards needed to facilitate the kinds of interoperability we seek. This will continue, and there is a lot of room at the top of this hierarchy!

By formal standards, we mean those accredited by an international standards body, such as ISO or ANSI. In the computer field in the United States, the main developer of such standards is the IEEE. The IEEE has had a number of key successes in the past, both in software, such as POSIX, and in hardware, such as Ethernet.

The role of formal standards will decline

However, formal standards are subject to a development process that is well known to be lengthy and unresponsive to timely development, despite attempts by the organizations to change their own processes. It does take a long time to develop, and then ballot, a formal standard, and that's just to get it to the point of being accepted within the standards development organization, much less the international community. The rate of change in the world right now is faster than the speed at which formal standards organizations can respond. The result may not necessarily mean that such standards will not be important. It's just that they may increasingly lag behind the state of the practice.

Although formal standards may not be leading the way as often, they may continue to have a role in providing recognition for the winners. Recognition as a formal standard could provide the new guy on the block with stability and longevity.

Consortia standards will increase in importance

Industry participates in the development of standards for one main reason: to be able to implement the standard and then seek an economic return on its investment. We see industry consortia becoming stronger and stronger. Some people will not be happy with this, because the balance of power shifts to the vendor, and the user community may lose power, but that's what it looks like on the horizon.

Industry standards are sometimes a marriage of convenience. They are typically specified more loosely than are formal standards, and this is done on purpose: to give vendors room for product differentiation. In fact, the standard may be written in such a way that you, as a consumer, may not be aware of a gap or a problem unless you are pretty knowledgeable.

Open source software will continue to gain attention

Open source software is software that is made available to others—source code and all—under a special license. The license includes a proviso that any modifications made are shared with the community. This is particularly attractive in situations when it is important to be able to bring a solid offering into even closer correspondence with one's needs. The leader in this field has been Linux, under the stewardship of Linus Torvalds.

Open source software is growing, particularly among those in what has been the traditional UNIX community. Several companies have gone into the business of marketing these products, in addition to participating in the free exchange of modifications. Open source software can be included in COTS products, so you may be using it without even knowing it. Given some of the benefits claimed for open source software, particularly in the significant reduction in time required to correct deficiencies and bugs, it is likely that this variation on COTS products will continue to gain attention.

We are seeing many large systems that include more and more COTS products. This is true even in the real-time domain. Where once consideration was given to a specialized operating system, now a POSIX operating system is accepted largely without question. The same is true in object technology applications. We do not see people putting forward a proprietary approach; instead, they are all riding on a COTS product. The advance of CORBA and COM (Component Object Model) certainly demonstrates this point.

COTS products will continue to drive systems development

This prediction has a second dimension. In terms of the infrastructure, such as networks or database components, the choices are being made largely in favor of COTS products rather than new development. But the applications, which ride on top of that infrastructure, are now the marketplace battleground. Part of the reason is to gain market share. But another part is the user's expectations for cost decrease from the use COTS products. It's an interesting happy medium.

Adage

"Who ever said capitalism and consensus had to go hand-in-hand?" (A colleague)

There has always been tension between the user community and the vendor community, and this tension is heightened by an increased emphasis on standards-based COTS products. The model of users significantly participating on an equal footing with vendors to develop standards is different from the model of vendors individually developing products to their own liking.

The struggle between users and vendors is being won by the vendors

To illustrate some of the increased shift of power to the vendors, one need only consider the legislative changes to the Uniform Commercial Code. In particular, we refer to the Uniform Computer Information Transactions Act (UCITA), which is supported by major hardware and software companies. If approved, this act would make some major changes by

- Allowing developers to remotely access your machine and shut down your software or to insert a time bomb that would remove a piece of software from your system
- Decreasing warranty considerations for users
- Decreasing opportunities for reverse engineering of COTS products

Another aspect of the user/vendor interaction is worth mentioning. We have often described the need for market research and keeping up with the market. But how can one project keep up with the dynamics of today's marketplace and probably tomorrow's as well? We see little collaboration among users to economically acquire all the knowledge they need about vendors and their products. For example, we see few mechanisms that help users share information. We've heard users suggest that they need a Web page that has product evaluation information. Forget the question of what information should be available, which is a bit tricky. The real question is, Who's going to do all this work?

Flexibility and creativity will be hedges against volatility

In the past, where has the basis of stability been for acquisition? Not so long ago, it was in the use of a build approach, exemplified by the waterfall development model. It was, therefore, the *development philosophy* embedded in a *simple acquisition process* that gave a project manager stability and control in the acquisition. Clearly, this approach was not perfect!

More recently, people have hoped to obtain stability through the use of standards-conforming COTS products. This is the shift from the build paradigm to the buy paradigm. However, the open, COTS-based market causes much more volatility than found in traditional developments.

So the shift from a build and waterfall approach to a COTS-based and evolutionary approach leads to an acquisition environment that is less stable than in the past. How do you deal with that volatility? We suggest two things.

First, a stable acquisition process is one key. If you have a sound process for dealing with upgrades to COTS products, you are more likely to minimize the instability introduced by those product upgrades. Stable processes can go a long way to giving you the foundation on which your acquisition takes place.

But stability of your acquisition process is not enough. Second, the process must also be sufficiently flexible and creative. Volatility and change can be viewed as opportunities. But to take advantage of those opportunities, you have to be flexible. You have to think more out-of-the-box and be creative when dealing with the external environment.

Get some of your best *technical* people to help you look at your acquisition process and see what they can come up with to make it more flexible and responsive. Remember, an ounce of prevention is worth a pound of cure!

16.2 For Government Project Managers

We have already seen the start of this in the past few years. In the DoD, for example, the number of military-unique standards and specifications has declined dramatically. By all accounts, most people have learned to accept this change but not without pain. In the past, the government tended to assume control of *how* an item should be developed. Now, the shift is to the government specifying *what*, not how, to develop.

Government-unique standards activities will continue to decline

A number of years ago, organizations in the government were actively involved in the development of standards. But these organizations have faded from the horizon: the Standard Army Vetronics Architecture (SAVA), the Navy's Next Generation Computer Resources (NGCR) program, and the Air Force's Modular Avionics System Architecture (MASA). There has also been a demise of the DISA Technical Architecture Framework for Information Management

(TAFIM) and the NIST Application Portability Profile, to name just a few. Where did they go?

The reasons for this decline are several. First, of course, there is the decrease in resources available to the government. It is a rarity for an individual project office to fund staff for standards work. A second reason is that the government, like others, is trying to follow the lead of industry. Of course, that assumes that there is a direction in which industry is moving that is sufficiently defined that someone can follow it!

Unfinished Debate

Two very senior military officers were in a meeting about standards and what role the government should play. One officer stressed that military systems have unique requirements different from those of commercial systems, so there was a special need for military-unique specifications. But the second officer responded by saying that "there are no require-ments unique to the military" and that "the requirements of industry are our requirements." His position supported harmonization of military and com-mercial needs. Recognizing that they were on the verge of a real argu-ment, rarely seen in a public forum, discretion carried the day, and the two officers adjourned to a private meeting to finish their discussion. Wonder how it ended.

In place of individual efforts like those we described, efforts are now underway to develop lists of standards, typically addressing a large domain. A notable example of this is the Joint Technical Architecture (JTA) [DoD 00c].

These efforts are reminiscent of a standards profile, except that they are not typically specified to the same level of detail as is a well-specified profile. For some rea-son, attempts are made to use these lists of standards as though they were an "architecture." But calling out a lot of standards, without addressing the fundamental issues of standards integration and the architectural context, is com-pleting only part of the job—the easy part.

Acquisition reform still sounds nice, but . . .

Acquisition reform has had some profound effects on how the federal government develops and maintains systems. Reform has included streamlining the acquisition process and greater reliance on industry to shorten acquisition cycles. But some areas still lag dangerously behind.

One of these areas is the remaining constraints on contracting. How can a process that often takes two years or more from start of work on an RFP to contract award be responsive when technology changes every two years? We also need to find more ways to build flexibility and incentives into our contracts to respond to the marketplace volatilities.

Another area that lags behind is budget cycles. Although long-term stability of funding is critical, there also needs to be a means to quickly respond to marketplace changes. Contingency funds are difficult to find or protect, but they may be necessary for success with open, COTS-based systems.

> **Some Things Don't Change**
>
> "In the old days, the government wanted to monitor everything a contractor did. Now, in the new days, the government still wants to monitor everything a contractor does. Why do you think metrics and risk management have become so important?" (A colleague)

16.3 Some Things We'd Like to See

The use of open systems and COTS products is fundamental to the acquisition of a system. But, as we've noted before, acquisition is performed in the context of a model. We have not seen well-specified descriptions of either currently popular acquisition models or, by extension, uses of such models in an acquisition context.

The lack of well-specified acquisition models means that a given approach may mean different things to different people. Most people are hard pressed to describe such models to any level of detail.

What does one learn from a well-specified acquisition model? First, the existence of a well-specified model means

A well-specified set of acquisition models

that it contains sufficient clarity and precision that one can reason about possible acquisition approaches. For example, we have noted that one of the major changes for an open, COTS-based approach is the need to respond to events from the external environment. A well-specified model is clear about how you will respond to these external events.

The second reason for a well-specified model is that we can gain an understanding of the fundamental characteristics of the model. From such an elaboration, one hopes to be able to gain *insight* into the overall acquisition process by considering its model. Furthermore, a well-specified model helps you understand how it can be reconfigured and tailored to meet the dynamics of today's environment. It's always easier—and more likely to be successful—to deal with change when you understand your options.

The material presented in Part Four of this book is intended to represent a start at development of the necessary models that a manager can apply.

Some serious work on cost estimation

We see most project managers developing plans, schedules, and budgets for out-years, although, in reality, they will tell you they have little confidence in the reliability of their numbers. They know this when they develop their estimates. The farther out project managers must predict, the more they wish they had a crystal ball. But the planning must be done anyway.

The flip side is that when things start to run into difficulty, it's easy to look around and cast blame. If the techies cannot meet a schedule, they did something wrong. But often, no one believed the schedule in the first place!

One good thing to come of this is the need for more risk management. Learn it and use it. Plan for and be ready to deal with change. It's coming!

Cohesive, multiproject, joint management

We've noted a number of times the importance of market research. We must recognize that there is a cost to performing market research and that many projects do not engage in substantive market research because they do not have the resources to handle it. One way to offset this cost in an organization is through a cohesive management approach. We mean cohesion in the context of multiple projects sharing the load of those acquisition activities that must deal with external events. The need for cohesion applies even when contractors are responsible for a portion of the market research.

Joint responsibility among projects has side benefits. Such an approach would help projects share information in a nonthreatening manner and help to develop strength in their common approach to how they will deal with the external environment. And a joint approach can help to remove some of the barriers posed by stovepipes.

16.4 And Finally

Way back in the beginning, we indicated that we felt that one of the most important characteristics of project managers—or any other manager, for that matter—was that they truly cared for their people. Whether it's the senior staff who are responsible for setting policy or those who have to implement that policy, they will all look to the project manager for leadership. In a dynamic acquisition environment, you need smarter, more capable people than ever before. Recruit, train, motivate!

Never, ever forget your people

> **Modern Truism**
>
> You lead people and manage work. Not the opposite.

Onward and upward!

Appendixes

The four appendixes in this part provide information that supports the chapters of this book: definitions in the glossary and acronym list and sample questions relating to open systems and COTS products. References are cited in Appendix D.

Appendixes in Part Six

A

Glossary

accredited The status of a standards organization when it is approved by an international standards organization or a member body of an international standards organization.

acquisition The set of activities performed to procure, develop, and maintain a system.

acquisition decision point A decision that determines whether the acquisition process will continue and which path will be taken.

acquisition framework A description of a general set of acquisition activities, acquisition events, and the relations among them, including timing properties.

acquisition model A particular description of acquisition activities, acquisition events, and the relations among them, including timing properties, based on an acquisition framework.

acquisition strategy A pattern of acquisition actions designed to accomplish the goals of a project.

architecture A representation of a system or a subsystem characterized by

- Functionality
- Components
- Connectivity of components
- Mapping of functionality onto components

attribute A qualifier or distinguishing characteristic of a service.

backward compatibility The ability of a new version of a product to work in place of an older version of the same product.

base standard An existing standard or an existing standard profile.

component A conceptual element of an architecture; a component has an interface specification and encapsulates functions and/or data.

component implementation An implementation of a component; in particular, this requires that the behavior and the interface to the component also be satisfied in the implementation.

concept development A process used to identify the functions of a system before and during the process of identifying system requirements.

configuration management A discipline applying technical and administrative direction and surveillance to identify and to document the functional and physical characteristics of a configuration item, control changes to those characteristics, record and report change processing and implementation status, and verify compliance with specified requirements [IEEE 91].

conformance The condition that exists when an implementation of a component fully adheres to a given interface standard.

conformance with extensions The condition when an implementation of a component conforms to a specification *and* also implements additional features that are visible as part of the interface.

conforming application with extensions An application that uses features specified in an interface standard *and* also uses additional features provided by an implementation.

consensus See group consensus.

cost profile The characterization of the cost of developing and maintaining a system as a function of time.

COTS product   A product that is

- Sold, leased, or licensed to the general public
- Offered by a vendor trying to profit from it
- Supported and evolved by the vendor, which retains the intellectual property rights
- Available in multiple, identical copies
- Used without internal modification by a consumer

data rights   The ownership of design information required to create or to modify a product.

de facto standard   A specification that emerges as a standard because of its product's popular use.

de jure standard   A specification created by an accredited standards development organization.

domain   The scope of functionality addressed by a reference model.

efficiency   The relationship between the level of performance of the software and the amount of resources used, under stated conditions [ISO 91].

entity   A grouping or set of services that are part of a reference model.

functionality   The existence of a set of functions and their specified properties to satisfy stated or implied needs [ISO 91].

glue code   The code written to fill the gaps between software implementations so that the integrated system will operate successfully.

group consensus   An activity that includes both

- The participation of multiple people or organizations
- A process by which consensus is achieved

hardware architecture   A specification of the mapping of functionality and connectivity onto hardware components.

implementation   A realization of a specification in terms of hardware and/or software. An implementation may be developed or procured, such as a COTS product.

informative Providing or disclosing information; instructive; used in standards to indicate a portion of the text that poses no requirements; the opposite of normative [IEEE 95].

integrated product team An interdisciplinary team composed of representatives from appropriate functional disciplines working together to build successful programs, identify and resolve issues, and make sound and timely recommendations to facilitate decision making [DSMC 98].

interface (1) A shared boundary across which information is passed. (2) A hardware or software component that connects two or more other components for the purpose of passing information from one to the other [IEEE 96].

interface-based approach The systems development process that focuses on the interfaces of the system components and how they work together.

interface specification An explicit specification of the required functionality of an interface.

interoperability The ability of two or more systems or elements to exchange information and to use the information that has been exchanged [IEEE 96].

legacy system A system that has been in place in an organization and has established processes associated with it.

maintainability The effort needed to make special modifications [ISO 91].

market analysis A set of activities that examine the results of a *market survey* to determine which are the feasible candidates.

market research The set of activities associated with *market surveys* and *market analysis.*

market surveys A set of activities whose goal is to determine what is available in the marketplace and what the features and characteristics of each product and vendor are.

militarized products Items that are designed and manufactured to military specifications [MIL-STD-2036A].

modification   Changes that alter the internal make-up of a product; for example, changing the source code of a software product.

monolithic standard   A standard with no specified options.

normative   Of, pertaining to, or prescribing a norm or standard; used in standards to indicate a portion of the text that poses requirements [IEEE 95].

open component   A component—part of an architecture—whose specification is open: fully defined, available to the public, and maintained according to group consensus.

open system   A collection of interacting software and hardware component implementations, and users

- Designed to satisfy stated needs
- Having the interface specification of components
  - Fully defined
  - Available to the public
  - Maintained according to group consensus
- In which the component implementations conform to the interface specification

open system architecture   A representation of a system characterized by

- A mapping of functionality onto hardware and software components
- A mapping of the software architecture onto the hardware architecture
- A representation of the human interaction with these components
- Interface specifications of the components that are
  - Fully defined
  - Available to the public
  - Maintained according to a consensus process

organic maintenance   Maintenance that is accomplished in-house rather than being contracted out.

paradigm   An example or pattern, especially an outstandingly clear or typical example or archetype [Webster's 93].

paradigm shift A fundamental change; a move from one paradigm to another.

performance specification A specification in which the item is treated as a black box and the interfaces to the item are specified [MIL-STD-2036A].

point-to-point integration A way of making one system or subsystem work with another system or subsystem successfully.

portability The ability of software to be transferred from one environment to another [ISO 91].

procurement The act of buying goods and services.

producibility The ease with which a product can be manufactured or otherwise created or developed.

profile A set of one or more base standards and, where applicable, the identification of chosen classes, subsets, options, and parameters of those standards necessary for accomplishing a particular function [IEEE 95].

protocol A set of syntactic and semantic rules for exchanging information.

reference implementation An implementation of a specification, most frequently a standard, which is assumed to be correct and is used to test other implementations.

reference model An abstract description of a system in terms of entities and services.

reliability The capability of software to maintain its level of performance under stated conditions for a stated period of time [ISO 91].

request for proposal A document that explicitly defines the elements expected in proposals that contractors submit to bid on a given contract.

roadmap A guide based on high-level activities that identifies key choices that are available.

ruggedized products COTS equipment that has been modified for military use. The modifications may be in the form of added parts, such as shields, power conditioners, and so forth, or in the form of direct modification of COTS equipment. Ruggedized products may be referred to as ruggedized COTS [MIL-STD-2036A].

service   A basic capability provided by an entity in a reference model.

service class   A set of related services that are often present in systems of the same type or in the same domain.

service definitions   The language documenting the connectivity of entities by explicitly defining each service. Service definitions are neutral with respect to implementation.

software architecture   A specification of the mapping of functionality and connectivity onto software components.

specification   A document that prescribes, in a complete, precise, and verifiable manner, the requirements, design, behavior, or characteristics of a system or system component.

standard   A publicly available document that defines specifications for interfaces, services, processes, protocols, or data formats and that is established and maintained by group consensus.

statement of work   A document that explicitly defines the work the contractor must perform to satisfy the contract.

strict conformance   The condition when an implementation of a component conforms to a specification and does not implement additional features.

strictly conforming application   An application that uses *only* features specified in the interface standard.

supplier   A provider of an off-the-shelf item. Thus, a *vendor* is a special case of a *supplier*.

survivability   The ability of an implementation to respond to events in its external environment and to maintain a specified level of quality.

system architecture   A specification of the

- Mapping of functionality onto hardware and software components
- Mapping of the software architecture onto the hardware architecture

- Representation of the human interaction with these components

tailoring Using mechanisms that a supplier builds into a product to allow it to meet the specific needs of a particular system. Tailoring does *not* involve changes to the internal aspects, such as source code, of the product.

upward compatibility The ability of the new version of a product to use the output of the old versions of a product.

usability The effort needed for use, and on the individual assessment of such use, by a stated or implied set of users [ISO 91].

vendor A company that creates and supports a COTS product. A *vendor* is a special case of *supplier.*

warranties Legal contracts that define how a product is expected to perform and the responsibility of the product vendor to address problems.

B

Acronym List

ACVC   Ada Compiler Validation Capability

AIA   Aerospace Information Association

ANSI   American National Standards Institute

AOAC   Association of Official Analytical Chemists

API   application programming interface

APP   Application Portability Profile

ASN.1   Abstract Syntax Notation/One

ASTM   American Society for Testing and Materials

ATM   asynchronous transfer mode

CALS   Continuous Acquisition and Life-Cycle Support

CANDI   commercial and nondevelopmental item

CASE   computer-aided software engineering

CDIF   CASE Data Interchange Format

CEC   Cooperative Engagement Capability

CGI   Computer Graphics Interface

CGM   Computer Graphics Metafile

CID   Commercial Item Description

CIO   chief information officer

COM   Component Object Model

CORBA   Common Object Request Broker Architecture

COTS commercial off-the-shelf

DAD Defense Acquisition Deskbook

DCOM Distributed Common Object Model

DFARS Defense Federal Acquisition Regulation Supplement

DII COE Defense Information Infrastructure Common Operating Environment

DII COE I&RS Defense Information Infrastructure Common Operating Environment Integration and Runtime Specification

DISA Defense Information Systems Agency

DoD Department of Defense

DODD Department of Defense Directive

DODI Department of Defense Instruction

DODISS Department of Defense Index of Specifications and Standards

DSMC Defense Systems Management College

ECMA European Computer Manufacturer's Association

EDIF Electronic Data Interchange Format

EIA Electronic Industries Association

FAR Federal Acquisition Regulation

FDDI Fiber Distributed Data Interface

FEDCAC Federal Computer Acquisition Center

FIPS Federal Information Processing Standard

FTAM File Transfer, Access, and Management

FTP File Transfer Protocol

GIF Graphics Interchange Format

GOA Generic Open Architecture

GSA General Services Administration

HTML HyperText Markup Language

HTTP HyperText Transfer Protocol

IEC   International Electrotechnical Commission

IEEE   Institute of Electrical and Electronics Engineers

IETF   Internet Engineering Task Force

IEWCS   Intelligence and Electronic Warfare Common Sensor

IGES   Initial Graphic Exchange Specification

IPT   integrated product team

IR&D   independent research and development

ISA   Industry Standard Architecture

ISDN   Integrated Services Digital Network

ISO   International Organization for Standardization

ITSG   Information Technology Standards Guidance

ITU   International Telecommunication Union

ITU-T   International Telecommunication Union Telecommunication Standardization Bureau

JPEG   Joint Photographic Experts Group

JTA   Joint Technical Architecture

JTC   Joint Technical Committee

MASA   Modular Avionics Systems Architecture

MIL-SPEC   military specification

MIL-STD   military standard

MP3   Media Player 3

NASA   National Aeronautics and Space Administration

NDI   nondevelopmental item

NGCR   Next Generation Computer Resources

NIST   National Institute of Standards and Technology

NSSN   National Standards System Network

NTDS   Navy Tactical Data System

NUWC   Naval Undersea Warfare Center

O&M   operation and maintenance

ODA/ODIF Office Document Architecture/Office Document Interface Format

ODP Open Distributed Processing

OSD Office of the Secretary of Defense

OSI Open Systems Interconnection

OSJTF Open Systems Joint Task Force

OSSWG Operating Systems Standards Working Group

OTA Office of Technology Assessment

OTS off-the-shelf

PAR project authorization request

PCI Peripheral Component Interconnect

PDES/STEP Product Data Exchange/Standard for Exchange of Product Model Data

POSIX Portable Operating System Interface

PSE programming support environment

PSESWG Project Support Environment Standards Working Group

R&D research and development

RDA Remote Data Access

RDT&E research, development, test, and evaluation

RFI request for information

RFP request for proposal

SAE Society of Automotive Engineers

SAVA Standard Army Vetronics Architecture

SCC Standards Council of Canada

SCSI Small Computer System Interface

SDO standards development organization

SEI Software Engineering Institute

SGML Standard Generalized Markup Language

SGOAA Space Generic Open Avionics Architecture

SMTP   Simple Mail Transfer Protocol

SNMP   Simple Network Management Protocol

SOO   statement of objectives

SOW   statement of work

SPAWAR   Space and (Naval) Warfare Systems Command

SQL   Structured Query Language

TAFIM   Technical Architecture Framework for Information Management

T&E   test and evaluation

TCP/IP   Transmission Control Protocol/Internet Protocol

UCITA   Uniform Computer Information Transactions Act

USB   Universal Serial Bus

VME   Versa-Module European[1]

VITA   VMEbus International Trade Association

VSO   VITA Standards Organization

WBS   work breakdown structure

XDR   external data representation

XML   Extensible Markup Language

---

1. Expansion of this acronym is no longer used.

C

Sample Questions

These are sample questions only, intended to suggest the lines of inquiry that might be useful. Tailor these questions, remove those that aren't relevant to you, and add others. Some of the questions are adapted from [NGCR 93]; others are from an Air Force document called *The COTS Book*, which unfortunately is not publicly available.[1]

C.1 Readiness Questions

C.1.1 System

1. *Is the current specification of the system modular?* Without a modular specification, it will be difficult to find your existing interfaces or to correlate them with what's available in standards and COTS products.

2. *For each component, are its interfaces to other components clearly defined?* Even with a modular structure, it will be easier going if the existing interfaces are defined well and completely.

---

1. Many of the questions for selecting implementations are very similar to those asked about standards—many of the concerns are the same. Another related document you might be interested in reading is *Buying Commercial and Nondevelopmental Items: A Handbook* [OUSD-A&T 96]. It is a successor to the original *COTS Book* and is available in the Defense Acquisition Deskbook [DAD] or online at *http://www.dsp.dla.mil/ documents/sd-2/default.htm*.

3. *For each component, are there special requirements that must be satisfied?*

   – Real time

   – Security

   – Safety

   – Availability

   – Fault tolerance

   Such special requirements may make moving to open, COTS-based systems for that component more difficult or less desirable.

C.1.2 People

1. *Are you and your staff receptive to change? Do you handle change well?* Few people or organizations are really "good" at change. But if there is openness to it and a willingness to try, chances of success are much better.

2. *Do you have the ability to adequately train your staff for open systems?* Training for everyone is critical. Make it the first move in your plan!

3. *Is your staff receptive to outside ideas and influence?* The "not-invented-here" syndrome will undermine your efforts.

4. *Can you identify someone who will serve as your champion within the program?* A champion may be such by title or by enthusiasm. It is very useful to have a peer who firmly believes in open systems and is committed to getting the most out of the paradigm shift. Enthusiasm can be contagious, and it is often much more effective than management decree.

5. *Does your contracting office tend toward conservative or liberal interpretations of the procurement regulations?* The willingness of your contracting personnel to interpret existing regulations in the spirit of the move to open, COTS-based systems will help a great deal.

6. *Are your contractors familiar with open systems and the effective use of COTS products?* If not, can they be

motivated to become familiar? Motivation might be provided through early hints, such as a request for information (RFI), that you are going to open, COTS-based systems and that contractors will be expected to be conversant with the concepts in their proposals, plans, and work. It might also be necessary to provide a setting in which it is relatively inexpensive (for you and/or for the contractor) to get needed training.

7. *Does upper management support the change?* The support of upper management is essential to success. Without it, you will not have the resources you need, and you may find that the tough decisions you will have to make will be thwarted at higher levels.

C.1.3 System Definition

1. *Are special features, such as security, safety, performance, or extensibility, critical?* If they are, you may find it more difficult to find appropriate standards and COTS products.

2. *What is the expected lifetime of the system?* A long-lived system has more time to make good on your investment in open systems and COTS products; a system that is to be retired soon is likely not to be worth transitioning.

3. *Might other projects use the same standards you are considering?* Open systems promote commonality and sharing. If other programs might be interested in the same standards you are, these should be identified and working relationships established with the project.

4. *What is the expected system's size/complexity, such as in lines of code and number of independent processors?* The larger and more complicated the system, the more difficult the transition will be. Knowing this will help you in your planning.

5. *How many copies of the system are expected to be deployed?* A one-of-a-kind system may be less attractive to transition to open, COTS-based systems; however, this is rarely the case. The more widespread the system, the greater the payoff may be.

C.1.4 Components

1. *How flexible are your system requirements? Are you in control? Can you act unilaterally?* This element is particularly relevant to interoperability with other systems, subsystems, and programs.

2. *How stringent are your requirements? Are you willing to adjust your requirements to better match available standards and COTS products?* It is very likely that existing standards and COTS products will not meet all your requirements. If you are not willing to compromise, you have little likelihood of success.

3. *What is the conceptual basis of your modularity? Do the "mental models" of your system match those found in the marketplace?* If your modularity cannot be related to the models on which current standards and COTS products are based, it will be difficult to transition your system by components. This shows another advantage of using common reference models.

4. *Are there any other effects of replacing existing interfaces with standards?* "Other effects" might include, for example, dependence of a component that cannot be changed to open systems on a nonstandard interface.

5. *Are any of your components so critical that you have to rule out openness on first principles?* For example, do you want a "shrink-wrapped software" giant controlling your nuclear warhead?

6. *How well do your component requirements match services provided by standards and available COTS products?* Even if your system is well modularized, if the interfaces and other component requirements do not align well with available standards and COTS products, your job will be more difficult.

7. *Might other projects use the same COTS products you are considering?* Open systems promote commonality and sharing. If other programs might be interested in the same COTS products you are, these should be identified and working relationships established with the project.

C.2 Standards

The term *standard* in all these questions applies equally to profiles and to simple—nonprofile, or "base"—standards.

C.2.1 Fitness

1. *Does the standard provide the functionality you need from it?* This question should be further elaborated in great detail by turning your interface requirements into evaluation criteria.

2. *Is the standard compatible with your security requirements?* Standards that incorporate security are rare. Most security considerations are determined by non-interface details of implementations, but it is possible for an interface to inadvertently create security problems, such as covert channels.

3. *Are there performance implications in the way the standard is specified?* Although there can be bad implementations of good standards, there can also be subtleties in a standard's specifications that will make it impossible to ever implement it with good performance.

4. *If the standard is an application programming interface (API), is it available for your language(s)?* Although it is possible for software written in different languages to work together, it is easier if the APIs are in the same language and require no translation.

5. *Are the standards under consideration consistent with one another?* The issue of mutual consistency of the standards is addressed in a profile.

6. *Are standards-based COTS products available on the hardware that is of interest to you?* For standards that will be implemented in software, availability of implementations in a form that your system can use is important.

7. *How compatible is the standard with the interface specifications currently in use?* This is another measure of how well the standard will match what is already found in your system.

8. *How acceptable will the standard be to your person-nel, including contractor personnel? What in-house expertise in the standard currently exists?* "User acceptance" can be foiled by a number of causes, such as that the standard

   - Is inconsistent with what is currently in use
   - Is based on a different methodology than that currently being used
   - Involves unfamiliar terminology or symbology
   - Represents a more difficult method of entering or extracting information
   - Allows less freedom in choice of operation

9. *If it is a requirement for your system, does the standard work well—or is at least neutral—in the context of a distributed system that involves heterogeneous hardware?* Planning ahead for heterogeneous network components is essential; a standard that cannot accommodate this kind of model should not be considered if your system requires heterogeneity.

C.2.2 Policy

1. *Does the standard support your organization's policies?* If your organization has already adopted certain policies with respect to standards, it is important that you be aware of those policies and that your choices conform to them.

2. *What is the stature of the sponsoring organization in terms of precedence of this standard over others?* If your organization's policies are not specific in stating which standards to choose, it is important to be able to judge and compare the organizations that are behind the standards you are considering. However, don't select thinly supported de jure standards simply because they are de jure standards.

C.2.3 Quality

1. *Is the specification public? Is it open?* You must assure yourself that the specifications being considered do indeed meet your required level of openness.

2. *Who defined the standard? Who has the authority to update it?* The pedigree of the standard helps determine its openness and its suitability to your purposes.

3. *When was the standard defined? Is it mature? Is the standard actively supported? How many organizations use it?* You may not want to choose a standard that is too old or too new. The existence of active support by a reasonably balanced group is a good indicator that the standard is still useful. Active support includes an active user's group or technical conferences, publicly available tutorials or training courses, and publications, such as textbooks.

4. *Is the standard stable? Has it had a history of upwardly compatible changes? How likely is it to change in the near term?* Some standards, like some products, can be updated in ways that are not compatible with previous versions. You need stability and compatibility of versions, while also trying to protect yourself from becoming locked into outdated technology.

5. *Does suitable documentation exist for at least the implementor and the user? Is the documentation of good quality?* "Good quality" in this case may mean not only that it is clearly written and complete but also that it is sufficient for inclusion in a request for proposal (RFP). In other words, can you get what you need from a contractor with it?

6. *Is the standard implementation independent? If it is a software standard, is it hardware independent?* This question refers to whether the specifics of a standard are wedded to a particular vendor's implementation.

7. *Is the standard extensible?* Extensibility has several aspects. You may be interested in how easily your program can add functionality to what is specified in the standard, thus creating a superset of the standard's specified functionality. (You may also be interested in

how easily you can subtract functionality, or subset the standard.) You may also be interested in extensibility in the context of how easy it will be for the standards group in charge of the specification to extend the standard itself with new functionality.

8. *Are conformance test suites available for the standard?* Be very careful in gathering information on the existence of conformance test suites. For example, a set of conformance test suites is available for IEEE/ISO POSIX.1, and some people assert that one is available for *POSIX*. However, this test suite does not provide any tests that address the other 20 POSIX specifications, such as POSIX.4, POSIX.5, and POSIX.13, and these conformance test suites may never catch up.

C.2.4 Marketplace

1. *How cooperative is the standards organization?* Remember that cooperation can be both a pro and a con. A very cooperative standards organization may take you farther from the marketplace if your requests are not in line with those of the rest of the community, whereas an uncooperative one may be unable to give you what you need.

2. *Is the standard technology independent? Does the standard embody state-of-the-practice technology? Is it based on lasting technology?* A standard that does not reflect any particular technology is preferred, but there are few of those. Although "lasting technology" may be an oxymoron, it is best not to lock yourself into a technology that is obsolete or will be soon.

3. *Is the standard supported by products that both implement and use the interface? Are such implementations available from multiple sources? How widely used are they?* For some kinds of interfaces, one implementation will implement the services and another will use them; this is typical, for example, with an operating system interface: An operating system implements the interface, and application software makes use of it.

For other kinds of interfaces, implementations will
both implement and use the interface; this is typical,
for example, with peers in a network that both implement and use a protocol. This is important for competition, as well as for protection from a vendor that
goes out of business or changes its business plans. It is
important for there to be products that implement the
interface, as well as products, such as applications,
that use the interface.

C.3 Implementation

C.3.1 Fitness

1. *Does the COTS product support your profile?*
   Because open systems means more than going to
   COTS products, it is essential that the implementations you choose, even if you build them yourself,
   conform to the standards selected.
2. *Does the COTS product meet all functional and typi-*
   cal nonfunctional requirements? This question should
   be further elaborated in great detail by turning your
   component requirements into evaluation criteria.
   Remember that, even though it might be cheaper, the
   product is no bargain if it doesn't meet minimum
   requirements.
3. *Can the COTS product meet special requirements,*
   such as real time performance, high availability, fault
   tolerance, or security? Again, even though it might be
   cheaper, the product is no bargain if it doesn't meet
   minimum requirements. Special requirements may
   often be the most difficult thing to achieve, but it's not
   impossible.

   These types of requirements will fall particularly on
   the implementations rather than on the standards. Not
   only must the individual implementations meet their
   requirements, but also you must be confident that the
   integrated system will satisfy its collective requirements.

4. *If it is a requirement for your system, does the standards-based COTS product work well or at least adequately as part of a distributed system that involves heterogeneous hardware?* Planning ahead for networking heterogeneous components is essential; a standards-based COTS product that cannot accommodate this kind of model should not be considered if your system requires it.

5. *Are the standards-based COTS products under consideration consistent with one another and with legacy implementations? Is substitution possible without major system impact?* You must assure yourself that the implementations not only meet your requirements individually but also can be combined effectively to meet the full requirements of your system.

6. *How acceptable will the COTS products be to your personnel, including contractor personnel? What in-house expertise in the COTS products currently exists?* "User acceptance" can be foiled by a number of causes, such as that the COTS products

   – Are inconsistent with what is currently in use

   – Are based on a different methodology or end user business process than that currently being used

   – Involve unfamiliar terminology or symbology

   – Represent a more difficult method of entering or extracting information

   – Allow less freedom in choice of operation

7. *Is it the lowest-cost alternative*

   – With regard to recurring and nonrecurring costs?

   – Over the lifetime of the item or system?

   As always, it is necessary to balance the cost against the requirements, the schedule impacts, support considerations, industry trends, and so on, in making the "build vesus buy " decision.

C.3.2 Quality

1. *How open is the standards-based COTS product? Does it support any standards in addition to those in*

your profile? Just because it is a COTS product does not mean that it is open! Even if the COTS product conforms to your profile, it may be important in the future that it implement other standards that you are not yet able to include in your profile. Consider

- Interfaces for sharing information with other components
- Interfaces/protocols for invocation
- User interface, if applicable

2. *What conformance data is available?* Preferably, a standards-based COTS product that already conforms to the standard(s) it claims to implement should be chosen. Be sure to check just how extensive the tests were that were applied and the level of conformance achieved by the standards-based COTS product.

3. *Does suitable documentation exist for use and for education and training?* The documentation that accompanies a COTS product can be as important as all the other things you can find out about it. Without good documentation, it will be difficult to make effective use of the product.

4. *What is the stature of the organization producing the COTS product? Can you live with the inherited support conditions? What are the contract repair/support considerations?* A well-established vendor with well-established support facilities is more likely to produce COTS products whose availability, quality, and support are more easily determined.

5. *How old is the COTS product? Is it actively supported?* The older it is, the more likely that it will soon become obsolete. On the other hand, if it is too new, it is more likely to still be encountering problems. Support for each COTS product should be readily available from the source that sold it or from other sources. There is usually a higher risk in using unsupported COTS products, as the support must usually be provided by the program itself.

6. *Is the COTS product stable? Has it had a history of upwardly compatible changes? Is it based on lasting*

technology? How likely is it to change in the near term? Are there good prospects for longevity and vendor support? Stability can be measured in terms of bug fixes, upward compatibility with previous versions, and the stability of the standard(s) implemented by the COTS product.

7. *Is the standards-based COTS product extensible? Is it subsettable?* You may need to know how easy it will be to customize the standards-based COTS product to your needs. For example, software that is written to be tailored by the consumer will be more suitable to your needs than something you would have to modify internally.

8. *Is the standards-based COTS product scalable?* You can count on demands on your system increasing in the future. An implementation that is not scalable may reduce the ability of your system to evolve with changing needs.

9. *Is the COTS product free of hardware or other implementation dependencies?* A software COTS product may be dependent on a particular platform or processor; a hardware COTS product may be dependent on a particular interconnection technology.

10. *Are the data rights and warranties sufficient and appropriate for your needs?* You may need sufficient data rights to facilitate integration and deployment. Warranties are especially important in determining liability and other legal issues.

C.3.3 Marketplace

1. *Does the COTS product embody state-of-the-practice technology?* You might not want a product based on outdated technology. You also might not want to take a chance on it if it is too new or experimental.

2. *How cooperative is the vendor? Is it willing to engage in customized maintenance agreements?* Remember that cooperativeness can be both a pro and a con: A very cooperative vendor may take you farther from the marketplace and cost you more money if your

requests are not in line with those of the rest of the community; a vendor may be unable to give you what you need. For example, you might need to negotiate for

- A new release every bug fix, although this is usually not desirable.
- Notice, under a nondisclosure agreement, of all bug occurrences.
- Special arrangements if the vendor stops supporting the product. Be aware that you won't get additional maintenance information unless you pay for it.

3. *Is there a competitive base for repair and support?* The opportunities for support are critical. It is possible to move to an open, COTS-based system only to find that you are locked into one vendor for support forever after. You may need to think about bridging the gap between what the commercial community provides and what you need.

4. *Is the vendor providing the product suitable for your needs?* Pertinent information includes
- Organization history
- Years in business
- Competitors
- Market share
- Privately or publicly held
- Parent organizations or subsidiaries
- Number of employees
- Customer base
- Financial condition
- Facilities
- Design support
- Lead time for the product
- Quality plans and procedures
- Existing supportability structures
- Conformance and interoperability testing

The combined answers to these and related questions should tell you whether this is a vendor with which you want to do business.

D

References

[Anderson 94]   Anderson, Julie. "Why Not Standardize When World Standards Day Falls?!" *Open Systems Today* 162 (October 31, 1994): 82.

[Boehm 88]   Boehm, Barry W. "A Spiral Model of Software Development and Enhancement." *IEEE Computer* 21(5) (1988): 61–72.

[Cancian 95]   Cancian, Mark. "Acquisition Reform: It's Not As Easy As It Seems." *Acquisition Review Quarterly* 2(3) (Summer 1995): 189–198.

[Clapp 91]   Clapp, Judith A., and Saul F. Stanten, *A Guide to Total Software Quality Control* (MTR11284), two vols. (Griffiss Air Force Base, NY: MITRE Corporation Air Force Materiel Command, 1991).

[DAD]   OUSD (AT & L). Defense Acquisition Deskbook. Available online at *http://www.deskbook.osd.mil/*.

[Dizard 96]   Dizard III, Wilson. "The Dark Side of COTS: Threatened Lawsuits Stifle Test Results." *Aerospace Electronics* 7(9) (September 1996): 1, 26.

[DoD 93]   U.S. Department of Defense. *Streamlining Defense Acquisition Laws.* Report of the Acquisition Law Advisory Panel to the United States Congress (AD-A262 699), January 1993.

[DoD 96]   U.S. Department of Defense. *Technical Architecture Framework for Information Management (TAFIM)*, volumes 1–8, version 3.0. (Reston, VA: DISA Center for Architecture, 1996).

[DoD 97] U.S. Department of Defense. *Information Technology Standards Guidance.* (Arlington, VA: Defense Information Systems Agency, 1997).

[DoD 99] U.S. Department of Defense. Memorandum for Contractor Performance Assessments. August 24, 1999.

[DoD 00a] U.S. Department of Defense. *Defense Standardization Program (DSP) Policies and Procedures.* DoD 4120.24-M. March 2000.

[DoD 00b] U.S. Department of Defense. *Best Practices for Collecting and Using Current and Past Performance Information.* May 2000.

[DoD 00c] U.S. Department of Defense. *Joint Technical Architecture*, draft. April 2000.

[DoD 00d] U.S. Department of Defense. *The Defense Acquisition System.* DOD Directive 5000.1. (Washington, DC: Under Secretary of Defense for Acquisition, Technology, and Logistics, October 23, 2000).

[DoD 00e] U.S. Department of Defense. *Operation of the Defense Acquisition System.* DODI-5000.2-R. (Washington, DC: Under Secretary of Defense for Acquisition, Technology, and Logistics, October 23, 2000).

[DODISS 95] U.S. Department of Defense. *Index of Specifications and Standards. Part 1. Alphabetical Listing.* (Washington, DC: Assistant Secretary of Defense (Command, Control, Communications, and Intelligence), Office of the Assistant Secretary of Defense for Economic Security, July 1995).

[DON 96] ASN (RD&A) Memorandum, Supportability Policy for Navy Implementation of Department of Defense Policy on Acquisition Reform, February 14, 1996.

[DSMC 98] *Defense Acquisition Acronyms and Terms*, 9th ed. (Ft. Belvoir, VA: Defense Systems Management College, Acquisition Policy Department, November 1998).

[ECMA 93] *Reference Model for Frameworks of Software Engineering Environments.* ECMA TR/55. European Computer Manufacturer's Association (ECMA), June 1993.

[EIA 93]   Electronic Industries Association. *EDIF (Electronic Design Interchange Format)*, (Arlington, VA: Electronic Industries Association, 1993).

[EIA 94]   Electronic Industries Association. *CDIF-CASE Data Interchange Format—Overview EIA/IS-106* (Arlington, VA: EIA Engineering Dept.) January 1, 1994.

[FAA]   Federal Aviation Administration. *Federal Aviation Administration Life Cycle Acquisition Management System.* FR Doc. 96-8245. (Washington, D.C.: 1996).

[FAR]   Federal Acquisition Regulations. Available online at *http://www.arnet.gov/far/loadmain.html/*.

[GSA 95]   General Services Administration. *C3, Inc., and Tisoft, Inc.* v. *General Services Administration and Unisys Corporation,* June 9, 1995. 13201-P, 13211-P. (Washington, D.C.: General Services Administration, June 30, 1995).

[Hissam 97]   Hissam, S. *Case Study: Correcting System Failure in a COTS Information System.* SEI Monograph Series. (Pittsburgh, PA: SEI/CMU, 1997).

[Hissam 98]   Hissam, S., and D. Carney. *Isolating Faults in Complex COTS-Based Systems.* SEI Monograph Series. (Pittsburgh, PA: SEI/CMU, 1998).

[IEEE 95]   Institute of Electrical and Electronics Engineers (IEEE). *IEEE Guide to the POSIX Open Systems Environment.* IEEE Std 1003.0-1995 (POSIX.0). (New York: Portable Applications Standards Committee of the IEEE Computer Society, 1995).

[IEEE 96]   Institute of Electrical and Electronics Engineers (IEEE). *The IEEE Standard Dictionary of Electrical and Electronics Terms,* IEEE Std 00-1996. (New York: IEEE Computer Society Standards Coordinating Committee, 1996).

[IEEE 98]   Institute of Electrical and Electronics Engineers (IEEE). *IEEE Standard for Information Technology—Standardized Application Environment Profile—POSIX Real-Time Application Support.* P1003.13 (POSIX.13). (New York: Portable Applications Standards Committee of the IEEE Computer Society, 1998).

[IEWCS 96]   Open Systems Joint Task Force. *Case Study of the U.S. Army's Intelligence and Electronic Warfare Common Sensor (IEWCS)*. (Alexandria, VA: Open Systems Joint Task Force, 1996).

[ISO 84]   International Organization for Standardization. *ISO/IEC 7498: Information Processing Systems—Open Systems Interconnection—Basic Reference Model*. (Geneva, Switzerland: ISO/IEC, 1984).

[ISO 91]   International Organization for Standardization. *ISO/IEC 9126: Information Technology—Software Product Evaluation—Quality Characteristics and Guidelines for Their Use*. (Geneva, Switzerland: ISO/IEC, 1991).

[ISO 95]   International Organization for Standardization/ International Electrotechnical Commission (ISO/IEC), *Basic Reference Model of Open Distributed Processing— ISO 10746*. (Geneva, Switzerland: ISO/IEC, 1995).

[Kaminski 94]   Kaminski, Paul G. Acquisition of Weapons Systems Electronics Using Open Systems Specifications and Standards. Memorandum, November 29, 1994. Available online at *http://www.acq.osd.mil/osjtf/policy.html*.

[Mettala 92]   Mettala, Eric, and M. Graham, eds. *The Domain Specific Software Architecture Program*. CMU-SEI-92-SR-9. (Pittsburgh, PA: Software Engineering Institute, 1992).

[Meyers 2001]   Meyers, B. Craig, and Patricia Oberndorf. *A Framework for the Specification of Acquisition Models*. Technical Report, CMU/SEI-2001-TR-004. (Pittsburgh, PA: Software Engineering Institute, 2001).

[MIL-C-44072C 90]   U.S. Army Natick Research, Development, and Engineering Center, Natick, MA. *Cookies, Oatmeal; and Brownies, Chocolate Covered*. MIL-C-44072C. April 30, 1990.

[MIL-STD-970]   Defense Standardization Program Office. *Standards and Specifications, Order of Preference for the Selection of*. MIL-STD-970. (Falls Church, VA: Director, Defense Standardization Program Office (DSPO), 1987).

[MIL-STD-2036A] Naval Sea Systems Command, Code SEA 03Q42, Washington, DC. *General Requirements for Electronic Equipment Specifications*. MIL-STD-2036A. Available online at *http://astimage.daps.dla.mil/docimages/0000\51\25\72575.PD6*. September 3, 1993.

[Nesmith 85] Nesmith, Achsah. "A Long, Arduous March Toward Standardization." *Smithsonian* vol. 15, no. 13 (March 1985): 176.

[NGCR 93] Next Generation Computer Resources (NGCR) Program. *Report on the Progress of the NGCR PSESWG*. (San Diego, CA: Space and Naval Warfare Systems Command, 1993).

[NIST 96a] National Institute of Standards and Technology. *Application Portability Profile (APP): The U.S. Government's Open System Environment Profile Version 3.0*. NIST Special Publication 500-230. (Gaithersburg, MD: Systems and Software Technology Division, Computer Systems Laboratory, NIST, 1996).

[NIST 96b] National Institute of Standards and Technology. *Standards Activities of Organizations in the United States*, Special Publication 806. (Gaithersburg, MD: NIST, 1996).

[NUWC 95] Naval Undersea Warfare Center. *New Attack Submarine Open System Implementation, Specification and Guidance*. NUWC-NPT Technical Document 10,414A, NUWC. (Newport, RI: NUWC, 1995).

[OMB 93] Office of Management and Budget, Washington, DC. *Federal Participation in the Development and Use of Voluntary Standards; Revised*. Circular A-119. October 20, 1993.

[OTA 92] U.S. Congress, Office of Technology Assessment. *Global Standards: Building Blocks for the Future* (TCT-512). (Washington, DC: U.S. Government Printing Office, 1992).

[Packard 86] President's Blue Ribbon Commission on Defense Management (Packard Commission). *A Formula for Action: A Report to the President on Defense Acquisition*. (Washington, D.C.: Government Printing Office, 1986).

[Perry 94] Perry, William J. Specifications and Standards - A New Way of Doing Business. Memorandum, June 29, 1994. Available online at *http://www.acq.osd.mil/osjtf/ssrwob.html*.

[Royce 70] Royce, Winston W. *Managing the Development of Large Software Systems*. *Proceedings*, IEEE WESCON, August 1970, pages 1-9.

[SAE 96] Society of Automotive Engineers, *Generic Open Architecture (GOA) Framework*. SAE Standard AS4893. (Warrendale, PA: SAE, 1996).

[SD-2] Office of the Under Secretary of Defense for Acquisition and Technology (OUSD (A&T)). *Buying Commercial and Nondevelopmental Items: A Handbook*. DoD Handbook SD-2, April 1996. Available online at *http://www.dsp.dla.mil/documents/ sd-2/default.htm*.

[SD-5] Department of Defense. *Market Research: Gathering Information about Commercial Products and Services*. (Philadelphia, PA: DoD Single Stock Point, Standardization Document Order Desk, 1997). Also available online at *http://www.acq.osd.mil/es/std/ndi*.

[Stovall 93] Stovall, John R., and Richard B. Wray. *Implementing the Space Shuttle Data Processing Systems with the Space Generic Open Avionics Architecture*. (Houston, TX: Lockheed Engineering and Sciences Company, under contract to NASA Johnson Space Center, 1993).

[Strickland 95] Strickland, Sharon, ed. "Charting a New Course." *The Standardization Newsletter* (Fall 1995): 4.

[USAF 89] U.S. Air Force. *The COTS Book* (out of print).

[Wray 93] Wray, Richard B., and John R. Stovall. *Space Generic Open Avionics Architecture (SGOAA) Reference Model Technical Guide*. (Houston, TX: Lockheed Engineering and Sciences Company, under NASA contract NAS 9-17900 to the Johnson Space Center, 1993).

[Wray 94] Wray, Richard B., and John R. Stovall. *Space Generic Open Avionics Architecture (SGOAA) Standard Specification*. (Houston, TX: Lockheed Engineering and Sciences Company, under NASA contract NAS 9-19100 to the Johnson Space Center, 1994).

Index

The SEI Series in Software Engineering

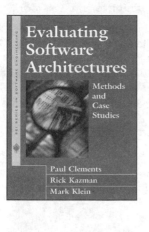

Evaluating Software Architectures
Methods and Case Studies
Paul Clements, Rick Kazman, and Mark Klein

This book is a comprehensive, step-by-step guide to software architecture evaluation, describing specific methods that can quickly and inexpensively mitigate enormous risk in software projects. The methods are illustrated both by case studies and by sample artifacts put into play during an evaluation: view-graphs, scenarios, final reports—everything you need to evaluate an architecture in your own organization.

0-201-70482-X • Hardcover • 304 Pages • ©2002

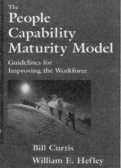

Software Product Lines
Practices and Patterns
Paul Clements and Linda Northrop

Building product lines from common assets can yield remarkable improvements in productivity, time to market, product quality, and customer satisfaction. This book provides a framework of specific practices, with detailed case studies, to guide the implementation of product lines in your own organization.

0-201-70332-7 • Hardcover • 576 Pages • ©2002

The People Capability Maturity Model
Guidelines for Improving the Workforce
Bill Curtis, William E. Hefley, and Sally A. Miller

Employing the process maturity framework of the Software CMM, the People Capability Maturity Model (People CMM) describes best practices for managing and developing an organization's workforce. This book describes the People CMM and the key practices that comprise each of its maturity levels, and shows how to apply the model in guiding organizational improvements. Includes case studies.

0-201-60445-0 • Hardback • 448 Pages • ©2002

Building Systems from Commercial Components

Kurt C. Wallnau, Scott A. Hissam, and Robert C. Seacord

Commercial components are increasingly seen as an effective means to save time and money in building large software systems. However, integrating pre-existing components, with pre-existing specifications, is a delicate and difficult task. This book describes specific engineering practices needed to accomplish that task successfully, illustrating the techniques described with case studies and examples.

0-201-70064-6 • Hardcover • 416 pages • ©2002

CMMI Distilled

A Practical Introduction to Integrated Process Improvement
Dennis M. Ahern, Aaron Clouse, and Richard Turner

The Capability Maturity Model Integration (CMMI) is the latest version of the popular CMM framework, designed specifically to integrate an organization's process improvement activities across disciplines. This book provides a concise introduction to the CMMI, highlighting the benefits of integrated process improvement, explaining key features of the new framework, and suggesting how to choose appropriate models and representations for your organization.

0-201-73500-8 • Paperback • 240 pages • ©2001

The CERT Guide to System and Network Security Practices

By Julia H. Allen

The CERT Coordination Center helps systems administrators secure systems connected to public networks, develops key security practices, and provides timely security implementations. This book makes CERT practices and implementations available in book form, and offers step-by-step guidance for protecting your systems and networks against malicious and inadvertent compromise.

0-201-73723-X • Paperback • 480 pages • ©2001

Managing Software Acquisition
Open Systems and COTS Products
B. Craig Meyers and Patricia Oberndorf

The acquisition of open systems and commercial off-the-shelf (COTS) products is an increasingly vital part of large-scale software development, offering significant savings in time and money. This book presents fundamental principles and best practices for successful acquisition and utilization of open systems and COTS products.

0-201-70454-4 • Hardcover • 288 pages • ©2001

Introduction to the Team Software Process
Watts S. Humphrey

The Team Software Process (TSP) provides software engineers with a framework designed to build and maintain more effective teams. This book, particularly useful for engineers and students trained in the Personal Software Process (PSP), introduces TSP and the concrete steps needed to improve software teamwork.

0-201-47719-X • Hardcover • 496 pages • ©2000

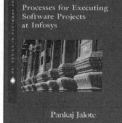

CMM in Practice
Processes for Executing Software Projects at Infosys
Pankaj Jalote

This book describes the implementation of CMM at Infosys Technologies, and illustrates in detail how software projects are executed at this highly mature software development organization. The book examines the various stages in the life cycle of an actual Infosys project as a running example throughout the book, describing the technical and management processes used to initiate, plan, and execute it.

0-201-61626-2 • Hardcover • 400 pages • ©2000

Measuring the Software Process

Statistical Process Control for Software Process Improvement

William A. Florac and Anita D. Carleton

This book shows how to use measurements to manage and improve software processes within your organization. It explains specifically how quality characteristics of software products and processes can be quantified, plotted, and analyzed, so that the performance of software development activities can be predicted, controlled, and guided to achieve both business and technical goals.

0-201-60444-2 • Hardcover • 272 pages • ©1999

Cleanroom Software Engineering

Technology and Process

Stacy Prowell, Carmen J. Trammell, Richard C. Linger, and Jesse H. Poore

This book provides an introduction and in-depth description of the Cleanroom approach to high-quality software development. Following an explanation of basic Cleanroom theory and practice, the authors draw on their extensive experience in industry to elaborate the Cleanroom development and certification process and show how this process is compatible with the Capability Maturity Model (CMM).

0-201-85480-5 • Hardcover • 400 pages • ©1999

Software Architecture in Practice

Len Bass, Paul Clements, and Rick Kazman

This book introduces the concepts and practice of software architecture, not only covering essential technical topics for specifying and validating a system, but also emphasizing the importance of the business context in which large systems are designed. Enhancing both technical and organizational discussions, key points are illuminated by substantial case studies.

0-201-19930-0 • Hardcover • 480 pages • ©1998

Managing Risk

Methods for Software Systems Development
By Elaine M. Hall

Written for busy professionals charged with delivering high-quality products on time and within budget, this comprehensive guide describes a success formula for managing software risk. The book follows a five-part risk management road map designed to take you from crisis to control of your software project.

0-201-25592-8 • Hardcover • 400 pages • ©1998

Software Process Improvement

Practical Guidelines for Business Success
By Sami Zahran

This book will help you manage and control the quality of your organization's software products by showing you how to develop a preventive culture of disciplined and continuous process improvement.

0-201-17782-X • Hardcover • 480 pages • ©1998

Introduction to the Personal Software Process

By Watts S. Humphrey

This workbook provides a hands-on introduction to the basic discipline of software engineering, as expressed in the author's well-known Personal Software Process (PSP). By applying the forms and methods of PSP described in the book, you can learn to manage your time effectively and to monitor the quality of your work, with enormous benefits in both regards.

0-201-54809-7 • Paperback • 304 pages • ©1997

Managing Technical People
Innovation, Teamwork, and the Software Process
By Watts S. Humphrey

Drawing on the author's extensive experience as a senior manager of software development at IBM, this book describes proven techniques for managing technical professionals. The author shows specifically how to identify, motivate, and organize innovative people, while tying leadership practices to improvements in the software process.

0-201-54597-7 • Paperback • 352 pages • ©1997

The Capability Maturity Model
Guidelines for Improving the Software Process
By Carnegie Mellon University/Software Engineering Institute

This book provides the authoritative description and technical overview of the Capability Maturity Model (CMM), with guidelines for improving software process management. The CMM provides software professionals in government and industry with the ability to identify, adopt, and use sound management and technical practices for delivering quality software on time and within budget.

0-201-54664-7 • Hardcover • 464 pages • ©1995

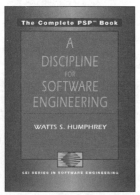

A Discipline for Software Engineering
The Complete PSP Book
By Watts S. Humphrey

This book scales down to a personal level the successful methods developed by the author to help managers and organizations evaluate and improve their software capabilities—methods comprising the Personal Software Process (PSP). The author's aim with PSP is to help individual software practitioners develop the skills and habits needed to plan, track, and analyze large and complex projects, and to develop high-quality products.

0-201-54610-8 • Hardcover • 816 pages • ©1995

Software Design Methods for Concurrent and Real-Time Systems
By Hassan Gomaa

This book provides a basic understanding of concepts and issues in concurrent system design, while surveying and comparing a range of applicable object-oriented design methods. The book describes a practical approach for applying real-time scheduling theory to analyze the performance of real-time designs.

0-201-52577-1 • Hardcover • 464 pages • ©1993

Managing the Software Process
By Watts S. Humphrey

This landmark book introduces the author's methods, now commonly practiced in industry, for improving software development and maintenance processes. Emphasizing the basic principles and priorities of the software process, the book's sections are organized in a natural way to guide organizations through needed improvement activities.

0-201-18095-2 • Hardcover • 512 pages • ©1989

Other titles of interest from Addison-Wesley

Practical Software Measurement
A Foundation for Objective Project Management
By John McGarry, David Card, Cheryl Jones, Beth Layman, Elizabeth Clark, Joseph Dean, and Fred Hall

A critical task in developing and maintaining software-intensive systems is to meet project cost, schedule, and technical objectives. This official guide to Practical Software Measurement (PSM) shows how to accomplish that task through sound measurement techniques and the development of a software measurement process. It provides a comprehensive description of PSM's techniques and practical guidance based on PSM's actual application in large-scale software projects.

0-201-71516-3 • Hardcover • 512 pages • ©2002

Making the Software Business Case
Improvement by the Numbers
By Donald J. Reifer

This book shows software engineers and managers how to prepare the *business* case for change and improvement. It presents the tricks of the trade developed by this well-known author over many years, tricks that have repeatedly helped his clients win the battle of the budget. The first part of the book addresses the fundamentals associated with creating a business case; the second part uses case studies to illustrate cases made for different types of software improvement initiatives.
0-201-72887-7 • Paperback • 224 pages • ©2002

Beyond Chaos
The Expert Edge in Managing Software Development
Larry L. Constantine

The essays in this book, drawn from among the best contributions to Software Development magazine's Management Forum, reveal best practices in managing software projects and organizations. Written by many top names in the field—including Larry Constantine, Karl Wiegers, Capers Jones, Ed Yourdon, Dave Thomas, Meilir Page-Jones, Jim Highsmith, and Steve McConnell—each piece has been selected and edited to provide ideas and suggestions that can be translated into immediate practice.

0-201-71960-6 • Paperback • 400 pages • ©2001

Component-Based Software Engineering
Putting the Pieces Together
By George T. Heineman and William T. Councill

This book provides a comprehensive overview of, and current perspectives on, component-based software engineering (CBSE). With contributions from well-known luminaries in the field, it defines what CBSE really is, details CBSE's benefits and pitfalls, describes CBSE experiences from around the world, and ultimately reveals CBSE's considerable potential for engineering reliable and cost-effective software.
0-201-70485-4 • Hardcover • 880 pages • ©2001

Software Fundamentals

Collected Papers by David L. Parnas
By Daniel M. Hoffman and David M. Weiss

David Parnas's groundbreaking writings capture the essence of the innovations, controversies, challenges, and solutions of the software industry. This book is a collection of his most influential papers in various areas of software engineering, with historical context provided by leading thinkers in the field.

0-201-70369-6 • Hardcover • 688 pages • ©2001

Software for Use

A Practical Guide to the Models and Methods of Usage-Centered Design
by Larry L. Constantine and Lucy A. D. Lockwood

This book describes models and methods that help you deliver more usable software-software that allows users to accomplish tasks with greater ease and efficiency. Aided by concrete techniques, experience-tested examples, and practical tools, it guides you through a systematic software development process called usage-centered design, a process that weaves together two major threads in software development: use cases and essential modeling.

0-201-92478-1 • Hardcover • 608 pages • ©1999

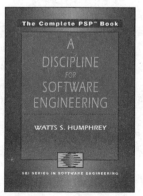

CMM Implementation Guide

Choreographing Software Process Improvement
by Kim Caputo

This book provides detailed instruction on how to put the Capability Maturity Model (CMM) into practice and, thereby, on how to raise an organization to the next higher level of maturity. Drawing on her first-hand experience leading software process improvement groups in a large corporation, the author provides invaluable advice and information for anyone charged specifically with implementing the CMM.

0-201-37938-4 • Hardcover • 336 pages • ©1998

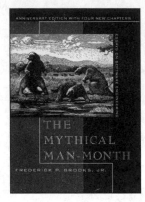

The Mythical Man-Month, Anniversary Edition
Essays on Software Engineering
By Frederick P. Brooks, Jr.

Fred Brooks blends software engineering facts with thought-provoking opinions to offer insight for anyone managing complex projects. Twenty years after the publication of this influential and timeless classic, the author revisited his original ideas and added new thoughts and advice, both for readers already familiar with his work and for those discovering it for the first time.

0-201-83595-9 • Paperback • 336 pages • ©1995

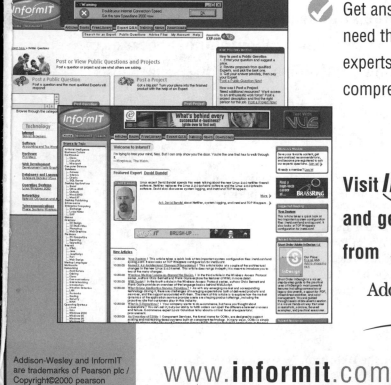